A
TIGER'S
HEART

Aisling Juanjuan Shen

A TIGER'S HEART

THE STORY OF A MODERN
CHINESE WOMAN

SOHO

Portions of this book appeared in altered form in
Pindeldyboz, Vol. 7 (2007) and in *H.O.W. Journal*
#1 (Fall/Winter 2007).

Published by
Soho Press, Inc.
853 Broadway
New York, NY 10003

Library of Congress Cataloging-in-Publication Data

Shen, Aisling Juanjuan, 1974–
A tiger's heart : the story of a modern Chinese woman /
Aisling Juanjuan Shen.
p. cm.
ISBN 978-1-56947-586-7 (hardcover)
1. Shen, Aisling Juanjuan, 1974– 2. Chinese Americans—
Biography. 3. Chinese American women—Biography.
4. Immigrants—United States—Biography. 5. Women—
China—Biography. 6. Sex role—China—Case studies.
7. Yangtze River Delta (China)—Biography. I. Title.

E184.C5S533 2009
305.48'8951073—dc22
[B]
2009005426

10   9   8   7   6   5   4   3   2   1

To China,
which forged me,
and America,
which found me

AUTHOR'S NOTE

ASIDE FROM MYSELF and my family members, the names of the people who appear in this book have been changed to protect their identities. If there is or ever was anyone by one of these names, he or she is not the person portrayed here. Similarly, the names of many of the businesses featured here have also been changed to protect the privacy of the employees and owners described in this book.

PROLOGUE

CHAIRMAN LIN IS telling me his plans to make his company one of China's biggest. Sitting across the oval oak table with his chin perched in his hands, he smiles sincerely. Two of his managers, in suits and ties, sit in leather chairs at his sides, all eyes focused on me. At the end of the long table, the heavy oil of the impressionist painting on the wall is gleaming in the afternoon sunlight coming through the picture windows. The fresh-cut yellow tulips in the vase sitting between us give out the first scent of spring.

This is my first time hosting a management team from China. I feel a little nervous. Gazing at the chairman, I tell myself to stay alert.

"We are planning to invest two billon dollars in Suzhou to build a couple of new plants." He points to a dot on the page.

"Oh?" I respond, leaning forward with interest. "I'm from Suzhou." Here in the faraway land of America, the familiar name warms me.

"Really? No wonder, Ms. Shen. The city is famous for producing sophisticated and pretty women."

"Well, I'm not from the city itself. I'm from a tiny village in the rural area around Suzhou. My parents are just illiterate peasants." I smile shyly. "If you had seen me fifteen years ago on the street of Suzhou, my fingernails were still filled with dirt," I say, probably telling him more than I should.

He chuckles and dismisses my words with a light wave of his hand. "Oh, come on, Ms. Shen." His expression tells me that he doesn't think this can be true. The same girl who he is now so eager to impress couldn't have been one of those dirty countryside people he ignores back in China. I remember standing outside a big factory in Suzhou fifteen years ago in drizzling rain, desperate for a job, when a boss just like Chairman Lin caught sight of me while walking to his limousine and ordered the guard not to let me through the gate. I stood there and watched him getting into the limo with its tinted windows, never giving me a second look, and then zooming away in a cloud of dust.

Flipping the pages of his presentation, Chairman Lin continues to speak about his grand expansion plan.

I nod my head from time to time, but my concentration is broken. My mind can't help but drift back to those early years. I think of planting rice shoots in the paddies with my bare feet deep in the mud. I can hear the mosquitoes buzzing around my ears and feel the leeches sucking the blood from my calves. I see myself later, wandering penniless in the streets. All I wanted at that time was a hot steamed bun. It was years ago, but it feels like yesterday.

This man, who once appeared on the cover of *Forbes*, sits here flattering me, while for my whole life I have begged one powerful man after another for a slice of opportunity. I'm in this gorgeous office in Boston's financial district dressed in a black suit, but just ten years ago I was literally homeless, wandering from city to city in China.

I tell myself that it would be silly to try to convince this multimillionaire that what I said is true. Even if I told people a fraction of the struggles I have gone through, few would believe me. I'm only thirty-three, but I've faced enough for a hundred lifetimes.

This is my story.

PART

I

THE SHEN HAMLET, where I was born, is a small rice-farming village in the heart of the Yangtze River Delta. Surrounded by rice paddies and fields of mulberry bushes on one side and bordered by a small river on the other, the hamlet had only about fifty villagers. My parents, the Shens, lived in the center of the hamlet. I was their first child. Old Auntie Feng, the toothless neighbor who had delivered me in our thatched shack, always said that the year and time of my birth, seven o'clock in the evening in September 1974, portended that I was a tiger coming out of its den—nothing but trouble.

And it did seem like I was trouble from the start. When I was a week old, my father took the family residence booklet and went to the commune office to report my birth so that we could get more land and monthly sugar coupons. The cadre behind the desk asked what my name was. Full of disappointment that I was a girl, my father hadn't bothered to choose a name for me yet. In haste, he said, "Hmmm. I don't know. Just call her Mei Yun."

My mother almost spit in his face and called him a pig-head when he returned. Family seniority was very important in the countryside. Not only was Mei Yun a dated name used only in Old China, but because my mother's name was Lin Yun, the shared second character made it sound like we were of the same generation. My father didn't say anything in response to her angry scolding. He just sat in silence in his usual spot behind the lime stove. My mother insisted on calling me Juanjuan, meaning "pretty," instead. I never liked the name Juanjuan. Later I changed my first name to Aisling, after I had moved to the United States.

I spent most of my infancy on the ridges between the rice paddies, crying and getting tired and sleeping and crying again, while my parents worked with all their might. Our region had very fertile soil, and almost all the villagers made their living working in the rice paddies.

The commune controlled all our land. It allotted blocks of fields based on family size and distributed seeds and fertilizer at the start of each farming season. Rice was planted and harvested twice a year, once in the early summer, once in the late fall. Safflowers were planted in the winter and harvested in the spring for vegetable oil. After each harvest, every family turned over the required amount of rice and oil to the commune and kept the rest for itself. For some reason, what was left was never enough to fill our stomachs.

At a meeting at the end of every year, the party secretary would hand a red envelope containing the yearly income to a male representative of each family. The red envelope was always very thin after all the deductions for the seeds, fertilizer, and debts the family owed to the commune. Sometimes it only contained a strip of white paper with a negative number on it.

My parents worked desperately because if the fields were left uncultivated, they would starve every day of the year instead of only some days. As the first son in the Shen family, my father was duty-bound to work the fields of his mother, Old Number Two, and of his youngest sister, Number Seven, in addition to our own. My mother had to help, of course, a fact that she resented to her bones. Though my parents tended to her fields and fed her, Old Number Two never helped with the housework and never took care of me like a normal countryside grandma. She just rambled around the village, sometimes disappearing for days.

My mother didn't like sharing our cramped thatched shack with Old Number Two and Number Seven either. Old Number Two had been my mother's enemy ever since my mom turned fifteen, when her widowed father, Lianshen, gave her away to become Old Number Two's daughter-in-law. Old Number Two had lost her husband a few years before and started to carry on with Lianshen, and she was able to persuade him to give my mother away without the betrothal gifts that were usually required. My mother barely knew my father, Yu Lin, at the time, but she had heard that the Shen family had nothing but the four mud walls of their thatched shack. Her hatred for Old Number Two only grew after she married into the Shen family five years later. The two women quarreled every day, and there was hardly any peace in the shack.

When I was almost four, my sister, Spring, came into the world. Shortly thereafter, the One Child Policy was introduced in China. From then on, a couple could only have one child and was only allowed a second if the first was deceased or handicapped. When I was young, I often wished that this policy had been enacted earlier, because then my sister would never have been born, would never have taken everything away from me.

Deeply disappointed that he would never have a son to carry on the family line, my father, who had never been very communicative, became even more reticent. He hardly made any noise, spending most of his time at home eating or sleeping, and sometimes you forgot that he was even living in the shack. After Spring was born, I was moved from my mother's side of the bed to his. Every night, my mother held my little sister in her arms and fell asleep, while I lay next to my father, who barely breathed. I grew unaccustomed to touching my mother, and whenever my finger accidentally brushed her skin, my muscles tightened.

My mother was always exhausted and muddy from working in the rice paddies, and she never smiled. If she had any energy left at the end of the day, she would use it on stamping with fury and swearing at my father.

I knew my mother was a pretty woman because the people in the hamlet said she was like "a flower in a pile of cow dung." So I looked at my father, five foot eight with small eyes and a small mouth on a flat, ashen face with droopy eyebrows, and I realized that he must be the cow dung. I felt sad, but then secretly a little happy, because the villagers said I didn't look like my father at all. I had a pair of thick eyebrows like my mother's. She was proud of her eyebrows. They made her look dashing and spirited.

I didn't know why she never talked to me and why she was never happy. Soon I learned that I had better keep quiet around her, because she was always in a bad mood, especially when she was lying in bed and moaning over the festering wounds on her shoulders from the pole she had to use to carry rice during the harvest. If I tried to talk to her, she would yell at me to shut up or get lost—or worse.

⎯

When I was six, my mother put a schoolbag she had made out of old clothes on my shoulders and took me to the local elementary school for the children in the surrounding eighteen hamlets. The government was encouraging parents to send their children to school for at least nine years, and the villagers were starting to warm up to the idea of letting their children learn instead of just working in the fields.

Before taking me inside, using a gentle voice that I rarely heard, my mother told me that I should be a dear, listen to the teachers, and study hard, because not every girl was lucky enough to go to school. "You see, Mama and Dad never went to school. Among the girls in the hamlet, only you and Peony are going to school." She knelt down in front of me and tidied me up. I said "uh-huh" softly, but I was nervous. What was school about, and what would happen now? I wished that my mother would explain it to me, or that I had the courage to open my mouth and ask.

Teacher Pang, the form teacher for first grade, welcomed us in a pleasant dialect, which I later learned was Mandarin, our national language. Her voice was sweet and soft, the way polished glutinous rice tastes in your mouth, and the skin on her face and hands was white and delicate. I liked her instantly. The skin of the people in the hamlet was like smoked pork, thick, dark, and hard, and when two or three people talked in our local dialect, it was like a dozen ducks quacking at the top of their lungs simultaneously. Even five-year-old girls used language like "fuck your mother's pussy." The Villages Committee had borrowed Teacher Pang and Teacher Shi for the fifth grade from Zhenze, a large town nearby. Because they were from an actual town instead of just a hamlet, they were "city residents." They were lucky enough to have gone to college for teaching and didn't have to work the rice fields their entire lives.

Sitting up straight in the classroom with my hands crossed behind my back, I watched through the open window as my mother disappeared in the distance. Feeling dazed, I turned to the big blackboard and the pudgy Teacher Pang. I had no idea that I, a small girl whom the world had shut out, was about to enter the most wonderful world in the universe, the one made of books, from which I would learn everything I would ever need in my life.

My home life, however, was still unpleasant. My mother couldn't live under the same roof as Old Number Two for one more day. She lost control at the sight or sound of her. In October 1981, my parents borrowed a hundred yuan from the Villages Committee, and with that and the savings they had somehow dug out from the space between their teeth over the years, they built a new brick house with the help of the villagers. The Villages Committee arranged for Old Number Two and Number Seven to move to a small brick room owned by the hamlet in front of our new house. Finally my mother and my grandmother lived separately.

My mother became calmer in the new house. She didn't scream all the time and instead used her natural voice more often, especially to Spring, who was almost four by then. As she grew taller, Spring became my mother's "pearl on the palm," so precious that my mother didn't know what to do with her. She grew up exactly the way my mother wanted her to be, completely the opposite of me. Thank Buddha, my mother said. Loud and outgoing, she was the most fearless child in the hamlet, and she spent her days running back and forth between the Big Poplar Tree at the entrance of the hamlet, where the villagers always gathered to talk, and home, reporting gossip. By contrast, I was simple and slow and afraid of other people. I seldom spoke and liked to hide myself in the corner where I would attract the least attention.

I was vexed about what was wrong with me and wondered why I couldn't be fast and brave like Spring. She always slipped out of my mother's arms after she fell asleep during the noon nap and searched the mulberry-bush fields for toads. With the big fire tongs and a gunnysack, she could always bring home lots of them. Then she would chop their heads off, skin them, and put this delicious treat on the table, making my parents love her all the more. I, on the other hand, was afraid of toads and even of small insects. I was so timid and frail that I couldn't slide the knife across a chicken's neck to kill it. I couldn't scrub the clothes clean enough on the washing board, which meant my mother always had to rewash them. I couldn't please my mother by stealing a pumpkin and covering it with grass in a basket to hide it like Spring did. Spring brought home lots of hard-to-come-by peaches from the next village's fields. Because she was fast, she was able to shake off the owner's chasing. She could catch the rabbit that we had raised and fed, grip it by its ears, and whack it against a poplar tree again and again until it was dead.

I could never make my mother smile. She told the villagers that not only was I ugly, but my personality was bad too. "She is just not lovable," she told her younger brother, whom I called Small Uncle.

As every bumpy day went by, I became more and more withdrawn. Sometimes I didn't talk for weeks, and I avoided the villagers in every possible way. Soon they started to call me a "sneaky devil" and my little sister a "precious angel." Nobody knew that at night I buried my head deep in the pillow and sobbed silently for whatever my mother and the world had done to me that day. Sleeping beside me, Spring's breathing was always peaceful and even. We now shared a small bed, across the room from our parents'. My father had built it when Spring turned six and was about to start kindergarten.

Every morning, by the time the Villages Committee had started to broadcast tips for keeping crops healthy from the speakers that hung on every family's walls, I had finished my bowl of congee and was on my way to school. I knew that later in the morning my mother would take Spring to kindergarten, and Spring would refuse to let go of her hands when they got to the door, and they both would end up crying. Spring hated school. Sometimes she would even run away from school and go back home.

I didn't understand how anybody could not like school, not like learning to speak like Teacher Pang or how to write Chinese characters or reading the beautiful Tang poems or even playing with numbers. For me, school was heaven, the only thing I enjoyed. Nothing could pull me away from it.

After school, instead of going out to catch cicadas, frogs, and eels with the other kids, I would study hard all evening until my father yelled at me to stop. "You're going to use up all the kerosene," he would say. I didn't mind working hard or being scolded, because school was the sweetest thing in my world.

My hard work paid off. At least I thought so.

After my last third-grade class, I ran home through the threshing ground and the fields. As Teacher Pang had instructed, I went to my father, who was sitting at the table in shorts, eating pickles with his congee, and handed him my report card. "Dad," I said shyly but with pride, "I got my grade report today."

"Oh, grade report." He picked it up and read it with difficulty.

I pointed to it and said: "I got a hundred in both Chinese and math."

He nodded his head, dropped the report to the table, and resumed his chewing. My mother, who was sitting on a stool against the front door sewing the sole onto a shoe, cast a sidelong glance at us but didn't say a word.

They just didn't care. I couldn't believe it. I turned around and ran out the back door to the small river behind our house. I stood at the half-submerged, moss-covered washing rock and gazed at the murmuring water. The drooping willows stirred its surface. I started crying. They hadn't even noticed my Certificate of Merit, one of only three given out in the class of forty. They had never come to the school since my mother had dropped me off on the first day, never met my teachers, never asked about my homework. They hadn't bought an umbrella to keep me dry on rainy days like other parents did. I didn't understand why they had given me life if they weren't going to treasure it. I studied extremely hard but still couldn't make my mother and father happy. I couldn't figure out what was wrong with me.

Then, the next evening, my parents suddenly started being nice to me. While they had been working in the fields, the villagers had told them about my Certificate of Merit. "How on earth did you parents raise such a smart kid?" they had asked.

My parents were overwhelmed by this unexpected honor. After all, for peasants, nothing was more important than face and reputation. So after they got home, my father scrubbed the wall next to the back door clean and pasted my Certificate of Merit on it. "This wall will be left just for certificates. Let's see if you can get one each semester and eventually cover the wall completely," he said to me, a rare smile on his face. My mother boiled me the one egg that our hen laid every day for a month after that, for nutrition, until the hen was sold.

I was immensely pleased and walked around with brisk steps, because, for the first time in my life, I had made my parents smile.

As I learned more Chinese characters, I became addicted to books. I searched for anything readable—newspaper scattered on the ground, wrapping paper with characters on it, gunnysacks with advertisements. I traded all my pocket money to my classmates for storybooks. I read while eating and was always putting my chopsticks in Spring's bowl by mistake, never realizing it until she yelped. I read while walking; I ran into walls and trees. I read while cooking and always overcooked the cabbage so it came out yellow. I was obsessed.

One hot day early in the summer, when I was ten, my mother

threw a roll of thin plastic strings next to my feet, handed me a straw hat, and said, "Even if you read all the books on the earth and you can rise into the sky, it still doesn't matter. A girl is a girl, and the matchmaker will only care how fast you can plant rice shoots when she looks for a husband for you."

I reluctantly put my book down, picked up the roll, and followed her to the paddies, where my respected ancestors, perhaps as far back as eighteen generations ago, had dripped with sweat and died.

The fields were bustling with activity. I looked around and saw many muddy and sad faces. Peony, my friend from school, and all of the other kids in the hamlet were there. After heaving a deep sigh, I kicked off my slippers, rolled up my pants legs, and stuck one foot into the watery earth. With a squish, the muddy water rose up to my knees and the mire covered my calf and filled the spaces between my toes. It was cold and slippery. I felt as if two hands had just pulled my leg deep into a huge dark hole in the center of the earth.

My father taught me how to plant rice shoots. They had already been uprooted from another field, and now bundles of them were placed randomly across the paddy for you to grab as you worked. Plastic strings separated the paddy into many long rectangular sections. Each section consisted of six columns. Standing in a section with your back bent and your legs spread between the columns, holding a bundle in your left hand, you pulled several rice shoots out of the bundle with your right hand and then planted them in the earth one by one, from left to right. Two next to your left foot, two between your feet, and two next to your right foot. You had to keep walking backward in a straight line so that you never stopped planting.

After managing to finish one section, I looked up. I saw the vast expanse of muddy water around me, waiting to be planted by hand, one shoot at a time. I felt helpless.

The sun was fiery hot. After finishing a couple of sections, I straightened up. I felt dizzy. My mouth was burning, and my back seemed like it was about to break in two. I dragged my feet out of the muddy water and went to the ditch nearby. I kneeled at its side and gulped down some dirty water. Then I saw Peony a few feet away, exhausted and filthy just like me.

We sat by the ditch and put our muddy feet in the water. "This is too hard. I don't like it," I complained.

"Yes, but everybody has to learn it. It's a peasant's fate," Peony said. "If you plant fast, you become famous. You know that girl Xiao Fang in the next village? She's only twelve, but she plants rice really fast. Everybody knows her, and her parents are so proud!"

Yes, I thought. I should learn to plant rice fast so that my parents will be proud of me too. I left the ditch and went back to the fields.

For the next two weeks, after getting home from school and finishing my homework, I went to the fields and joined my parents to plant rice until dusk. Spring was too young to go to the fields, so she ran around the hamlet all day like a homeless kid. Gradually I learned to plant rice fast; by the time all the planting was done, I could go almost as fast as my mother. I was proud of my performance. My parents must be happy with me, I thought. Their eyes seemed softer when they looked at me.

The week after the planting was done, my father went to the fields with the insecticide sprayer on his back. The rice shoots needed to be sprayed with pesticide regularly while they were growing. In the evening, he came back wrapped in the stifling smell of pesticide and wearing a gloomy face.

He stared at me with anger and told my mother that the rice shoots in the sections I had planted were either dead or had hyperplasia because I had plunged them too deep into the earth.

My mother glared at me. "What a useless thing."
I lowered my head. I couldn't believe that my hard work had been for nothing. I had planted them so deep because I wanted to be sure they'd stay in the earth and not float in the water and so that I could speed up the planting, as my parents wished. Scared and ashamed, I buried my head in my book to hide my tears.

Two months later, the harvest season came. My father gave me a sickle and took me to the paddies again to cut the ripened rice shoots. Most of the water was gone from the paddies, but the dirt was scattered with puddles everywhere. The tall rice shoots were densely packed, and the fields were hot and humid like a food steamer. The rice leaves had sharp edges, and soon my hands were full of bloody cuts. With the scorching sun above my bent back, everything was dark in front of my eyes. I was certain I was going to faint, but I gritted my teeth and told myself that I would not lag behind. Using all my strength, I stayed in the fields cutting like a robot. But the next day I got a fever, and the local doctor had to come to our house and put me on a glucose drip in order to help me regain my strength.

After the drips were done, my mother thanked the doctor, saw him off, and then came to my bed. She shook her head and sighed.

"She isn't good at anything," I later heard her telling my father in the kitchen. "What's she going to do with her life?"

I lay in bed quietly, trying not to make any noise. I didn't understand why I was born so useless. Why couldn't I do any decent fieldwork to help my parents? I condemned myself despairingly.

This time, my father was extremely disappointed. He didn't talk to me for days. My mother started to call me a "soft-shell crab." Whenever she saw me, she grumbled and swore. "You can't plant rice shoots; you can't wash clothes; you can't cook cabbage," she complained. "What man would want a weakling like you?"

The hardest part of the harvest came after cutting the shoots. They were bundled, transported to the threshing ground, and piled up, waiting to be threshed. With the bamboo carrying pole on their shoulders, my parents shuttled between the fields and the threshing ground. There was only one threshing machine for every four hamlets, so once our turn came, my parents had to work all through the night. When the sky turned bright in the east, my father would put the unpolished rice grains into big wicker baskets and carry them home.

While my parents were threshing, I was on summer break from school and was left at home to cook, look after Spring, and feed the ducks in the pen. The rice grains were spread all over the ground in front of the house. They needed to be in direct sunlight for a couple of days before being bagged so that the moisture from the fields wouldn't destroy them later. Every hour, I went out into the blistering sun and turned over the grains with a wooden spatula so that they got an even amount of sun. In between times, I read my books while Spring played alone.

One afternoon at three o'clock, when the speaker on the wall started to broadcast the second round of the day, telling me it was time to start cooking dinner, I reluctantly put down the book I was reading and walked to the lime stove. I knew that at this time of year my parents were like two packs of dynamite and the slightest mistake would detonate them. I really didn't want to land myself in trouble.

I filtered the polished rice grains and poured them into the wok on the stove. Sitting on the stool behind the stove, where hay was piled up against the wall, I lit the fire and pushed some hay into the chamber. Soon steam began to rise from the cracks in the wok cover. My mind wandered back to my book.

I couldn't stop speculating about what would happen to the characters next. Finally I grabbed the book, returned to the stool, and started reading.

Before I realized anything had gone wrong, a flame leaped up from the chamber of the stove to the hay against the wall. Spring, who had been playing with rice grains next to the stove, started to cry in fear. I looked up and saw the flames rushing at me. All I could think to do was to yell to Spring, "Go get Peony!"

Peony rushed in, lifted a bucket of water, and threw it on the fire. She kept refilling the bucket with water from the vat we kept in the kitchen until at last the fire was put out. Spring stood to the side, too shocked to say anything. Peony looked at me and panted, "Don't worry. It's an accident, and it didn't burn anything. Your parents won't blame you." Then she left.

I stood next to the front door, covered with ashes, and waited for my parents' arrival. I didn't believe Peony. Her parents were different from mine. They never scolded her for anything. I knew I had gotten myself into big trouble and my parents wouldn't let me off the hook so easily. I felt like a criminal about to be executed.

Soon my father walked in with two baskets full of rice grains wobbling on his carrying pole. When he saw the stretch of burnt rice on the ground and my ashy face, he dropped the baskets and shouted, "Why don't you just burn the entire house down, you good-for-nothing?"

He grabbed his carrying pole, held my arm firmly, and began to strike me heavily on the hip, ranting angrily the whole time.

My mother, returning from checking the ducks, roared at me with rage:

"Why are the ducklings dead?"

I suddenly realized that I had been so wrapped up in the book I'd been reading these past two days that I had forgotten to feed cabbage leaves to the baby ducks. Panic-stricken, I burst into tears. I moved my lips to say something to defend myself, but I realized that I had no excuses.

"She can't do anything," my mother told my father. "Even a dog knows to watch the door. What good is it to raise her? It's better to just beat her to death!"

Harder and faster the pole hit me on my hip. I saw Spring leaning against the door and watching quietly, looking a little scared. A couple of nosy neighbors stuck their heads out of their windows. Gradually my fear turned into anger and shame, and I threw off the hand on my arm and charged to the back door, howling, "I don't want to live any more."

I ran without stopping until I was standing on the moss-covered tip of the washing rock. I wondered if I should just jump into the river and kill myself. My life was a tragedy. Perhaps only a solemn death would end my miseries. My parents would live with the guilt for the rest of their lives.

My mother had followed me to the river. She saw the tears in my eyes and my angry stare. Standing on the bank a few feet away from me, she pointed at the water and said, "Why don't you jump? Why don't you just jump, if you're that brave?"

The storm in my mind came to a standstill. I calmed myself. I would never do anything that would make her happy. If she wanted me dead, I wouldn't give her the satisfaction. She went away when I didn't respond.

I stood on the rock until darkness surrounded me, until all the lamps in the nearby houses were off and all the laughter and conversation had faded away. Then I made my way back to the house and slipped into my bed. The wounds on my hip burned like fire. For the first time, I felt hatred. It was running through my body, cold and clear.

THE YEAR I turned thirteen, China was like a giant dragon awakening from a long sleep. Three years earlier, Deng Xiaoping, the paramount leader of the country, had called for the reform of the Chinese economic system and the opening of Chinese markets to the West. A small portion of the Chinese people along the east coast was encouraged to get rich first, in order to bring along the rest of the country. The wind of reform blew all over this ancient country, where for thousands of years businessmen had been condemned as villains. Now businesses of all kinds sprang up like bamboo shoots after a spring rain.

Located just a hundred miles from where the Yangtze River empties into the East China Sea, the county of Wujiang, which contained hundreds of hamlets including the Shen Hamlet, was changing. Just the previous year, electricity had come to the village. Suddenly, the peasants seemed to have woken from a deep sleep and turned into restless animals locked up in cages. Everybody was trying to find their way out, looking for opportunities to make money. Township enterprise and specialized households emerged overnight.

The Villages Committee set up a big textile factory next to the Shen Hamlet, and the party secretary, Beiling, maneuvered his way into the job of director. He could hire anyone he liked, and right away everyone in the Shen Hamlet fought to lick his family's boots to get a job. They did it in secret, of course. No one wanted to be thought of as a shameless toady.

As the villagers made more money, two-story cement houses started to go up all around the hamlet. Crammed between them, our small one-story house became a place where the sun didn't shine. Spring and I were told to stay at home because we didn't have the face—the status, the prestige—to go out and see people. Our mother was embarrassed because we couldn't afford a two-story house.

But the door couldn't shut out the world. Once or twice every summer, my mother would go to the nearby canal and trade a little rice to the men on the boats for some watermelon, one of our few luxury goods. One day an old woman from the village peeked through a crack in our door and saw Spring gnawing a watermelon almost to its rind. Immediately, the entire hamlet knew—our family was so dirt-poor that the kids ate melon rinds!

"Why is that old woman with one foot in the grave so nosy?" my mother shouted, angry and ashamed. "But we aren't going to go and beg that son of a bitch Beiling. That bastard is nothing but trash," she told my father.

Overhearing this, for the first time in my life I looked at my mother with admiration. Yes, we were poor, but it was still beneath our dignity to beg Beiling to take care of us.

Since I was little, I had stayed away from Beiling and his family because we belonged to two different worlds. They threw out rotten meat every day while we survived on soy sauce and rice for months; they waved their hands and hundreds responded, but nobody would care if we starved to death. Beiling was said to have slept with every woman under his power, and his illegitimate children were as many as the stars on a clear night. No woman had ever stood up to Beiling. Instead they swallowed their knocked-out teeth because if Beiling was pleased, he could help your family to rise up to the heavens. If he wasn't, he'd knock you down to hell.

It seemed that Beiling liked me when I was a little girl. In the evenings when he strolled through the hamlet with his hands behind his back, he would peek through our half-open back door and give me a glance before quickly walking on. Immediately I would move away and hide myself in the bedroom, as if he were the god of plague. If he ran into me on the asphalt road in front of the hamlet and nobody was around, he would stop me and try to strike up a conversation. His triangular eyes would smile at me, and I would feel scared and sick, my clenched fists shaking slightly at my sides. I would lower my head and run away as fast as I could.

Inside our small, moldy house, my mother kept grumbling to my father, her punching bag, about not being able to afford a two-story house. My father responded with silence, his head and shoulders drooped. My mother's desperation escalated day by day, until she couldn't do anything else but wail and weep.

"Why can't you do some business or do anything? Why are you so useless?" I heard her moaning to my father one night after Spring and I had gone to bed. She banged the table occasionally with her fist.

My father's muffled voice eventually emerged. "I don't know how to do business. I just can't. I only know how to care for the rice fields, and we don't know anybody who would help us." He paused for a moment and then spoke more forcefully. "Even if you hound me to death, it's no use."

My mother cried even louder. "You bastard, during these many years we've been married, have you ever bought me anything? *Anything?* Even a pair of socks? I have injuries and aches all over my body. Have you ever opened your mouth once and asked me, 'Are you okay?' O, Buddha, what wrong did I do in my last life that you put me in this lousy family, gave me to this lousy man?" I heard her storm into the bedroom, stuff some clothes into a cloth sack, and then go out the front door, crying. Spring and I sat up in our bed nervously. I knew she was stumbling to the bus station in Zhenze, hoping to get on a bus that would take her to a better place. She had done this before.

"Don't you know better?" my father roared at us. "Get up and follow her!" I got out of the bed, put on my shoes in a hurry, and charged out the door.

I trailed my mother all the way to the old, shabby bus station where the lime walls were graffitied with chalk. It was closed, of course. A street lamp illuminated the big iron lock on the gate. I realized then that my mother wasn't going anywhere; she sat on the cement block under the lamp outside the station and started to weep again.

Gingerly, I moved closer to her and stood beside her. Her wailing made me want to cry too. I just couldn't understand why life was always so hard. Exhausted, she finally stopped weeping. She turned to me and said weakly, "Let's go home."

We dragged our feet back to the house. My father was lying on my parents' bed, facing the wall, as still as a dead man. That night I dreamed of coming back to the hamlet one day with thousands of yuan in my pocket and making my parents cry with joy. Now we had enough money. Now they wouldn't fight any more, and we'd have a happy family from then on. I smiled in my sleep.

Around the time I started junior high, a visitor came and stirred the Shen Hamlet. His name was Honor, and he lived in the nearby Lao Hamlet. He had been a young man when he was discharged by the People's Liberation Army, and it was said that when he arrived home, he found that his eccentric widow mother had already arranged a wife for him, a woman who was not quite right in the head, who meant to say "fuck your mother" but always ended up saying "fuck my mother." Now they had a fourteen-year-old girl and a twelve-year-old boy, and this woman still hadn't learned how to cook stir-fried cabbage or iron Honor's pants.

Honor had recently made a fortune buying tons of cheap raw cocoon silk from the poorer areas north of the Yangtze River and selling them to the textile factories near the Shen Hamlet. His newly built two-story house on the other side of the river had glazed tiles and was enclosed by a magnificent wall. The house faced Beiling's villa almost directly.

The people in the Shen Hamlet welcomed him with huge, sincere smiles. When Honor pulled a stack of dazzling new bills out of his wrinkled suit pocket and started to hand them out as if they were worth no more than toilet paper, the crowd cheered. Their eyes twinkled like the eyes of owls in the night as they chased after the flying bills.

Eventually, Honor came to our door.

My mother often worked the overnight shifts in the tiny textile factory the village had recently built, but she was home that night. Honor sat down next to me at the table in the central room and said hi. I gave him a polite smile and continued to do my homework. My mother put a cup of tea in front of him and sat beside him. He grasped the teacup with both hands.

"My old comrade-in-arms, now a factory owner, is very generous and gives me as much raw silk as I want," Honor said, beaming.

"Wow," my mother sighed. In the light of the kerosene lamp, I saw her blush.

Honor then reached over to Spring, who was sitting on a small stool, and put her on his lap. He pulled out a ten-yuan bill from his pants pocket and squeezed it into her hand.

Honor started to come almost every night when my mother was at home. He usually stayed for dinner. The big grass carps or bundles of lean pork he brought with him always made my mother smile. The expensive cigarettes he offered softened my father's taut face. After dinner, my father, Spring, and I would go to bed and my mother would stay up with Honor in the central room. From the bedroom, I listened to their low laughter as the light from the kerosene lamp danced on the wall

One day a couple of months after Honor started to visit, I came home from school and my mother was gone. I didn't see her the next day either. On the third day, I had to ask. "Dad, where is Mama?" I said.

"She's on a business trip," he told me casually. "Her textile factory gave out bolts of cloth as salaries, so she's gone with Honor north of the Yangtze River. The market for cloth is said to be better there."

I didn't say anything, wondering how my father, who cared about his reputation more than his life, could be so calm when he told me that his wife was on a business trip with another man. This was unheard of in the countryside.

My mother returned ten days later, looking radiant. She wore a new blue silk blouse decorated with small white patterns, like the clouds in the sky. We happily sucked at the litchi nuts she brought back, a precious fruit that was produced only in the South, which in ancient times had been shipped three thousand miles on horseback to Beijing to make the Tang Emperor's most beautiful concubine smile. Later, Spring, still the apple of our mother's eye, showed me a picture of our mother walking from a boat onto a small dock, carrying a briefcase and smiling like a real businesswoman. I looked at the picture for a while and felt confused about what was going on with my mother. I noticed a flashy silver watch on her wrist in the picture, but I didn't ask Spring why she wasn't wearing it now.

My mother went on many trips with Honor. Whenever the villagers asked, "So, your mother is on a . . . business trip?" I would say "Uh-huh" and walk away.

While she was not around, our house became light, as if it was made of paper. When my father and I had to talk, he would stutter and flush, and I would never waste one extra word. We secretly wished that my mother would come back soon.

Finally, in October 1989, when I was fifteen, floor slabs and cement were purchased; the builders were contracted; and we were ready to build a two-story house in the front of the hamlet. Honor, infinitely resourceful, had obtained the many red stamps from the Villages Committee required for us to use a new piece of land.

It was clear to everyone in the hamlet that we never could have paid for the house without Honor's help. The villagers started to refer to my mother as a "pussy-seller" and my father a "wife-seller." Whenever I walked by the Big Poplar Tree, people would give me strange smiles. Hearing their ear-piercing laughter, I would keep my head as low as possible and wish there was a hole in the ground where I could hide. There was no bigger shame in the whole world than having your mother called a whore.

We moved into the house about a month after the building began. There were three rooms on each floor and a kitchen attached to the first floor in front of the building. It had cement floors and pure white lime walls. The stairs were wide and strong, just as we had always wished.

The bedrooms were upstairs. Spring and I took the center

room. My father moved my parents' old bed into the east room, away from the stairs. My mother put a new bed in the west room, where the stairs led directly.

My parents slept on separate beds in separate rooms for the next ten years.

Nobody talked to each other in the new house for months. It was like a thousand-year-old tomb. Spring seemed to have changed overnight, becoming like me, sad and quiet.

I lived my days and nights like a walking corpse, drifting silently from place to place. I sat in the classroom, listening to the sounds of my internal organs. The teacher's voice became vague background noise wafting in from far away.

One afternoon, my form teacher called me into her office with a stern expression on her thickly powdered face. I knew why. I had scored badly on the last mock college entrance examination.

Sure enough, she struck her desk with her palm, pointed her finger at me, and began scolding, pausing dramatically between each sentence. "Did you see how you scored on the exam? What the hell's happened to you? Do you want to go back to the paddies and plant shoots? If you keep going like this, forget about college."

On the bike ride home, I started thinking seriously about my education, which I had been neglecting. Words like "career" and "ambition" rarely entered my mind. They were too abstract and modern. I was only a fifteen-year-old peasant girl; I had never had many extravagant wishes. Every morning when I woke up, my only desire was that it would be a peaceful day and that my mother and father wouldn't fight. But at this moment I began to think about my future. I knew that I didn't want to marry a peasant in one of the local villages and work in the rice paddies my whole life. More clearly still, I knew that I didn't want to live in my family's house even for one more day. I would do anything to get myself out of that endless hole of miseries. If going to college was the only way, then why was I letting the opportunity pass me by?

I refocused all my attention on schoolwork. Every day, I stayed in the classroom as late as possible. When the power in the town went out and my classmates whispered to each other in pairs in the flickering candlelight, I sat in the corner alone memorizing English words. The girls giggled continuously about the new wool coats they had bought, about the movie tickets some boy had just tucked into their notebooks, and about how many looks the handsome geography teacher had given them during the last class. I covered my ears. My world was too narrow for any of these luxuries. I was sure no man would ever want me. I was short, ugly, and quiet, I thought. My own parents didn't even like me. Whenever jealousy or sadness crept up in my heart, I pushed them down immediately and told myself that I wasn't born lucky or pretty like those girls. I came into this world with unfairness. But I was going to prove that I was different, and some day I would shock everybody and become the brightest star in the sky.

When he wasn't out on business trips, Honor still came to our house almost every day, despite the sneers he got from my sister and me. He always had a smile on his face and talked softly to everybody, and he started to do more and more for us. He brought food from the market every day, bought us coal and gas, did house repairs, asked me about school, gave us money for clothes, and got medicine for my mother's various ailments, snacks for Spring, and books for me. Gradually we became friendlier to him and started to expect him every evening. After dinner, sometimes I would stay at the table and listen to my mother, Honor, and Spring chat idly. I seldom looked straight into Honor's eyes. He was still the man who was ruining my family—while simultaneously supporting it—but I was growing more accustomed to the situation and sometimes I almost believed that this strange family, which had two men and one woman, was normal.

—

At the end of May 1991, two months before "Black July," when all the high-school seniors would take the national college entrance exam but only a half percent of us would squeeze across the narrow bridge to colleges and universities, my form teacher was kind enough to pay us a visit.

She told my mother that a student like me, one from a poor family and a mediocre high school, should make a teachers college my top pick. She recommended Changshu Senior Specialized College, which she said not only would waive tuition but would also give free housing and food coupons. In her cheerful description, this school sounded like cake falling from the sky. My mother nodded her head like a chicken pecking at rice. She was overwhelmed by the unexpected favor that this flashy city woman was showing to her ugly daughter.

Finally I spoke up. "Maybe I can try another teachers college a little further away too?" Changshu College was in the city of Suzhou, only an hour and half's bus ride away. I wanted to go much farther from home.

Displeasure flickered in my form teacher's heavily lined eyes. She looked like a panda. My mother gave me an angry look. "What do you know? Of course Teacher Chen knows what the best school is for you."

Just like that, my teacher and my mother decided my future. Not until years later did I learn that teachers colleges like the one they picked for me were still vocational schools. They were usually the best choice for kids from poor families because no one else was willing to be a teacher, the lowest-paid civil servant. Even worse, most teachers trained in vocational schools like mine were assigned to remote areas after graduation.

After my form teacher left, I was weighed down by anxiety. I knew that there would still be some living expenses to pay, even in a not-so-elite college, and I wasn't in the habit of discussing such things with my mother. The next evening, though, Honor told me that he would be delighted if I went to college and that there was no need to worry about anything else. I wanted to say something to him, but I couldn't bring myself to respond, not even to say thank you. He must be a noble person God has sent to help me, I thought, and I didn't understand why I was too stubborn to accept him.

Honor told me he had bought a condo right in front of my school, which I could use to study for my exams. He spoke to me very softly, as if I were a doll made of glass. I took the key from him silently.

I shut myself in the condo during the one-week study period before the exams, not caring about the classmates knocking on the windows, not caring about their laughing eyes and questions about the owner of the condo. July 1991 was unusually hot. I couldn't eat or sleep. I was restless and agitated, like a small animal before an earthquake. I stripped off all my clothes, held a book in my hand, and paced the room for the entire night, thinking of my father's sad face, my mother's sharp voice, Honor's sallow fingertips, my classmates' sly smiles, and the handsome geography teacher's eyes. Everything I could think of, I thought over twenty times. By the time I was sitting in the exam room, I had banished all my anxiety. I felt as calm as if I had just taken a tranquilizer.

At the end of August, the mailman finally handed me a letter from Changshu Senior Specialized College. My hands were shaking a little bit as I tore it open. On a small paper strip, in Song style, the most common Chinese character style, it read:

Dear Comrade Shen Juanjuan,

You have been admitted to Changshu Senior Specialized College in the English class of 1991. Please report to the school in the city of Suzhou on August 29.

Yours truly,
School Admission Office

Enormous happiness shot through my chest. For a few seconds I could barely breathe. My mother and father would finally see my worth.

I walked into the kitchen. "I got in!" I announced.

Spring jumped up from the small stool she was sitting on and rushed toward me, pleasantly surprised. "Really, Jiejie?" she shouted, using the term for older sister. My mother turned from the stove, a big smile on her sweaty face. My father remained expressionless at the table. Over the next few days, he only pulled up one corner of his mouth to show his good mood when people came to congratulate us.

The villagers seemed to have forgotten the scorn they had heaped on us in the past. They scattered around our kitchen, sitting or squatting, all talking at once about how truly amazing it was that two illiterate parents had produced a college daughter, how lucky I was to be the only one out of almost a hundred students to go to college, how long ago they had realized that this girl was a smart kid with a grand future. My mother nodded her head to everyone, proud and elated. She seemed to have forgotten that for the past several years she had been hiding herself in the house to get away from these people.

"I was so worried before, because she couldn't plant rice shoots," she chirped. "Now it turns out that it wasn't necessary, because she'll never have to go near the paddies." Everyone laughed and kept saying yes.

I cared about none of these things—my parents' faces, my grand future, my reputation for intelligence. The only thing I cared about was that I could finally leave the hamlet, leave this home, after nearly seventeen years of nothing but nightmares.

PART

II

ON AUGUST 29, 1991, shortly before my seventeenth birthday, I became the first person ever to leave the hamlet for college. When I got up that dawn, I didn't feel the slightest bit nostalgic. All I wanted was to get out as soon as possible.

After a fierce fight with the other passengers to get through the door, my mother and I, soaked with sweat, finally made it onto the bus. There was only one bus trip daily from Zhenze to Suzhou. It was always so crowded that some people practically hung in the air the whole trip, but my mother had thrown our luggage through a broken window to claim a spot, so now we sat on those sticky seats, awaiting departure.

At 5:59, one minute before the bus was scheduled to leave, Honor's tall, skinny figure appeared outside the window, the chubby bus driver walking contentedly behind him, a Grand Gate cigarette dangling from his lips. Under everybody's admiring eyes, Honor got in and took the passenger seat next to the driver. This spot was usually reserved by the driver for his acquaintances. He would throw you off the bus if you sat there without permission. Honor coughed once and then turned toward the back of the bus for a quick glance at us. I shrank back to avoid his eyes.

Panting heavily, the bus made its way slowly onto the asphalt road. Outside the window, rows of two-story houses surrounded by rice paddies and mulberry trees skimmed past my eyes. Everything looked so familiar. Everything I had always wished to forget was now disappearing behind me. I had thought I would be rapturous at this moment, but I felt a pang of sadness. I lowered my head, blinking back tears. Then a strong smell of industrial chemicals mixed with dried urine drifted under my nose. I reminded myself that I should be happy to say good-bye to this place, my so-called home, a place where people peed anywhere they wanted and made the earth smell like a giant latrine at the height of the summer. So what if my mother said there were a lot of bad people in the cities? I didn't see how they could be worse than the Shen Hamlet. I was excited to be going to Suzhou, a sophisticated city that people called "heaven on earth" or the "Venice of the East."

As old as China itself, Suzhou was located on the south side of the Yangtze River, a place where fish and rice were abundant. Ornately carved stone bridges spanned the many narrow rivers that crisscrossed the entire city. Low houses built on the water and surrounded by gardens were hidden at the ends of small zigzagging lanes. But what the city was really famous for was its girls, who were known for their slender figures, their large liquid eyes, and for speaking the softest dialect in the country. Even my mother, who didn't even know who our president was, was telling the fat woman who was resting half her hip on my mother's small shoulder, "Yeah, Suzhou is famous for its pretty girls."

I knew she must be in a good mood, since she was striking

up a conversation instead of rolling her eyes and elbowing the fat woman away.

I turned toward the dusty window and caught sight of my reflection—a chubby bucket-shaped body in a taut plain white shirt, a short neck, a rustic ponytail and bangs, and a pair of round glasses with brown frames that almost covered my entire face. I looked away, depressed.

The bus bumped over a crack in the asphalt road, and my mother's bare arm touched mine. Even in the scorching heat, her skin was cool and slippery, like a snake hidden in green leaves. I writhed on my seat.

She turned to me and asked softly, "What's wrong? Is the skirt too tight?"

"Nothing," I mumbled and stared resolutely out the window. It was true that the denim skirt Honor had bought me was a little too tight, but that wasn't why I had turned away. I still wasn't used to how my mother had been treating me since I had gotten into college, as if I were an ancient vase that had been buried for centuries and had suddenly been dug up by accident and found to be priceless.

An hour later, we arrived in the clamorous city of Suzhou. I looked around curiously. It was my first time in a city. Ancient buildings with ornate eaves and tiled roofs stood next to tall modern buildings with shiny windows. Poplar trees lining both sides of the cobblestone street cast leafy shadows on the rows of parked bicycles on the sidewalks and on people's faces. I followed closely behind Honor as we walked through the crowd. Dodging the endless stream of traffic, I sweated nervously.

We hopped in a rickshaw, and Honor gave the driver the college's address. After speeding through a maze of alleys, the rickshaw finally dropped us in a stone slab lane, at the end of which lay my new school.

Through the arched stone entrance, I examined my college,

my home for the next two years. There was a circular yard so small that a soccer ball kicked lightly at one end would easily reach the other. Around the yard were three cement buildings and one red brick one and three trees—two poplar and one jasmine. A person carrying a thermos in each hand was walking by the bicycle shed in front of one of the cement buildings, his head lowered. At the center of the circle was a shabby playground painted a faded yellow. This was very different from the college I had imagined. I had pictured a big green park filled with lively young students holding books in their hands, walking and chatting.

"Let's go find the dorm. Hurry!" my mother barked.

Pull back the disappointment right now, I ordered myself, and I hastened behind my mother. After all, this was my dream come true. I shouldn't be wallowing in self-pity.

At the end of a long corridor on the second floor of the dorm, we found my assigned room, number 207. It was quiet and empty, except for the four iron bunk beds standing on the mottled wooden floor and the big spiders hanging from webs in the corners.

My mother, who had the cotton padding for my bed folded into a square block on her shoulder, pushed me through the door. "Go," she said. "Grab the bed next to the window in the corner. It's the best one. Go!"

I hesitated. We were the first to arrive. Was it necessary for us to fight for a bed? It was just a bed, after all. I walked in, feeling embarrassed. I saw my name on a paper strip pasted on the iron pole of the bed my mother had pointed to. The beds were preassigned. I put my plastic bags on the bed and didn't say anything.

While we were busy making up the bed, two of my roommates arrived one after the other. A small girl with freckles all over her tiny face took the bed above me. She extended her hand to me and spoke in a resounding voice. "Hi, I am Chen Xin. Call me Jenny. It's my English name."

I liked her instantly. I shook her hand a little shyly. "I am Juanjuan. I don't have an English name yet."

As Jenny and I were getting to know each other, a gaunt girl with a loose ponytail came in and took the bunk bed across from me. She smiled and introduced herself as Kate. From the innocent smile on her flat face, I could tell right away that she was an easygoing person, someone who didn't always think before speaking. Blinking her long eyelashes, she asked me curiously, "Is that your father? You two don't look alike."

I knew she meant Honor, who was busy putting my belongings away: thermos behind the door, toothbrush on the table, slippers under the bed. Pretending that I hadn't heard her question, I quickly looked away from her and turned my back to her, because I didn't know how to answer. For a moment, I wished that this man in a tidy, dark gray suit, who now, with one knee on the bed, was hammering a small nail into the wall for me to hang my clothes on, *was* my father. For years, my real father hadn't moved a finger for me. My heart twisted when I forced myself to admit it, but Honor, a man whose face I had imagined punching to bits millions of times, had been taking care of me like a father. At this thought, guilt leapt up in my chest. *No, he is not your father!* a sharp voice inside admonished me. *Not only is he not your father; he ruined your family. Don't ever forget it.*

Without straightening her arched back, my mother casually answered Kate while making the bed. "Oh, he's her uncle."

I stood there, relieved, but also feeling a little disconsolate.

After putting a string bag of apples next to my pillow and squeezing a hundred-yuan bill into my hand, Honor urged me to be a good student and then left to catch a train north for a business trip. As usual, staring at his slightly bent back moving toward the door, I bit my lips, wanting to say something nice but remaining silent. After he left, my mother finished unpacking my luggage and straightening up while I stood around curiously checking out my roommates. She wanted to take the bus home as soon as she was finished. I agreed to accompany her to the station.

I watched her standing in line at the bus terminal. She turned her head and looked at me as she shoved the tall middle-aged man who was pressed up behind her. I heard her worried voice yelling for me to be careful.

I clutched the rusty railing and cried out, "Mama!"

She turned around again. I saw that her eyes were filled with tears. She glowered at me as if she were angry that I had made her cry, and then she disappeared into the vast space behind the wooden gate where the buses waited. It felt like I would never see her again. I started to cry.

—

The jasmine tree outside the classroom on the second floor of the red brick building was blossoming that autumn as I started my college life. The sweet, refreshing smell filled me with hope for the future. I had become one of God's superior children—a college student. The government now guaranteed me a job for the rest of my life.

But the education we received was far worse than I had expected. We didn't have the freedom to choose our subjects. Instead they were imposed upon us: English Reading, Listening Ability, Oral English, Chinese Literature, History of the Chinese Communist Party, Moral Principles, and Methods of Teaching. We went to the same classes every day in the same classroom, and two years later we would be assigned by the government to remote locations in all different counties as junior high school English teachers.

Still, I never felt like joining in when the other students complained about having wound up there instead of at a normal four-year college. I told myself that since I was there already, I should accept it and try to do as well as I could. In fact, grades were the only thing I cared about, the only way I had of distinguishing myself from others. Here the teachers didn't announce the students' grades out loud in class as they had in my old school, but you always heard about other people's scores through the grapevine. I was only happy if I was one of the top three in the class and was secretly jealous of the students who got better grades. I was perhaps the only person in the class who was so competitive. Most students stopped studying as soon as they entered college, because they would have jobs no matter how poor their grades were, but I was used to competing with others. Life was a war to me.

The seven girls in Room 207 got along well. Coincidentally, we were all from poor peasant families in the surrounding counties. We elected the conscientious and perpetually energetic Jenny as class monitor. We joked that she was what Chairman Mao had described as the sun around eight or nine o'clock in the morning—the hope of China. Fish, a tall girl with a fleshy body and a freewheeling personality, became my closest friend. She called me Tiger, my birth animal, and soon everyone else did too. Though I wasn't sure whether deep down I was really ferocious like a tiger, I accepted it happily.

Every night at nine o'clock, after everyone came back from the required evening solo study sessions, the lights in the dorms were shut off. In the dark, the girls in Room 207 didn't talk much. Instead, we lay inside our mosquito nets and listened to the girls in Room 208 across the hall chatter loudly about the boys in our class. Being an English teacher was widely thought to be too feminine for men, so there were only seven boys in our class of thirty. They all shared a room downstairs. Thus these guys, whether handsome or ugly, became the pandas in the zoo, seven national treasures for the girls in the class to scramble for. The girls in Room 208 were way ahead of us in getting their attention. They came from small towns instead of peasant hamlets like us. They wore lipstick and high heels and walked like willows swaying in the breeze. Bubbling with enthusiasm, they quickly became friends with the boys and fiercely guarded them from other girls. We sneered at the vapid 208 girls and seldom talked to any of the guys.

Never thinking a man would fall for me, I came and went from the classroom like a quiet cat, sitting in my seat with a stiff back and listening to the jarring flirting and laughter of the other boys and girls.

But one day when I walked into the classroom, a boy named Chi gave me a friendly smile from his seat. I quickly avoided his eyes. Not until I had walked to my chair and sat down did I realize that my heart was beating like a drum. Why would he look at me? Standing six feet tall with two bushy brows over a pair of big eyes and a dashing long nose, he had been voted the most handsome guy in school by the 208 girls. It seemed impossible that he would deliberately pay attention to me.

I thought about Chi all through the class, not coming to my senses until Professor Fan gave me an unsatisfied look. I was usually the one who timidly gave him the correct Chinese meaning every time he threw out an English word, a skill for which my classmates hated me. During breaks, much to my embarrassment, fat Professor Fan would sit next to me and show me the *Time* magazine his broadcaster daughter had sent him from the United States. He told me I should go study in America, because it was so much nicer there that even the moon was rounder and brighter than the one in China. I would nod my head to him cordially, but deep down I would laugh to myself.

Professor Fan was so naïve. America, the real heaven on earth, was impossible for a peasant girl like me to even dream about.

After class, I walked outside to the corridor, leaned over the cement railing, and tried to cool down. I needed to stop thinking about Chi. Probably the look had meant nothing. Snowflakes were falling thickly. It had been a long time since we had had such a heavy snow. The first red blossom of the newly planted winter plum was gorgeous against the white. There was an old Chinese saying: a snow year, a rich year. My father will be happy with the good harvest, I thought.

Chi came outside too, followed by two girls from Room 208. The girls grabbed the snow piled up on the railing and started to throw snowballs at each other, laughing hysterically. I walked farther away from them. I was trying to push away the unexpected homesickness that was engulfing me.

A hand appeared under my nose, a candy wrapped in colorful plastic lying in the palm. "Want one?" I raised my head and saw Chi's smiling eyes under very long lashes. I took his offering and ran back to my seat without saying anything. I felt the heat of his palm on the candy.

The next day was a Saturday. One of my roommates, Jean, told me that a guy from the same county as her, Gu, and Chi had invited us to see the snow-covered Tiger Hill. I put on my best khaki coat, brought a pair of black gloves, and headed out with her.

Though usually a popular tourist destination, Tiger Hill was deserted that day. We seemed to be the only four people in that world of ice and snow. Gu and Jean wandered off. Under the black umbrella Chi was holding, we walked silently with some distance between us. I dared not look at his handsome face and his soft eyes. On the top of the hill, he reached out his hand to me. My fingers touched his. The dancing snowflakes caressed my face, and I felt like I could barely breathe.

"Why didn't you ask me out directly?" I said.

He looked at me and smiled shyly. "I don't know. I was scared. It's my first time asking a girl out."

My heart was melted by this incredibly good-looking yet bashful man. I fell in love with him. Nobody had ever looked at me so gently or spoken so sweetly to me before.

From then on, we searched for each other's shadows everywhere, in the cafeteria, the classroom, and the playground, and then we would blush and turn our heads when we found each other. In the evenings we stayed in our seats patiently in the classroom until we were the last two remaining in the candlelight. Then we sat in the dark and just gazed at each other. Sometimes he would light a cigarette and I would watch his face in the misty moonlight. We dared not stay in the classroom too late, since the school forbade dating, so we would wander together into the sleeping city night after night.

We just walked and walked, never tiring. Neither of us needed to talk. In the harsh winter wind, he wrapped the long white mohair scarf I had knitted for him around both of our necks and held me tightly. I wanted to be with him every second of every day.

Fish wasn't happy that I spent so much less time with her now.

"Tiger, now I see that you're one of those people who care about love more than friendship," she complained to me half jokingly one day while braiding my hair. I had let my hair grow, and instead of wearing a ponytail, I had Fish make small braids on the sides and wore them like a headband. I was trying my best to look decent for Chi.

"I'm sorry, Fish. But you don't know. . . ." I covered my face with my hands and moaned, "I love him so much that my heart hurts. He's my first love."

Fish rolled her eyes. "I just don't know why you love him.

He's not that special. He's so quiet and introverted. Does he have good grades? No, he has the worst. Does he play basketball well? No, he doesn't even play."

"Can't you see how handsome he is and how ordinary I am?" I said earnestly.

Fish shrugged. "Frankly, I don't think he is that good-looking. And, Tiger, you are not that ordinary-looking."

The Spring Festival of 1992 was approaching. Chi and I were a little worried because it meant that we would be apart for a month while we were on vacation. We were also anxious about being separated after graduation. One night we sat quietly against a tree trunk by a river in the city, thinking about these tough times ahead. He caressed my shoulders for a while and then finally spoke. "Don't worry," he told me. "I'll speak with my uncle. He's a powerful man, and he'll have both of us assigned to my county so we can stay together." His county was Taichang, very far away from my home county, Wujiang. According to official policy, we would be assigned to our counties of origin.

His voice sounded uncertain but soothing. I pictured my future in that strange county with him, a man I was crazy about, and I found it a little difficult to believe. It seemed unreal, like the incredibly round, bright moon hanging in the corner of the sky. But I nodded my head.

That Spring Festival was the longest but easiest one I had ever experienced. My parents' bickering became senseless noise to my ears, like the cooing of the chickens and the oinking of the pigs. The awkward dinners with Honor were easier to take. It was just like watching a ridiculous play on stage. I was calm and peaceful, although I missed Chi terribly. Spring was in junior high school by then and had grown taller than me almost overnight. She was quieter and nicer to me than she had been as a child, and she didn't mind at all when I borrowed her new coat to wear at college.

The first night of the spring semester, Chi and I spent a large portion of our monthly allowances and bought two movie tickets. We hid ourselves in the last row and kissed each other frantically for the entire movie. I had never thought that I could love someone so deeply and completely.

4

ENGROSSED IN MY love with Chi, that spring semester was the happiest time of my life. Soon it was April and starting to get warm. On his way home from a business trip, Honor visited me at college. As usual, he brought me fruits and snacks, and then he asked if I needed clothes for the warm weather. In the department store, I boldly picked a tight wool dress and some black stockings, two expensive and fashionable items I would never have thought of wearing before.

On a pleasant day the following week, I put on the dress and stockings. "Tiger, you look so pretty," my roommates said. "Did your uncle buy it for you?"

"No, I bought it myself," I said.

They had noticed the awkwardness between Honor and me long ago, and I always avoided talking about him.

A couple of guys from other classes whistled from the second floor as I walked briskly to the classroom in the spring breeze. My face flushed red instantly. I had never garnered this kind of attention before. I gathered my courage, raised my head, and looked up. I saw many faces looking down, and in the corner I saw Chi's gloomy one. My smile faded. He looked angry.

That night when we were the last ones left "studying" in the classroom, he didn't move closer to my seat like he usually did.

"Are you upset?" I walked over to him, worried.

He didn't say anything.

"What did I do wrong? Is it because of my dress? Is it too tight?" I stepped closer. Of course he didn't like seeing his girlfriend dressed so flashily in public. He was such a reserved person. I should have thought of this.

He gave a noncommittal grunt in reply. I had hit a nerve.

"Who bought you the dress?" he asked after a minute.

I hesitated for a second. "My uncle," I told him limply.

"The man who always visits with your mother?"

"Yes," I admitted. I knew he was waiting for me to tell him more, but I just couldn't open my mouth to tell him about my mother the "pussy-seller" and my father the "wife-seller." I thought he wouldn't love me as much if he knew about my shameful family.

I looked at him desperately, afraid that I would lose him. "I'm sorry, I'm sorry, I won't wear it again, I promise." I put my arms around his neck and apologized repeatedly. He sighed and then he seized me by the waist and pulled me onto his lap.

We kissed each other until his hesitant hand groped its way under the dress and touched my chest. "I looked it up in the dictionary," he murmured. "In English they're called 'nipples.'"

I wondered foggily why a guy would look that up. I was lying practically flat in his arms. His hand moved to my stomach and then paused. I saw his blushing face in the shadows of the window lattices, and his eyes were filled with eagerness, irresolution, and questions. I knew I would do anything for this man, the first person in my life to give me love. It was like a disease growing inside me that made me willing to give everything I had.

I put his hand on my knee and gave him an encouraging look. When his hand reached where it wanted to go, I felt both of our bodies tremble. His fingers on my skin were like an electric current, and a feeling of pleasure instantly spread all over. All was quiet and still except for the crickets chirping in the flower terrace downstairs and the excited panting in the English classroom on the second floor.

He unbuckled his belt and put my hand underneath his shorts on his flat stomach. I slowly slipped my hand down until I touched the center of his universe. I put my hand around it. It was hard yet smooth. It felt beautiful, just like the rest of him.

He carefully moved a few chairs out of our way, spread a layer of newspapers on the floor, and put his coat over them. The cement still felt cold under the coat. When he lay down on top of me, I held his lean body tightly. He felt strong and warm and safe. I closed my eyes, telling myself that I would never ever regret this.

He moved a few times on top of me, and then a waft of warm breath blew into my ear. "I don't know how to do this."

I moved my arm awkwardly in the air. It hit the wall below the blackboard and came back to the floor with chalk dust all over it.

"I think you need to support your body with your arms on the floor, and not entirely on me," I suggested. I didn't know anything about it either except what I'd seen when I was five and had woken up in our big bed to find my father moving on top of my mother. As soon as they noticed me, my father had giggled to my mother and then lifted the quilt over their bodies.

He tried a few times unsuccessfully, until finally he turned over, exhausted and discouraged. "It looks easy in the movies. I don't know how to do it. Forget it."

We lay still on the floor, staring at the flat tile ceiling in the dim moonlight. I wanted to tell him not to worry, but my mouth felt taped shut.

The embarrassment of that night remained between us, though we never mentioned it. Chi became quieter, but he still dominated my world. The physical intimacy made me love him even more. We went to movies whenever we could afford it and made out the entire time. I wished that he would try to make love to me, but he never attempted it again.

Gradually the differences between us surfaced, but I swallowed all my unhappy thoughts and tried my best to please him, naively thinking that the love between us would last for all eternity.

"Do you think you can learn to speak Mandarin?" I asked a couple of months later, while we were walking down the street. I was sounding him out carefully. He was the only student in the class who refused to learn Mandarin and insisted on speaking his rustic local dialect. Mandarin was our national language. Teachers were required to know it. Without saying anything, he jerked his arm away from mine and stalked off ahead of me, angry.

He didn't like to study and missed classes all the time. He thought that no matter what, he would be assigned somewhere awful after graduation, so he did as little work as possible, like most of the students. I didn't picture a different future for myself, but I was still a "good" student, obsessed with grades.

"With a cigarette after a meal, I'll be happy as a god," he always sighed contently.

"So you'll be happy being a teacher your entire life?" I asked him one day.

"I'm not ambitious like you. I'm just ordinary," he snapped, displeased. I looked at him ardently and thought to myself that a man with such a beautiful face couldn't be ordinary, no matter what he thought of himself.

I thought he was unhappy just because he didn't like college or was irritated with the hot weather. I was so head-over-heels in love that I had never ever even considered the possibility of him wanting to break up with me. I didn't see it coming at all, the humid Sunday afternoon when he asked me to meet him in the classroom. Cicadas were twittering in the poplar trees outside the classroom. After a long silence, he spat out, "Let's end it like this." I was shocked. Feeling like a knife was piercing my heart, I sat across the table and gawked at him, speechless, for a long time. His face looked thin and sallow, as if he hadn't slept for days. He wouldn't meet my eyes.

"Why? Don't you want me any more?" I felt like I had been dumped by the whole cruel world.

"No reason." He lowered his taut face.

"You said you would love me forever."

"Feelings change." He spoke lightly, but to me his words seemed heavier than a mountain. No, feelings can't change, I thought. Your love for me can't change. Can't change. It just can't.

"Tell me if I did something wrong, please."

"It's not your fault."

"Are you falling in love with another girl? Is she pretty? Of course she's prettier than me, isn't she?"

"No, I'm not. We're just not right for each other. I won't date for two years. I promise."

He sounded like a man who was just recovering from a serious illness.

I felt like I was living in hell for next several days. When Jenny reminded me to eat, I followed her to the cafeteria like a robot. She had to carry my bowl, fill it with rice and vegetables, put in front of me, and order me to eat.

But I didn't. I just rambled nonsensically to her. "Why did he break up with me? What did I do wrong?" I clutched her arm. "I want him back. Do you think I can get him back? Tell me how I can get him back."

Jenny whisked rice into her mouth, looking at me sympathetically. After she finished chewing her last mouthful, she sighed. "Look, you need to eat, and then you can go get him back."

"Whatever, Tiger," Fish interjected. "You should've dumped him anyway before he had the chance to do it to you. Now don't cry. You go find a better boyfriend and let Chi cry."

I barely heard any of their words. For me, it was the end of the world.

I still went to classes every day the week after the breakup, but Chi was never there. I sat through the classes silently, but on that Thursday during Listening Ability class I started to shake uncontrollably at my station while the earphones on my head played an excerpt from the BBC news. Jenny, sitting next to me, was frightened and whispered to me to go and rest; she wouldn't put my name on the absent list.

I staggered to the deathly quiet dorm building. I paced the corridor on the first floor, staring at the unlatched door of the guys' room, behind which I knew Chi must be hiding. Eventually I ran wildly upstairs to Room 207 and slammed the door behind me. I marched back and forth in the room like a mad soldier. I lifted the thermos and started to pour hot water into one of the aluminum cups on the table. Then I put it back down and squatted on the floor, sobbing to myself hoarsely. I knew I needed to do something to ease this pain, so enormous that I couldn't handle it. I lifted the thermos again and poured the boiling water on to my wrist. Soon the skin turned red, and magically the roaring pain inside me started to vanish.

There were bubbles all over my wrist when I sat down next to Fish in the cafeteria for lunch. I smiled with bloodshot eyes and said that I was so stupid for having burned myself while pouring water. She gave me a penetrating look and then she said casually while placing some rice in my bowl, "You burned yourself on purpose, didn't you?"

I forced an embarrassed smile to the concerned Room 207 girls sitting at the table. Then I concentrated on the rice bowl, not raising my face.

—

I wrote a very long letter to Chi, recalling the happy memories we had shared and begging him to give us another chance because I really would die without him. I ended this last sentence with three exclamation points.

The next day, I arranged to meet Chi that night, behind the cement moon gate next to the playground, where the gymnastic bars stood in the grass. All sorts of feelings welled up in my heart when I saw him. He looked surprisingly wan and his hair was a mess. So the breakup had not been easy on him either. Hope rose in my heart.

He played with a small rock with the tip of his foot. I asked if he had read my letter. He nodded.

After a long silence, I took a deep breath and asked him in a quivering voice, "Do you think we can have another chance?"

"I don't think so," he said simply.

I burst into sobs. "Why are you so heartless?" I shrieked.

I had brought all the letters and pictures we had given each other, and now I tore them apart and hurled the pieces at him. He dropped his head and stood still in the moonlight, looking helpless.

Finally, I realized that it was over.

I will never love again, I swore to myself as I ran back to the dorm. Love was all lies and betrayal.

For my remaining year at college, I lived like a shoddy actress, putting on a bad show for Chi, my only imagined audience. My sole goal was to prove to him that I could live very well without him and that in giving me up he had made the biggest mistake of his life. I hid the scorching pain inside myself and wore a happy face in front of people. I searched constantly for things to do, not allowing myself to be free for one minute.

I bought a small blue violin, and every afternoon I biked to lessons, even though I didn't know how to read music. I took Japanese lessons every night for three months and then in the next month forgot all the syllables I had learned. I joined the basketball team, even though all I could manage to do was push and shove people without any respect to the rules. I took dancing lessons, and I took the bus every weekend to Suzhou University with Fish, the only girl in our room who dared to dance with strangers and have fun. I would sit nervously on a bench in the big sweaty-smelling dance hall packed with people, praying some guy would ask me to dance with him, but at the end of the night I always realized that nobody could compare to Chi.

I hung out with the boys from Suzhou University, pretending that I wanted to help their relatives with English or that I was there to learn kung fu, and I often found myself in their playground at the crack of dawn, flirting with some guy. Muddle-headed and driven by a relentless anger, I let a couple of lusty guys touch me, never paying attention until my underwear was pulled down to my knees.

I failed the Moral Principles class. I had never gotten a score below 90 before. I couldn't help grinning to myself. Did this mean that now I was a person without morals? Even if it did, so what? Good morals wouldn't bring Chi back to me. Good morals couldn't decide which school I would be assigned to the next summer. Good morals could not change my fate to be an English teacher working for minimum wage until the day I retired. I had been born to a peasant family without any powerful friends or relatives. I was doomed to be assigned to the most remote school with the worst academic reputation.

Everyone in our English class dreamed of becoming a travel guide or a secretary or an interpreter in a joint-venture company instead of a teacher. I thought if I found a job like this, I wouldn't have to become a teacher. This would be the best proof to Chi that he had been an idiot to have left me. At that point, I didn't even care whether it was a governmental job with benefits or a job in the private sector that offered no guarantees at all.

Graduation was only a few months away, so on afternoons after classes ended, I started to wander among the octagonal pavilions and tall pagodas in Suzhou's ancient gardens, striking up conversations with tourists with blond hair and blue eyes. My broken and heavily accented English often scared away those foreigners with cameras hanging around their necks, but not always. Some tourists were nice and gladly spoke with me. I could never forget a kind old couple from California named Erica and Peter. Erica sat with me on the rocks facing the lotus flowers in a pond, and we talked for a long time. For many years afterward, no matter where I drifted, her letters from the other side of the Pacific Ocean would always reach me when I needed a kind word the most.

On weekends, I trudged along by myself in the suburbs, holding the classifieds and knocking on the doors of any joint-venture company I could find. They all looked the same—spacious factory buildings, machines roaring, workers in uniforms pushing huge carts, and the human resource ladies in suits, with cold faces, telling me that they didn't need any workers without a bachelor's degree. I was graduating with an associate's degree.

Spring was a season of drizzles in Suzhou. When I dragged my feet out of those factory gates, my hair was always wet and the road in front of me was always muddy. When I got back to the dorm, I couldn't always just collapse on my bed as I wished, because sometimes my mother would be sitting on it. She or Honor or both of them visited me once every month, a painful ritual. The happiness brought by the food and clothes she gave me quickly passed, and then for the next hour I'd sit next to her, listening to her babbling about my father's stupidity. "He's just like a bead on an abacus—never do anything unless you move it. And he still allows his mother, that old dying witch, to spread rumors about us. Sometimes I hate him so much that I just want to chop him up with a knife. . . ."

I would stare at my mother's tears quietly and imagine putting my hands around her neck and choking her just to get her to shut up. I realized that no matter how far away I got from the village, I would never be able to escape my mother's crying and moaning, and I felt desperate at this realization. But I pressed down my agony and let her vent. As I grew older, it seemed that my mother had gradually begun treating me as a crutch. I didn't want to hurt her by refusing this role, though God knows how hard it often was for me. She was the most difficult problem in the world. No matter how good I was at math, I couldn't solve it. Sometimes I wished that I could just point my finger at her, my father, and Honor and magically turn them into three small, quiet clay figures.

After she left, I'd look at the food resting on the table, duck my head under the covers, and cry.

July 1993 arrived, the month of graduation. Everyone became moody, busy with packing, yelling at each other impatiently.

Once in a while, you would hear a girl who had just broken up with her boyfriend running and screeching in the halls.

In the classroom, people passed around memento books in which you were supposed to leave your contact address, the most handsome signature you could write, and a few sentimental sentences. I signed every book mechanically, and occasionally picked the biggest blank space on the page and jotted down things like "May you have a big and fat son very soon!" I felt like a bored movie star. I hadn't bothered to pass around a memento book of my own. I thought it was all so superficial, until I saw Chi's name on the cover of one blue book. Suddenly the pages felt burning-hot. I couldn't believe he was so mellow and happy that he was passing around a stupid memento book while I was still tortured day and night by my unending love for him.

I passed the book along without signing it. I was certain I would never get over him. I had dreamed many times that he had come back to me, saying he loved me, and I kept dreaming it for many years. Although his face gradually became blurry, he had become a secret buried in my heart, an icon carved into my bones.

On the day I was scheduled to move out of the dorm, Honor and my mother came to Suzhou to try to solicit help from some potential backers to get me a decent job assignment. We squatted in the shadow of a tree, waiting for my Small Uncle. One of his former battle companions was a doctor in a big hospital in Suzhou who might be able to introduce us to some powerful people in the educational system. Small Uncle had promised my mother that he would come and help.

But he never showed up. In the end, he had decided not to face the heat and the unpleasant task of begging people. The three of us squatted there for hours, and by the end of the day we were sunburned and looked like three red lobsters. Disappointed, we went back to the hamlet.

Throughout August, Honor and I, bearing cases of popular nourishment drinks, visited all the teachers and clerks he knew in the Educational Bureau. Bowing and scraping, we grinned broadly at those reluctant stern faces and begged them to help to assign me to a good school in a good location. My smiles gradually became stiff as I realized that all our efforts were going to be for naught. Without a few stacks of money to give the top leaders in the Education Bureau, my fate was entirely at the mercy of others.

As expected, at the end of August, while I was sitting listlessly on the side of the asphalt road, watching the local police bullying the passing cars, the mailman handed me my job assignment letter. I walked back home and started to pack, trying to turn a deaf ear to my mother's histrionics. "Oh lord, why is she assigned to such a place? Why is he such a useless father?"

The next day, I reported to Hope Middle School. It was located in the town of Ba Jin, in the opposite end of Wujiang County. It was such a poor place that the birds were said to be unwilling to shit on it.

"THIS IS WHERE the middle school assigns you to live, Teacher Shen."

"Thank you." I smiled to Ms. Xu, a woman of about fifty, originally from Shanghai, who was now one of the leaders of the middle school.

I moved my eyes from her big golden front tooth to where her long fingernail was pointing. Her loud, scratchy voice echoed in the vast classroom, which looked like it had been abandoned for years. There was nothing but a wooden bed standing in one corner and a dilapidated table that had once been a school desk. Now half of one of its legs was missing.

"Little Shen, don't hesitate to talk to me if you have any questions. All right?" Ms. Xu laughed heartily. Her high-heeled leather shoes clicked out the door, which had been pieced together from several rotten, mossy planks.

I looked at my classroom-dorm and let out a deep sigh. How was I going to make a home out of this huge, empty square box? I stood there for a while until finally I thought, I need to deal with this.

I took out the broom my mother had squeezed into my luggage and started to sweep the floor. I wouldn't have expected so much dry dirt on a cement floor. After a few strokes, I was almost choked by the clouds of dust. I ran downstairs to a rock sticking out of the river behind the building, scooped up a bucket of water, ran back, and poured it all over the floor.

Two hours later I sat on my bed, stretching my legs and looking at the new home I had just made for myself. It was quiet at the moment, except for the ringing bells of the bicycles going in and out of the old gate next to the building. This classroom building, which had been abandoned by the school when it moved to a new location a couple years earlier, was a few minutes away from the teacher's compound where almost all of my colleagues lived. A blue mosquito net was spread above the bed; a small electric stove with wires wrapped in black tape sat on the table; and all the windows were pasted over with layers of fresh newspaper. I couldn't afford curtains. I stared up at the bulb swaying slightly in the middle of the room. It was just too bad that I couldn't reach high enough to clean it. Its long, thin wire was covered with dust and spiderwebs.

I decided to check out the town and went first to the small convenience store around the corner.

The middle-aged woman behind the counter smiled at me as she poured a handful of rice onto the scale's small aluminum plate. "Oh, you must be the new middle school English teacher!" she exclaimed. Seeing my questioning face, she explained, "My husband is the vice principal of your school."

I smiled weakly. Great, I thought. So one of my bosses would know how many kilos of rice and how many bags of salt I was buying every month.

On the sides of the town's central street, hawkers in towel

turbans were crying for customers to buy their fresh green vegetables. There were four clothing shops, one hardware shop, one barbershop, and one decent-looking restaurant. Small piles of cement or bricks or trash were scattered here and there on the ground. Compared to Zhenze, this town looked backward and undeveloped.

Thinking I should make myself look decent now that I was a teacher, I walked into the barbershop and sat down in the only chair in the shop. A dusty fan was whirring above me. With a pair of scissors in hand, the friendly barber looked at me in the mirror. "You must be the new English teacher in the middle school," he said.

I felt like I was being spied on. "How do you know?"

"Oh, I heard there was a beautiful new college grad assigned this year. This is a small town. Everybody knows." He smiled eagerly.

A beautiful girl? Me? What a liar! I thought. Nobody knew better than I did that the word "beautiful" wasn't appropriate for me.

Okay, I told myself, taking a deep breath. I was going to have to accept the fact that everyone in this town would recognize me the moment I met them. I smiled bitterly to myself at this sad reality. I had worked very hard to escape my village, and I had ended up here, in a small town where the people were just as nosy as they were in the Shen Hamlet.

"Hey, Teacher Shen, wanna have a picnic with me and my friends some day?" the barber asked.

"Oh, sure." I smiled politely to the egg-shaped face in the mirror.

While far from the teacher's compound, my new room was close to the river. With rats running around wildly, boats honking, waves lashing at my ears, and newspaper rustling, my eyes were wide open most of the night. The next morning, the first day of my teaching career, I summoned up all my courage and followed Principal Chen, an old man with a pair of presbyopic glasses and a face full of bumps and hollows, to the desk of Big Shen, the head of the English Department.

I spoke as politely and sweetly as possible to Big Shen, a stick-like, middle-aged man who was wearing both his shirt sleeves and his pants legs rolled up. "Please don't hesitate to instruct me in the future," I told him. I remembered the lecture my mother had given me before I left home about how I ought to be modest and diligent in the outside world. I knew that my future was in the hands of people like Principal Chen and Big Shen, both of whom could make changes to my personal file. If either happened to be in a bad mood one day and put down something weird in that confidential folder, which was sealed and stored somewhere secret, I would never get a promotion, never be able to move out of my dreadful living arrangements. Like the Book of Life and Death in which the god Yama inscribes your fate, you would never see this folder, which the government kept for every person—but it controlled your future.

"Oh, don't worry," Big Shen said. "There is really not much to learn. Just prepare your lessons well, and—"

Without finishing his sentence, he dashed out of the office, jumped over the waist-high cement fence, ran to the nearby path, pulled a boy off his bicycle, and dragged the screaming boy into the office. He did this all in a matter of seconds.

"You little bastard, got a duck egg for the exam. Aren't you ashamed? I told you to copy those words a thousand times each. Where are they?" He roundly cursed the boy, who hung his head like a caught thief. He then took a ruler out from a drawer. It was the longest ruler I'd ever seen. He wouldn't really use it on the boy, I thought. It was just to scare him.

"And now you want to run away. Not so easy. Spread your palm."

Big Shen turned to me and switched to a softer tone. "Here is a lesson—forget that crap the college taught you: be nice to students; become their friends; whatever. They'll ride roughshod over you if you do that. These little brats, they won't listen to you at all if you don't show them some color."

The ruler struck the boy's palm fast and hard. I winced. I was relieved when the electric bell rang, signaling the beginning of the next class. I grabbed my notebook and a box of chalk and ran toward the classroom building.

I paused at the door of the sixth-grade classroom, where I knew there were fifty students quietly waiting for me to give them their first English lessons. My legs were shaking. At barely nineteen, I was myself still a child. How could I teach these teenagers who were only a few years younger—but often much taller and bigger—than I was? But I was a college graduate, I remembered, and I calmed myself down. I could do this.

I inched a few steps forward, took a deep breath, and entered the classroom, feeling like a soldier going into battle.

"Good morning, teacher!" All the students stood up quickly, chanting in unison, giving me a start.

"Good morning, students!" I replied, walking to the podium.

The classroom then became very quiet. I took a brief glance at them and then placed my notebook on the dusty podium. Fifty students in identical blue uniforms sat stiffly with their hands crossed behind them. Fifty pairs of eyes were fixed on my face.

My fingers turned the pages of my notebook so quickly that it almost flew out of my hand. I heard my shaking voice. "Hi, I'm your English teacher."

There was a long pause. I swallowed hard and struggled to remember the speech I had practiced a hundred times.

"And now let me tell you a story about how I made friends with an American couple and tell you why English is so fun to learn." I looked at the students occasionally while telling them how I had met Erica and Peter. All of them were listening attentively, immersed in my story. I turned to the blackboard and slowly and carefully wrote down the letters A through G.

"Read after me," I said. "A. . . ."

When I returned to the teacher's office after the lesson was over, I collapsed in my chair.

"So, how was it?" Big Shen smiled.

"Oh, God!" I sounded feeble, like a fast-leaking balloon. I couldn't believe I'd made it through my first class. I fooled those kids, I thought to myself happily.

With three or four lessons to teach to two classes of students every day, a month went by before I knew it. At the end of the month, I received my first pay: 250 yuan. On my way to visit my parents, I was quite excited thinking about what this money could buy: twelve chickens, or twenty-five bags of fertilizer, or maybe a rice cooker.

Like a good kid from the countryside, I gave my mother 230 yuan to keep for me so that I wouldn't spend it all. Proudly, she wrapped the bills in a handkerchief and put it in the bottom of a drawer, saying she would save it for me now and give it back as dowry for my wedding, which shouldn't be long from now, perhaps three or four years?

As usual, her happy face didn't last. It turned sullen again, and now the new wrinkles on her forehead and at the corners of her eyes made it look even more unpleasant. "I don't know what to do with Spring. Can't plant rice, can't raise silkworms, doesn't want to work in factory. A good-for-nothing. What is she going to do?"

Well, that's thanks to you for spoiling her all these years,

Mama, I thought. But I kept my mouth shut. She would explode with anger if I blamed Spring's problems on her.

"Do you know anybody in your town who she can learn some skills from? Like a tailor or a barber, something? Oh Lord, why can't that useless monkey do something? Why do I have to worry about everything? Why is my fate just like that cleaning towel in the drugstore, so bitter?"

I couldn't stand to hear her moans and groans. My elation over the paycheck was fading fast. "All right, I'll ask around," I said. I left in a hurry, amazed that my mother still had this magical power to turn my joy into distress.

The barber in Ba Jin, Master Liu, said yes instantly when I asked him whether he could take Spring as his apprentice. "I'll teach her everything and treat her like my own sister," he promised.

My mother would be happy that her older daughter could take care of her younger daughter now, I thought to myself that night while lying in bed. In that big room, I felt so small and insignificant. I almost liked the idea of Spring coming to live with me.

A couple of days later, Spring took the bus to Ba Jin and moved in with me, and we started our lives together without our parents for the first time. Without our mother's complaints, we lived peacefully together, though we seldom exchanged deep thoughts. Spring seemed happy with going to the barbershop every day and learning how to cut hair. Sometimes when we were lying in our bunk beds at night, Spring would tell me about something she had seen during the day. "People here talk differently from the villagers in our hamlet, Jiejie," she'd say. Or, "The women here still wear towels around their heads. They look so silly."

Listening to her giggling, I would smile in the dark. For the first time in my life, I felt that I was really Spring's older sister.

I couldn't make up for the demented childhood we'd had, but at least I could help her future a little bit. I didn't know when it had happened, but strangely I had become the strong one, and now it was Spring who needed protection.

About two months after I started teaching, I gave my students their first exam. I couldn't swallow my meal after getting the results—five zeros and twenty-one failures. What had gone wrong? Was it true that I needed to drag them by their ears or have them stay two extra hours after class and copy the words a thousand times like all the other English teachers did? There was an old saying: sticks produce filial sons; rulers make obedient students. But I didn't believe I had to be so brutal to make them listen to me. I couldn't brandish the ruler. I was only a few years older than them, and I just wanted to be their friend and develop their interest in the English language.

The second exam was another disaster, and now fully half of my students could not complete the daily task of memorization. Boys in the back seats started to hit each other during classes. Some girls were doing their math homework in my English class, because the math teacher didn't allow her students to have lunch unless they submitted their homework on time. A few times, I got so mad that I threw pieces of chalk at some boys who were whistling. That shut them up, but only for a little while.

One day when I walked into the classroom, a broom fell from the top of the door onto my head. The room erupted in laughter and then suddenly became still at the sight of my dust-covered head.

"Who did this?" I screamed, red in the face and trying very hard to hold back my tears.

Nobody answered. I felt betrayed, like a farmer who had saved a frozen snake only to have it bite him as soon as he had warmed it up on his chest.

There was a stubborn and naughty boy in the class, Feng, who believed that anyone who dared to contradict a teacher was a hero. He always stared at me provocatively during classes and sat with only one leg of his chair on the floor. I was certain he was behind this. After giving him a few useless angry looks, I lost my temper and pulled one of his ears, howling at him to get out of the classroom.

Everyone was shocked, and some girls even cried out, when his fist hit my chest with a thump. I reeled back, hearing my chest buzzing like a lute string. Too stunned to say anything, I threw the pointer to the ground and ran out of the classroom.

"I don't want to teach any more," I cried to Principal Chen like a little girl.

"How dare this little bastard hit his own teacher. It's unheard of!" Principal Chen gasped, twisting his hands, shaking his head, and looking at me sympathetically.

"I want him expelled." Knowing that I was the only college graduate in the entire English Department, I whined like a spoiled child demanding a candy.

"Yes, definitely, we should expel him." Principal Chen nodded his head.

As I sat bent over my desk that afternoon with red eyes, feeling sorry for myself, I heard a timid knock. In came a peasant woman with a towel wrapped around her head, her face dry and wrinkled like a walnut. Under my confused gaze, she slowly placed a string bag of cabbage and chopped goose meat on the floor next to my desk.

"Teacher Shen, I know the little bastard deserves to die, and you, as a teacher, have every right to have given him a lesson. He shouldn't have hit you. I'm so sorry."

As she twisted the corner of her mouth, the wrinkles on her face deepened, reminding me of the ditches in the rice fields. I realized that she was Feng's mother.

"But please don't have him expelled. That will ruin his future. Please."

Her miserable face reminded me of my own mother, an illiterate peasant woman who was used to begging everyone for everything. I forced myself to give her a smile and told her not to worry. After she left, I went to Principal Chen's office and told him that I no longer wanted to give Feng the harshest punishment.

In the end, the school gave Feng a demerit in the form of a public notice on the big blackboard next to the entrance. He kept quiet after that. So did I. I became like an old comrade who had taught for years and possessed neither passion nor ambition but only craved a quiet life. I walked with heavy steps and a drooping head for weeks.

Very soon, the sparse leaves on the few trees at the school started to fall and the cold wind from the north carried them off. I put on my sweater and biked to the school every morning. It was deep in autumn, a season that always brought out the loneliness at the bottom of my heart. My deserted classroom-dorm became even quieter and dimmer, like a place the world had completely forgotten. Spring only came to the room to sleep every night. Master Liu's parents, who lived at the back of the barbershop, liked her very much and always had her stay for dinner—also a perfect excuse to keep the shop open late.

Lying on my hard wooden bed one night, I clutched a letter from Erica in my hands, gazing at her tidy handwriting and the American-flag stamp with the wavy blue postmarks.

"Juanjuan, my dear friend, I understand your loneliness and frustration at being in a small farm school, but just remember, you have a very long way to go in front of you. Sometimes people like to be a big fish in a small pond instead of a small fish in a big pond. Ask yourself, what do you want to be? Be strong and happy, my friend." Her words comforted me, but the truth was that I didn't know the answer to her question. What did I want to be?

Master Liu didn't want to give up on his invitation for me to go on an outing with him. Feeling like I owed him, since he had taken my sister on as an apprentice, I finally agreed. But I regretted it even before our bus pulled into the big lot in front of the Grand View Garden, where the greatest novel of all time, *A Dream of Red Mansions,* was said to have taken place. His smiles and soft looks made me feel like I had come out of a pool full of eels—grimy all over. I tapped my foot rapidly on the floor and looked out the window.

"I've always wanted to make friends with a female teacher, a government worker. This is great." He yammered incessantly, walking close behind me with a huge Canon camera swaying in front of his chest like a pendulum. I kept walking fast, not caring if he kept up, eyes shifting between the road and the dried plum trees on its side.

After sightseeing, we went to dinner at a crowded restaurant in a boat floating on the artificial lake in the garden. As I stretched my chopsticks toward the fish steamed with scallion shoots, one of the men who was sharing the same table with us caught my attention; he had blue eyes and the longest nose I had ever seen. His face made me think of a horse. He was staring at the head in the brewed whole-chicken soup, which was staring back at him, and holding his chopsticks in mid-air. When he looked up, he saw me and smiled, and we struck up a conversation.

In my broken English, I told him about my frustration with being stuck in Ba Jin. "Yeah, it's not easy being in a small town. You know, companies in Shanghai need people who can speak English. You might want to poke around there." He spoke carefully and slowly to me, and I nodded my head thankfully. Master Liu pricked up his ears and looked at us curiously, trying to be involved. I didn't care to interpret for him.

The Chinese guy sitting next to him in a gray suit, an interpreter-type, shot a sideways glance at me and then another at the horse-faced man. He nudged the Westerner's arm and said, "Come on, Paul. We need to get back to the city."

He was obviously a city guy, and he looked at me like I was the plague, an impertinent girl from the countryside who still had the color of dirt on her face.

Paul was a consultant for a company called Solutions Computer Inc., and he left his business card on the table. I watched his tall back disappearing out the cabin door and then chuckled to myself. I could never imagine myself being in Shanghai, the most modern city in China. I tucked the card in my pocket, wondering if I would ever set foot in that city. It was only a two-hour bus ride away, but it seemed as far as the moon.

6

ONE EVENING WHEN I was sitting in my room alone, Ms. Xu showed up at my door smiling from ear to ear and told me that Principal Chen wanted me to join him in the JinSheng Building, the official entertainment center of the town. I readily agreed to go, eager to break the monotony of my endless days of teaching.

Deafening karaoke music being sung in a husky voice blasted my ears as soon as I pushed open the heavy wooden door of the dark ballroom in the JinSheng Building. A disco ball hanging from the center of the ceiling rotated quickly, throwing colorful patterns around the dimly lit room. I spotted Principal Chen and Ms. Xu sunk into big leather couches, along with Mayor Huang, his secretary, and another thirtyish man. On the dance floor, I saw the red-faced Vice Mayor Li and Zhang, the dean of our school, each clutching the waist of a female teacher, wobbling all over the wooden floor. It seemed that they had soaked themselves in mao-tai at dinner, and now it looked like even their toes were drunk.

"Come here, come here, Little Shen." Principal Chen stretched his arm in my direction and beckoned me with two fingers. "Mayor Huang, Boss Pan, let me introduce you to Teacher Shen, a young and competent teacher."

Mayor Huang, who walked with his hands crossed behind his back and a solemn face when inspecting our school during the day, gave me a drunken smile and patted the space on the couch next to him. I went and sat between him and the thirty-ish man, Boss Pan. I felt a little intimidated; after all, I had never been to a place crowded with powerful men like this.

Boss Pan shook my hand firmly with both of his and kept saying hello. Beaming back at his pear-shaped, pockmarked face, I wondered what role he played in this ballroom. He signaled for the waitress and ordered another glass of beer, and I realized that his presence made perfect sense: politicians always joined up with businessmen for their entertainment; otherwise, who would pay the bill? Tonight's partying would probably cost the equivalent of months of my salary.

After several rounds of dancing, Vice Mayor Li called me over to the karaoke stand and asked me to sing a love song with him. Emboldened by the alcohol, I took over the microphone and sang loudly in front of an audience for the first time my life. When there was a pause in the lyrics, I glanced at the crowd. I saw everyone watching me and listening intently and Boss Pan standing in a corner with a look of admiration in his eyes. Everyone clapped loudly after I finished, and I smiled, excited and flattered.

For the entire night, Boss Pan ran around in circles, making sure that the tea cups were always full, that the fruit kept coming, and that the music played smoothly. When he finally took my hand and glided with me onto the dance floor, it was the last song of the night. He tried to keep his stocky body, clad in a brown jacket and gray pants, an appropriate distance from mine. I was relaxed enough to listen to him talking over Vice Mayor Li's loud and hysterical rendition of "Loving Birds Going Home Together."

"Wow, you're terrific—a teacher at such a young age and a college grad too." I couldn't detect any falsity in his fervent voice. "I am glad I met you. If you need any help in the future, just ask. I know Mayor Huang well."

"Thanks," I said, flattered by this praise from a successful businessman who had good relationships with the mayors. I had learned from Ms. Xu that he owned a big welding factory in the next town and was the youngest millionaire in his business circle.

"You are an educated person, not like me. I'm a bit of a bore. I can't even read a few characters. But I have given my daughter a good name, Yu Shi. Yu is pure as jade. Shi is like a poem. What do you think?"

All of a sudden the music stopped and people surrounded us, shaking hands and saying their good-byes. Not used to social occasions like this, I didn't feel like I belonged. I ran downstairs quickly to the foggy streets outside. I walked home alone, thinking Yu Shi was a very good name for a girl and regretting that I would never have the chance to tell Boss Pan this. I found myself attracted to this ordinary-looking but charming and successful man. But it didn't matter, I thought: we would never cross paths again.

To my surprise, a week later Boss Pan called the only phone in the middle school and asked to speak to me. I ran to Principal Chen's office, not knowing who the caller was.

"Little Shen, I'm treating some business friends tonight in my town, and I am wondering if you'd be kind enough to join us. You had such a good voice and sang so well the other night."

Shocked by the boldness of this married man, I hurriedly said yes and hung up the phone. Principal Chen had been giving me curious looks. "Oh, it was an old classmate from Suzhou, just saying hi," I told him as I walked toward the door.

I sat on the stairs to my dorm that night, completely bored, wondering if the phone call was just a joke. But while I was giving free rein to my imagination, Boss Pan suddenly appeared at the bottom of the stairs, giving me a start.

"How did you get here? Bike? Your town is almost twenty kilometers away!" I blurted out, too surprised to keep my voice down. I felt happy to see him. I would have gone anywhere with him, just to escape the dreadful loneliness I was feeling.

"No, motorcycle. I parked over there and walked. I wanted to see you too badly." He came toward me, smiling broadly.

"Walk with me out of the compound. I don't want everyone to hear us," I said, always nervous about my reputation in this small backward town. Thankfully, Spring was working late at the barbershop.

Later, at his friend's karaoke club, we sat side by side on a couch and talked the entire night.

"My wife is a peasant woman, so uneducated. She can't help me with anything in my factory. I don't know what to do. I need an intelligent and pretty friend like you, someone I can talk to." He threw his head back, frustration all over his face. Believing everything he said, I nodded my head shyly and felt a rush of sympathy. I thought it was fate that Boss Pan had come into my empty life. I was so hungry for love and attention. I knew I wasn't in love, but I felt close to him.

Two weeks later, he appeared again in the dark like a ghost. With his helmet in hand, he pushed open the unlatched plank door, calling my name. I sprang up and shoved him out into the hall, shutting the door behind us before Spring, who was spreading a sheet over her bed, could see him. I had never tried very hard to be a good role model for her, but I didn't want her to see me with a married man.

Sitting on a motorcycle wedged between him and the driver, a friend of his who had a belly as big as Santa Claus's, I raised my head and enjoyed the autumn wind blowing into my face as we zoomed down the asphalt roads between fields. He drew my face toward him and kissed my cheek and my red nose. I turned around more and leaned my body against him.

"I want you," he whispered.

"I don't know. I've never done this before," I bleated.

He stopped kissing me. "Get out of here. Are you a virgin?"

"Uh-huh." I turned back around, blushing.

"No way. I don't believe you." He paused. "I don't know if I should sleep with you then. You'd probably never want to leave me if we did that. I might have to get a divorce." His arms encircled my waist again, and he laughed playfully in my ears. My heart jumped. I knew he was just joking, but suddenly I had the dim hope of having a family with him one day. It felt safe to be with him, a successful and mature man.

A month after meeting Boss Pan, I was on a bus to the city of Wujiang. He had made plans for us to spend the weekend together, he'd told me on the phone the day before.

My mind was in a whirl. There was a voice in my mind telling me to get off the bus, to stay away from this married man. But when a person is hungry enough, he'll eat poisonous berries. I thought I now understood what my mother felt like when she was on a bus to a strange city to meet Honor. People always said that daughters resembled their mothers. My whole life, I had tried to be as different from my mother as possible. I knew what I was doing was wrong, and I condemned myself, but I couldn't stop it.

Boss Pan and I spent the entire afternoon with his friends at the dining table, toasting loudly and drinking in gulps, singing karaoke and dancing and flattering each other. I was the only female drinking and dancing partner, and my head felt heavy by the time the sun went down.

Boss Pan's Santa Claus–bellied friend threw a cotton quilt into his arms and made a sly suggestion: "Why don't you two just cuddle tonight over in my storage place across the street?"

Boss Pan giggled and then laughed more playfully when he saw my reddening face. I knew what was coming, and I found myself nervously looking forward to it.

After shutting the garage door, we saw nothing in the gloomy light of the dusty room but piles of raw textile materials, a chipped desk, and a few chairs. It was not exactly romantic. Boss Pan put six chairs together in two rows facing each other, so that there was space for both of us to lie there. "Sorry, Little Shen," he said. "I'm afraid we will just have to make do with it tonight."

We lay down on the chairs with our clothes on. He wrapped his arms around me. We lay silently in the dark for a long time, and then I heard him breathing in my ear. "I don't know if I should do it," he said. "Shall we do it?" Feeling the heat from his body, a strong desire rose in me.

Before I could answer, he had already unbuckled my belt and rolled my pants down to my knees. I heard the hard wood creaking under my back as he quickly climbed on me. My backbone hurt, and I wanted him to slow down, but I was too shy to say anything. Without taking off his pants, he quickly entered me, causing a sharp pain. He wiggled a few times on top of me; before the sharp pain had faded away, he stopped and rolled off. The whole thing lasted only a couple of minutes.

Soon he started to snore. I lay in the dark, baffled, trying to figure out how I felt after losing my virginity to a married man. Sex wasn't as enjoyable as the books made it sound, I thought, disappointed. It was so quick, painful, and cold. Eventually I dozed off.

The next morning I turned over the quilt and examined it secretly while he was putting on his jacket.

"What are you doing?" He smiled at me.

"Nothing." I dropped the quilt, puzzled by my fruitless search for blood, thinking that if I lived in Old China my mother-in-law would be driving me out of the door by now. If a bride couldn't produce a cloth with bloodstains after her consummation with the groom, she brought huge shame to the family.

After that night, Boss Pan no longer called the school or showed up in the dark outside my dorm. I felt a little lost because I missed him, but I was also relieved. As each night passed, my conscience bothered me less and less. I thought I would soon forget that I was a shameless woman who had carried on with a married man.

By the time people in the school started donning heavy cotton coats for the winter, I thought my life was completely back to normal, and I could start all over and be a good person like every other teacher in the school. But then one night a mysterious pain attacked me in my sleep.

It felt like a long needle was drilling into all my internal organs. I curled into a ball. The sharp pain made goose bumps break out all over my neck. I was bleeding. Eventually, I couldn't take it for any longer. I got out of bed and went to the night-soil bucket, where I could sit, making the pinching a little softer and the bleeding easier to control. I kept moving back and forth between the bed and the night-soil bucket until finally I was completely worn out and just stayed on the bucket.

Spring woke up once in the middle of the night. "Jiejie, anything wrong?" she asked sleepily. "Nothing," I groaned, and she went back to sleep. I sat there until the dawn broke through the newspaper on the windows.

The pain boiled and simmered in me for three more days. I knew that I needed to go to a doctor immediately. I also knew that I couldn't go to the hospital nearby—the news would be all over town in ten minutes. Plus I didn't even have enough money to pay a doctor.

That Saturday morning, Spring and I went back to the Shen Hamlet. She had finished her apprenticeship at the barbershop and was going home to stay. After paying for the bus fare, I only had a few pennies in my pocket, but I didn't dare to ask my father for money. He was especially sulky and reticent that day because my mother was away with Honor.

At last, Spring broke the silence for me. She looked at me and then at our father and said, "Dad, Jiejie is sick."

Reluctantly, my father pulled thirty yuan out of his pants pocket. "Go to Zhenze hospital," he said. "Give me what's left when you come back," he added tonelessly.

On weekends there was only one doctor in the gynecology department.

After fiddling inside me with her cold instruments for a while, she had me sit on the old wooden stool next to her desk.

"Married?" she asked while writing on my medical records.

I was too embarrassed to answer. She gave me an impatient glance.

"Oh, no, but I have a fiancé," I lied.

"You must have had sexual intercourse with him, then." She looked at me with a stern face and said scornfully, "You reckless young people. You know our country advises you not to have sex before marriage."

I sat quietly, dropping my head and pressing my thumbs into each other.

"Go downstairs for a urine sample check." She tossed a small thin piece of paper onto the desk.

Waiting outside the window of the lab, I stared at the girl

doing the work on the urine samples and wondered why the doctor wanted me checked for pregnancy. It had never occurred to me that this was a possibility.

The girl handed me a small paper strip through the window. I grabbed it and saw a "+" stamped in faint blue ink. I took a deep breath. Thank God, I thought. A positive sign was always good. No pregnancy.

But after the gynecologist read the results, she looked grim. "You're pregnant. What do you want to do now?"

I froze.

"I can do the abortion for you. You're lucky; I'm the only one here today, and usually you can't get it done without a marriage certificate. It costs sixty yuan. Wanna do it?" She tried to appear indifferent, but her eager voice gave her away. She really wanted to make this side money.

"Oh, I need talk with my fiancé." Still reeling from the news, I turned on my heels and got out of that white room fast. When I reached home, I handed my father the rest of the money and told him that it had been nothing serious. He took the cash and didn't say a word.

Worried sick, I called Pan right away and asked him to meet me in an alley in his town the next day. I didn't feel at all happy to see him this time. With my hands in my coat pockets, I walked in silence beside him, trying to figure out how best to phrase my news. The bell on his bike jingled as he pushed it along the bumpy slab stones.

"So, how have you been?" he said.

"I'm pregnant." I spit out the words, feeling like the female lead in a poorly written drama.

He jumped back. "No way! This must be some sort of mix-up!" he said incredulously.

I threw the medical records at his chest and kept walking.

"Oh God," he groaned. "Are you sure it's mine?"

I stopped, turned around quickly, and glared at him. It seemed that the melodrama was being played in the most cliché way. Now the male lead was going to deny his responsibility. How ridiculous.

"It was my first time," I said and started walking again.

He forced a smile. "Oh, well, we can't prove that."

My eyes blurred. I wanted to turn around and punch him, but I just kept going, the space between us increasing. I was furious at him and even angrier with myself.

He jogged up to me. "All right, all right, let's go to Wujiang tomorrow, and I'll find a way to deal with it."

—

The next day was a Monday. After getting a leave from the school, I took the bus to Wujiang and met him at his potbellied friend's place. He talked with various friends for hours and couldn't find anybody who knew any doctor at Wujiang Hospital. I sat to the side quietly during these conversations.

A friend of a friend of someone eventually brought lunch for people in the room. After he finished eating, he stood up. "I have to go take lunch to my aunt working in the hospital too," he said.

Pan's eyes glittered. He quickly took out a cigarette, handed it to the guy, and encouraged him to sit for a couple more minutes. Then he leaned toward the man and whispered, "Hey, Brother, you think you can introduce your acquaintance in the hospital to me? Little sister has some trouble here. . . . You know. We don't have a marriage certificate."

I saw the friend smile with a knowing look. I hung my head, downcast, half-wishing I were trapped in a pigskin net being drowned. That was what they did to women like me in Old China.

On the way to the hospital, I sat on the rear seat of Pan's bike, which he pedaled with some difficulty. We didn't talk to each other at all. The bike bumped over the stones in the road, making me feel sick to my stomach. Suddenly I was scared. I didn't really want to end this small life inside of me. I held Pan's waist tight with my arms, put my head against his back, and began begging him. "Let's keep it, please. You always said you wanted a boy. Maybe this is a boy."

Continuing to pedal, he replied, "Little Shen, I want a boy, but I can't. You know the One Child Policy, and my family, the factory. It's too difficult."

His words poured over me like a bucket of ice water. I knew he was right. I didn't blame him; I blamed myself. I was nineteen, and I had been ridiculously stupid to sleep with this smooth-tongued married man.

Sitting on the waiting bench in the operating room, I stared at the over-washed white curtain in front of me, which separated the room into two sections. On the other side of this curtain, a woman was having an operation and screaming.

It reminded me of when I was younger, when the pigs we had raised during the year were butchered for Spring Festival. The butcher always came very early, at three or four in the morning, hung the pig upside down from a tree, made a small cut in its neck, and then started to blow into it through a thin bamboo tube. When the pig became swollen like a balloon, the butcher started to skin it. Its squealing was so sad and shrill that I always blocked my ears.

My mother and father would probably skin *me* alive if they knew I was here, waiting to abort the baby of a married man, I thought dryly. Maybe they wouldn't have actually gone that far, but they definitely would have beaten me.

"Shut up, will you? If you knew it was going to be so

painful, why did you do it with your husband?" I heard the
doctor say to the screaming woman.

"Sorry, doctor," the woman apologized weakly. "The birth
control loop fell out. We didn't want another child. Sorry."

I realized that anesthesia wasn't used for abortions. I swore
to myself that I would not let one scream slip out of my mouth
while I was on that table. This would be my punishment for
sleeping with Pan so recklessly. I deserved it.

A middle-aged peasant woman limped out from behind the
curtain, still groaning and grimacing. "Neeext!" a voice yelled.

Sterilizing the tools in alcohol with her back to me, the
nurse, a woman in her late twenties dressed in white overalls,
bellowed, "Here for abortion?

"Take off your pants!

"Lie on the table!

"Put your feet into the loops!

"Move your butt a little down. Down. I told you down!"
Now she was sitting next to the table, facing me.

I heard a click and then I felt warm. A bright light shone
down on me.

A cool blade touched my skin, and before I realized what she
was doing, the blade was sweeping quickly all over my most
private area.

"Jeez. You're bleeding. Why didn't you tell the doctor you
were bleeding?"

So it wasn't normal to bleed for days during pregnancy. But
how was I to know? Biology wasn't taught in school, and I had
never seen a gynecologist before in my life. And even if I had
known, how could I have mentioned this to the doctors there?
I had been smuggled into this operating room.

"Stupid country girl!"

I heard the sound of clothes rustling and someone pulling up
a chair next to the nurse. It must be the doctor, I thought. A

long iron rod was abruptly inserted into my body. The abortion had started.

The rod, an ordinary iron rod, suddenly became the whip in Satan's hand. It danced in my abdomen. My body felt like a piece of gum being chewed, twisted, split, and then blended back together, over and over again. The operating table under me kept sinking, pulling me into an enormous pitch-black hole, and I clutched the edges, wanting to yell out that the table was collapsing. I gnashed my teeth, pushing away the dizzy spells. Everything was darkening in front of my eyes. Every second seemed to stretch out forever.

I thought if the pain didn't die soon, I would die from it.

Suddenly, the rod was yanked out of my body, and the roaring beast inside me calmed down. I inhaled sharply.

I heard the doctor click her tongue and then murmur with frustration, "Hmm. . . . It's not clean yet. Still something there."

Without the slightest hesitation, the rod invaded my uterus again, scratching aimlessly and then scraping its edges and turning it over and over like food in a wok.

It was going to stop very soon, maybe the next second, so—just hold it; hold it, and hold it, I told myself.

"This girl is quite strong. She hasn't screamed yet," I heard the doctor saying to the nurse, sounding a little surprised.

"Jeez, it's not very clean yet. . . . Hmmm. . . . Should be okay." The doctor pulled the rod out of me, and then I heard her pushing away the chair and standing up.

"Done!" the nurse cried.

I pulled my pants up, crawled down from the table, fished out my shoes from under it, and left the room on trembling legs. Pan, who had waited on the bench outside, came to me and held my arm. We moved toward the hospital gate together. I saw the blurred reflection of my yellow face in the window glass, looking like a jaundice patient's, with sweat drops as big as soybeans dripping down my forehead.

Pan squeezed three thin boxes wrapped in red paper into my hands. "Here are some nourishment drinks. The doctor says they're good for you. It's supposed to make up for the blood you lost."

It was chilly. Looking out at the traffic on the street, he took sixty yuan out of his jacket pocket and squeezed the cash into my hand.

"Little Shen, I gotta go back to the factory now. You go back to the school on your own, okay?" And then he was gone.

I stood on the corner of the street alone, looking at the poplar trees with naked branches, the buses passing by with speakers blasting, people walking with their necks drawn into their coats, and I didn't know where to go. I got onto the first bus that stopped in front of me. I felt numb.

The next day I appeared in the classroom in my usual light green coat with my usual faint smiles, a diligent People's Teacher, a moral model for my students. But I knew I had changed forever.

I never told anyone that I'd had an abortion when I was nineteen, not my mother, my father, my college friends, or my colleagues, nobody. If I had told anyone, the rest of my life would have been ruined. I would be a broken shoe who would never find a husband, who would be spit at by people forever. I would have brought disgrace and sorrow to my parents, who would have cursed me and beat me. I swallowed all my pain and told myself that it had never happened, and I didn't allow myself to think about it even for one minute. Eventually, I thought, it would just blow away like flying ashes and smoldering smoke.

I WAS LIKE a hibernating animal that winter, shrinking into myself in my room and secretly licking my wounds. I rarely stepped out into the backward town, and in the middle school, where every teacher was living the same mundane life, I couldn't find anyone I could confide in. No one ever visited me. After work, I would shut my plank door and then spend most of my evening lying in bed, staring at the window and watching it getting darker and darker outside. My books were tossed all over the cement floor. Students' papers and exams were scattered about on the table. I had lost all interest in life.

I didn't understand how Boss Pan could just walk into my life and then walk away with my innocence. I had had hopes that he would love me, marry me even, and I had given him the most precious thing I had.

I often touched my abdomen and could hardly believe there had once been a life inside. It was gone so quickly, just like Pan. I felt devastated yet relieved. I knew I had never loved either of them. I didn't miss them, but I felt as if they had taken a big chunk out of me.

In the poisonous silence of those lonely nights, I saw that I was splitting into two people. By day, I was an elevated and upright teacher; but when the sun went down, I became an anguished, angry girl who just wanted to destroy everything, including herself.

The New Year came. I returned to the Shen Hamlet. My mother insisted that I go to the barbershop in Zhenze and get my hair done. You are an honored teacher now, and you should make yourself look decent and different from us country folks, she told me. I sat in the chair and let the barber put a ridiculous amount of styling gel on my hair so that it stood up on top of my head like the Eiffel Tower. I looked at myself in the mirror and then turned away.

Outside the window, garbage blew in the wind. I watched a man in a beat-up leather jacket come into the shop, bringing a gust of cold air with him. He sat down, and soon the barber's apprentice started to blow-dry his hair. The stranger prattled in a loud voice over the noise of the dryer about how he was going to motorcycle to Wujiang in the afternoon. That was thirty kilometers away, and it was freezing out. Everyone in the shop thought the idea was ridiculous, but he shrugged them off.

The stranger caught my eye a couple of times. I kept my head low and ignored him. He was not bad-looking, I noted. Suddenly a desire for revenge overtook me. Before I even realized what I was doing, I turned to him and asked, "Hey, Big Brother, mind giving me a ride? I'm going back to Ba Jin this afternoon, and I can catch a transfer bus in Wujiang."

An hour later, I was sitting on the back seat of his motorcycle, and we were speeding down the asphalt road. Nobody wanted to be on a motorcycle in January when the sharp wind cut your face. Certainly nobody wanted to be on a motorcycle driven by a stranger. But I didn't care. I moved closer to him and put my hands in his jacket pockets. The leather was cold as ice when it touched my skin, but strangely it made me smile. I didn't know what exactly I wanted. It just felt like there had been a small flame toying with my heart and nobody in the whole world cared. I was alone now, so I decided to play with it.

I took the stranger to the karaoke club where Boss Pan and I used to go. We snuggled together on the same leather couch where I had sat on many other nights, and we sang "Loving Birds Going Home Together." The thought of Pan's friend who worked at the club telling him that I was with another man made me feel triumphant. I was just a People's Teacher who couldn't risk going to Pan's factory to cry and scream. But I had my own body, the only thing that belonged to me, so why not wreck it, I told myself. I was already a broken shoe anyway.

I didn't plan the night out, but I ended up taking him to my dorm room and offering him the bunk bed above mine. There were a couple of minutes of silence after I turned off the light, and then I heard his voice wavering in the darkness: "I want to come down."

When he crawled into my bed and climbed on top of me, I didn't feel anything. He started to take off my clothes. I didn't refuse. He moved his hand around gently and slowly touched off the desire in my body. It was still painful when he penetrated me, though, and the pain didn't have time to go away before he finished off on my stomach. I frowned at the slimy fluid and wiped it away. Then I hugged him. I hadn't enjoyed myself, but I realized that this was what I needed—to be close to someone, to lie in someone's arms, even if I didn't know the person.

Yet in the morning, I felt ashamed. Thankfully, he left at

dawn, telling me he'd come back that night. As I biked to the school, I saw the bad me—the slut—scampering off the street like a frightened rat. As soon as I finished giving my lesson, I hopped back on my bike and pedaled to the local post office. I grabbed the public phone and dialed the number he had left. A clear and soft voice answered at the pager station. I told the lady hastily, "Please send 'Don't come tonight, or ever.'"

That night, I returned to my empty dorm room. I stood in the middle of the floor and couldn't stand the sight of the bed where my bad side had taken control of me. I knew I couldn't live here any more. Sooner or later, something, whether it was the deadly lonely quiet nights or my troubled thoughts, was going to drive me crazy.

The next day, I requested that the school move me to one of the brick rooms behind the abandoned classroom building, even closer to the water's edge. These rooms were so run-down and sunken into the riverbank that nobody wanted to live there except for the acidic female Teacher Wang. The school approved my request immediately.

After pulling all the weeds from the bottom of the walls and the gaps between the bricks, I stood a thin bamboo board upright in the middle of the room, separating it into two sections. My tottering desk went in the front section, and I purchased a petroleum gas stove to go with it. The rear section became my bedroom. I was happy with my new home, even though the floor was so uneven on top of the muddy ground that I could barely make my bed stable. I had to be extremely careful, walking around, to avoid turning my ankles.

Though the honking boats seemed to be sailing only an inch from my head, I slept soundly that first night, something I hadn't been able to do for a long time. In my new room, hidden from the world, I was able to breathe freely again. Nobody, neither Boss Pan nor the stranger, could find me here, and I could just hide in my cave and fight the bad me—the slut.

But I underestimated her strength. I couldn't forget the sound of karaoke, the smell of rice wine, and the flashing disco ball that Boss Pan had gotten me used to. They became especially alluring in the evenings in my dark, damp brick room by the water. Loneliness was swallowing me up like a beast. Finally one night I wandered to the only club in town. As a young unmarried teacher, I was welcomed by people and invited to sing a song for free. The applause at the end of the song intoxicated me.

I started going to the club almost every night. Though I couldn't always afford to pay for songs to sing, time flew by for me in the smoke and clamor. Boss Pan began to fade from my mind. I became familiar with the local businessmen, as well as the hoodlums who hung out in the club. I smiled to the businessmen and ignored the hoodlums, but my eyes couldn't stop chasing after them secretly, even though I knew I should have been looking for a good man, someone with whom I'd be proud to be seen in broad daylight.

A man soon caught my attention, a strange man who only appeared in the night, walking soundlessly on his heels. He had bangs that covered his temples, and he had longer fingernails than any woman I knew. His oddness entranced me. I'd hear him singing Leslie Chueng songs, all of which I knew by heart, in his rich, deep voice, and my body would tingle. No one else at the club could ever sing Chueng's songs as well or pronounce Cantonese as clearly as he did. His name was Hao. He was the son of a rich businessman, and he was known as a bad seed.

I hid in the club's shadows and watched him singing. He stood in the spotlight, with one hand clutching the microphone and another holding a burning cigarette. Once in a while, he'd turn his pudgy body and run his eyes over the audience.

I wondered if he had ever noticed me, with my short frame and massive glasses. But maybe it would be better if he didn't. After all, what could he—a man who idled away his time, paid no attention to his wife, and was sleeping with the daughter of the club owner—bring me except blue ruin and tears?

But then one night he followed me home from the club. I wasn't surprised when he came into my room, and I did nothing to stop him. He started to strip my clothes off before my fingers could touch the linen string to turn on the light. He pinned me down on the bed. My body stiffened as soon as he entered me. As he moved his hips, the bed and the four bamboo posts holding the mosquito net wobbled. He was too big for me, and his thrusts were too forceful. I felt like there was a baseball bat inside me. I clenched my fists and hissed through my teeth, wishing every pounding were the last.

"You're like a dead fish," he mumbled to me, frowning.

I forced a sorry smile. He wasn't happy with me, and I didn't want to spoil his mood. I was glad to have someone who wanted to be with me.

The bamboo creaked and he moaned loudly. Ms. Wang, the eccentric teacher who lived on the other side of the brick wall, must have heard, I thought, panicking. Tomorrow the entire town would know that I had slept with a hooligan. I would be a broken shoe forever. Finally the bed came to a standstill. The night regained its tranquility. I listened carefully, but I didn't hear a peep from next door.

Hao collapsed next to me with his mouth open, panting. I moved over and put my head on his chest. We didn't say anything for a while. Soon I began to sob. I started to tell him everything about me, the hamlet, my emotionless father, my loveless mother. I forgot that I barely knew this man, forgot my worries about being overheard, and wailed stridently. He covered my mouth with his hand, hushing me. He wrapped his arm around my shoulder and caressed me.

Gladly I became his secret mistress, or more precisely, one of his secret mistresses. He came to see me once in a while from then on, but only after dark. When I heard someone tapping on my window in the deep of the night, I would leave the bed and open the front door for him.

I tried my best to be a good mistress to him. I never asked about his whereabouts. When he visited, I lay mute in the darkness and endured the painful rituals and his complaints. I didn't mind, as long as I could sleep in his arms for the rest of the night. In the club, we pretended to be strangers. At the ends of many nights, I saw him zoom away with other girls on his motorcycle, girls who all had figures more slender and skin whiter than mine. I would walk home alone those nights, upset, but I always ordered myself to cool down and be happy that I was lucky enough just to be one of his concubines. I wasn't really sure why I was attracted to him. Maybe it was his haughty-yet-noble manner, or the way he sang like Leslie Chueng, or perhaps it was just that he was the only one in that deathly still town who was willing to listen to me.

—

I spent the time when Hao wasn't around condemning myself for my affair with him. Between this and his secret visits, a few months went by in no time. Then, one day while I was grading homework in the office, Small Uncle called and told me that Spring was in the emergency room of Suzhou No. 4 Hospital, more dead than alive.

"She rode a motorcycle into a tree." Small Uncle's voice was unusually slow. My mother, he told me, was north of the

Yangtze River, on a vacation with Honor, but she had been contacted and was rushing back.

When I reached the hospital, it was completely dark. I found my way to the patient unit. As soon as the ominous smell of sodium carbonate pervading the hallway came to my nose, my muscles tightened as I remembered my own hospital visit, which suddenly didn't seem so long ago. I stopped and took a deep breath.

I burst into sickroom number 3. I quickly glanced at each of the heads lying on the dirty pillows, searching for my sister's familiar face. I didn't see her. After thoroughly searching the other three sickrooms on the same floor, I still couldn't find her. I ran back and forth down the dimly lit hallway several times, not knowing what to do. I felt like I was losing my mind, engulfed by the clamor of the busy nurses and the sick, sobbing patients.

Finally, in the corner of sickroom number 3 farthest away from the door, I spotted my father's bent back in his old navy blue jacket. I ran toward him. On the bed he was standing next to, I saw my sister's head, swollen and covered with wounds, almost entirely unrecognizable. I put my hand over my mouth. For a minute I stood there gasping at her distorted features, and then I started crying.

As I've said, I had never liked my sister when we were growing up. She was the little witch sent to torture me. I cursed her thousands of times as a child, this evil being who had taken everything away from me. But now, at the sight of her swollen, damaged face, I felt for her as I never had before.

I fell to my knees and clutched the edge of the bed. I saw her matted hair sticking to the blood on her face. She groaned but didn't wake up.

Covered with charcoal dust, my father stood in the corner, mopping tears from the corners of his eyes with the bottom of his jacket. I couldn't believe it. My father was crying. The zombie father who had barely talked to us for ten years was actually crying.

He did have feelings after all. I don't hate you any more, Dad, I thought, no matter what you did before.

"Dad," I called him gently, with tears in my eyes.

"That son of a bitch. I'm going to kill him " He choked and couldn't continue.

So there was a man involved. I wanted to ask him who it was, but I couldn't speak either.

Soon it was midnight, and the hospital became quiet except for the sound of snores as patients fell asleep. My father and I sat on the floor in the dark, fully awake and alert. We knew the real storm was yet to come, as my mother would soon arrive on the overnight express train from the north. We didn't exchange a word, longing for and yet dreading the pounding of those familiar footsteps down the hall.

Finally the door swung open. My mother entered with a travel-worn face and wide-open, panicky eyes. She spotted us and then flew to the bed like an arrow. In the moonlight shining through the windows, she looked at Spring's face and immediately clamped her palm over her open mouth. She pivoted around and dashed back into the hall. I followed. In the corridor's pale yellow light, I saw her throwing her head back and banging it hard against the wall, trying to muffle her crying by covering her mouth. But then she gave up and let out her hoarse wails.

"Why? Why did this happen? Why did I leave her alone at home?"

The doors of the sick rooms swung open and people stuck their curious heads out to watch. My mother was shaking and crying out as if she were the one who had almost killed my sister. I wanted to step forward, put my arms around her, and cry with her, but I stayed where I was. The enormous sorrow she was feeling echoed mine, but I was also full of anger, thinking about where she had been while her daughter was nearly dying.

My father appeared quietly in the hallway with red eyes. At the sight of him, my mother started throwing out accusations. "Why did you let her out, you son of a bitch? Why didn't you keep an eye on her?"

"How could I know what she was doing? What kind of irresponsible mother are you? That son of a bitch sweet-talked her into riding the motorcycle at night," my father swore angrily.

"That son of a bitch! O Buddha, why did this happen? That fool is married and has a kid. She's only seventeen. How is she going to face the future, now that everyone knows she is a pair of broken shoes?"

They were biting at each other like two dogs again. I turned around and went back to Spring's bed. I just wanted my sister to come back to life.

To everyone's relief, two days later Spring, who at one point had been pronounced dead, twitched her puffy fingers and slowly opened her swollen eyelids.

"Don't blame Jian. He's not a bad guy," she murmured immediately to my mother.

"You knucklehead. Is this the only thing on your mind, after a near brush with death?" My mother pointed her finger at Spring and reprimanded her loudly. "Don't blame him? You idiot. He walked away with a few scratches, and so far even his soul hasn't showed up at your bed. Who is going to pay for the hospital bill? How are you going to find a husband in the future?" Her scolding slowly turned into choked whines.

Spring lay in her bed and listened to my mother's grieving quietly. Her silence absorbed all the noise and cries in the room like a sponge. You could hardly tell she was breathing.

"I don't care if his father is a tycoon or what. I'll settle accounts with him even if I have to crawl on my knees to the Villages Committee," my mother declared.

I stepped back into the corner and hid my face, dreading what was to come. I realized that Spring's accident was just the first shot of a bloody war.

Spring stayed in the hospital for almost eighty days, each one filled with my mother's tears, swearing, and scolding. Soon after my sister limped out of the hospital gate with the help of a cane into the summer's fierce heat, my mother's long battle of appeals and sobs to the cadres in the Villages Committee began. She often stopped a cadre on the road and pleaded with him to help. She cried and begged them to talk to Jian's father, who owned a factory, and to persuade him to offer us some financial compensation. The cadres always turned a deaf ear to her, since she was just an ant who dreamed of shaking a big tree.

Afterward, she would come home and sit in the cement front yard, scrubbing dirty clothes and crying and berating Spring for being such a disgrace and bringing so much shame to the family. The crying and moaning dragged on deep into the fall. One day, when the leaves were almost all on the ground, my mother finally came home with a thin stack of yuan in her hand.

It wasn't just the money; it was the principle, she said. But for this thin stack of bills, she had shed so many tears, knelt down to the cadres so many times, and endured countless insults and so much ridicule. Life was so unfair to us because we were poor, lowly, and powerless. There was no such thing as justice.

Spring's body was still swollen like a balloon, and her face was so puffy that her eyes were almost hidden. I hoped that the memory of the pain and numbness in her limbs was carved into her bones and would stop her from doing anything foolish again.

—

Bad things always come in pairs. The secret relationship between Hao and me was finally brought to the surface by Ms. Xu, who was in charge of every aspect of the lives of the female teachers at the school. There is not a wall in the world that air doesn't leak through, people say. Apparently my activities were now fodder for gossip.

On a hot day in the summer, she stopped my bike as I was on my way home. She chatted with me, smiling, as we walked together, and I nodded to her occasionally.

Out of the blue, Ms. Xu said, "Little Shen, I heard a rumor that you are very close to a scoundrel in the town called Hao. Of course, I said this couldn't be true, right?" She looked at my eyes, trying to sound me out. "You are a young, prosperous teacher. He's married and a good-for-nothing. It's not possible that you two could be together."

I looked at her unflinchingly and laughed. "God, why do people make these things up? I've only met him a couple of times at the club."

She kept looking at me expectantly. I raised my head and continued, trying to sound as sincere as possible: "How could that be possible? What am I, stupid? Wreck my future for such a rascal?"

Her over-powdered cheeks relaxed. "Good, good, Little Shen. I know you're a good girl and wouldn't make any political mistakes. Of course you know how important your reputation is for your future."

Hao came that night, and I told him about my encounter with Ms. Xu. He listened quietly, taking a drag from his cigarette occasionally. While exhaling the smoke through his full lips, he said cheerfully, "No worries. I'm leaving for Shanghai soon anyway. My father is building a new factory there, and I am going to be the manager."

"Oh, really?" I squeezed out a smile. "Congratulations!" I added flatly.

He doesn't appear at all sad about leaving me, I thought bitterly. But then, what was I? I was just one of his mistresses. I should have expected this the minute he barged into my life. By now I should be used to men coming and going, I told myself, and I put on my happy face.

I didn't see him again until the end of August, when he and a group of friends came to the town's newly opened pub, where I was working as a cashier during the summer. I sat behind the cash register in the dusky light and stealthily watched the box with tall chairs and chiffon curtains where Hao was holding a girl in his arms and enjoying himself with his friends. My mood was as dark as the corner where I hid myself.

Just that day, Principal Chen had warned me: "I heard you are working at the pub. They don't need you to collect money. Good people in the town never go there; only hoodlums hang around there. You are a teacher, a model to our future generations. You should pay more attention to the impression you make in public."

I knew that he was right. Just half an hour earlier, a hoodlum had caught me and grabbed my chest. I didn't know why I wanted to work in the pub, why I wanted to be close to hoodlums, why I wanted to be bad and why in the end I couldn't be truly bad—truly bad people didn't lash their consciences every minute of the day, as I did.

Hao was saying good-bye to his friends and promising to call them from Shanghai. He passed my cashier desk next to the door without stopping, without giving me a look or saying good-bye. He disappeared out the door.

Just like that, another man had gone in and out of my life

as carelessly and breezily as an airborne feather. I was alone again.

As if a box of bees had been set free in my chest, I fluttered around the pub for the rest of the night. My shift finally ended. I walked out of the pub feeling restless. Frogs were singing gleefully in the rice paddies that lined the road.

I spotted Gold Hill, one of Hao's best friends, sitting on his motorcycle smoking a cigarette. Hot-headed yet loyal, he was one of the town's top hoodlums. He was very different from Hao. While Hao was stocky, reticent, and mysterious, Gold Hill was athletic, dauntless, and always on a rampage. I walked up to him and asked him whether he could talk to me. He looked at me with knowing eyes and smiled. Then he threw his cigarette away, pointed at the rear seat of his motorcycle, and told me to hop on. I saw his four-fingered hand, and for a second I hesitated. I knew how he had lost his index finger. It had been lopped off by a kitchen knife during a gang fight. But I got on the motorcycle anyway. It would cool my burning heart down just to talk to him about Hao, I told myself.

The moist but dusty summer breeze blew into my face as the motorcycle streaked down the small countryside roads. The night was so serene, the wind was so free, and finally the tears I had been holding in were flowing down my cheeks. I had feelings for Hao, I realized. I had thought I didn't care any more, but I was wrong.

We stopped at a small cliff next to a rice paddy. I quickly got off and ran toward the stream under the cliff. I went into it, shuddering in the water and letting myself sink down into it, trying to extinguish the fire in my heart, not caring that I had never learned how to swim.

Gold Hill climbed down the cliff to the riverbank. He reached his hand out to me.

"I want to swim. Let me swim." I smiled sweetly at him and stepped away from his hand further into the water.

He shook his head and then sat down on the ground. He crossed his legs, shrugged, and said to me, "Why are you doing this? You know Hao doesn't care."

His words hurt. I sank myself deeper into the chilly water. "Hey, you want to see me topless?" I asked half-jokingly.

"What are you doing?" he said with a baffled smile as he watched me taking off my clothes.

Though I hadn't had a sip of alcohol that night, I felt as if I was drunk. Gold Hill waded into the water, pulled me out, and led me up the slope. I followed him like a lost child, and then, at the top of the cliff, I collapsed onto the muddy ground. I wrapped my arms around my knees and sat beneath the stars, shivering and crying.

Gold Hill sat next to me, held me in his arms, and started to kiss me. I sobbed dizzily while he caressed my body, this man who was more a hoodlum than Hao.

I took him to my room that night. We lay inside the mosquito net on my hard wooden bed, side by side. The usually talkative Gold Hill was quiet. Eventually, without saying a word, he rolled over and started to undress me. Surprisingly, despite his appearance, he was gentle and tender when he caressed me. Then he slowly entered me, and the physical pleasure brought by his movement gradually eased my pain. Afterward, I put my head on his chest, like I used to do with Hao, and closed my eyes. I didn't tell Gold Hill anything about my family. He was nobody, I told myself, just someone I had grabbed hastily to fill in the spot left empty by Hao. At this point, I didn't even care what kind of man I was with. I just wanted someone to hold on to.

Life continued as before, with only one difference—now it was Gold Hill, not Hao, who tapped on my window.

TIME PASSES QUICKLY in a small town where people don't use their calendars except to note holidays. Soon it was the summer of 1995, and I had been at the school for two years. I was only twenty-one, but I didn't feel young at all. On the contrary, I felt old and drained, like the sugarcane dregs kids dumped at the side of the road after sucking out all the juices. When the safflowers started to open their buds, in hopes of throwing off my depression, I decided to take a trip to Shanghai and to visit Paul, the horse-faced American consultant I had met at the Grand View Garden two years earlier.

I got up at dawn and crept off the school grounds. I trotted along the miry ridges, which smelled of soil and manure, criss-crossing the safflower fields and avoiding the main road leading to the bus station. Very few cadres rose this early to bike to their offices in town, but I still couldn't take the chance that one of them might see me. Nor did I want to be seen by the gossipy farmers in towel turbans on their way to market with loads of fresh vegetables on their shoulders. I didn't want my leaders to know about me going to Shanghai. "Keep your mind on your work, Little Shen," I could picture Ms. Xu advising me sternly. "It doesn't look good if people see female teachers from the middle school running around."

I took a deep breath and let the chilly morning air fill my nostrils. I sighed heavily at the sight of the rows of village houses rising up beyond the fields. Two years—it had been almost two years since I had become a teacher in this town, a position I would have to hold—and a place where I'd have to stay—until the day I died. This seemingly benign town had unleashed a devil in me. That devil had turned my world upside down, and I didn't know how to make him leave. I had allowed a married man to impregnate me. I had let Hao and now Gold Hill sleep with me. Why did I spread my legs to any man, like a whore? Surrounded by golden safflowers, I wondered why I felt so worn out from my seemingly simple teaching life. It was as if I had slipped into a river two years ago and had since been flapping in the water, struggling to get out.

Two hours later, the bus entered Shanghai, one of the largest cities in China. It dropped me off under a huge overpass and then zoomed away, leaving a tail of black exhaust. Every car and motorcycle on the road seemed to be running toward me and everyone seemed to be honking at me. The passersby all gave me strange looks—what was this scared-looking country girl doing just standing around? I felt as if I had washed up on a desert island. I stood on the sidewalk, holding the piece of paper with Paul's address on it, not knowing what to do. When the cars stopped before the painted white line in the road, I steeled my nerves and started to walk toward the bus stop across the street, praying that I had chosen the correct signal for "walk." I hadn't. Before I reached the middle of the road, I heard tires skidding and then strings of loud curses flying from car windows. "Are you looking to die, country bumpkin?" someone shouted. I stumbled across five lanes to the island in the middle of the road and took shelter there, frightened like a duck in a thunderstorm. I put my hand against a column to support myself.

I decided to do what I had seen on TV—get a taxi. I held out my arm to the flying cars. Luckily, the Shanghai taxi drivers would stop anywhere, even in the middle of a road. A red cab pulled up, causing a series of deafening honks. The cab started off again as soon as I had crawled into the passenger seat, and we soon merged into the traffic. The driver, his white-gloved hands holding the wheel steadily, didn't move his head when he asked curtly, "Where?" Panting out Paul's address, I realized this was my first time in a car. The experience would cost me a quarter of a month's salary.

Half an hour later, the cab dropped me off in a new brownstone neighborhood hidden amid trees and flowers. I found Paul's apartment on the second floor of his building. I paused for a moment, composed myself, and then knocked cautiously on the door. To my surprise, a young Chinese woman answered. Paul appeared behind her shoulder, a warm smile on his long face.

He came out and shook my hand. "Come in, come in. This is my wife, May."

"Thank you for inviting me over," I stuttered nervously to Paul and May in English.

May nodded her head politely, a grin on her thin, freckled face. I said hi to her awkwardly and didn't know where to look. I had never been good at interacting with women and was especially uncomfortable with a city woman married to an American. She was most likely superior to me in every way.

May turned around, walked to a rosewood table in the living room, sat down in a leather chair, and continued reading the book my knock had obviously taken her from. "Let me show you around," Paul said. "Let's start with the kitchen." He led me away from the living room. I followed him rigidly.

I nodded my head and smiled nervously as Paul showed me the various items in the apartment that had been shipped directly from the U.S.: the Sealy king-size mattress, the Harley-Davidson Fat Boy, the Braun coffeemaker with Starbucks coffee beans. Occasionally he would ask, "Have you heard of it before?" and I'd shake my head, embarrassed by my ignorance. Everything I saw seemed to have fallen out of an American movie.

Afterward, we sat down at the polished rosewood table and Paul brought coffee over in elegant porcelain teacups. I held my cup daintily with one hand and covered the stain on my over-washed beige cotton dress with the other. I had scrubbed the stain for a long time the night before, but the cheap soap hadn't helped much. Now the stain seemed to be growing larger and more eye-catching by the minute. I felt ill at ease in this exquisite apartment under May's casual glances.

Perhaps Paul sensed my nervousness, because soon we were in a taxi speeding through the tunnel that connected the main city with the new Pudong Development Area. The Oriental Pearl TV Tower, the world's third-tallest TV tower, had recently opened to the public, and Paul suggested taking me there for sightseeing. May sat in the passenger seat and stared out the window, completely blasé. Eager to express my appreciation, I cleared my throat and said painfully in English, "May, you are from Shanghai?"

"Oh, no, I am from San Francisco," she replied in a flat tone without turning around. My face turned red instantly with embarrassment at my obtrusive question. San Francisco, a place where the sunshine was said to be brighter than in China. How ignorant of me to assume that she was from Shanghai.

"So what do you want to do in the future, Juanjuan? I know you don't like teaching," Paul said, breaking the awkward silence.

"I don't know."

"Oh, well, don't worry. You are too young to know what you want. I don't think you'll figure that out before you turn . . . uh . . . twenty-five." He turned to May for confirmation. "Right, honey?"

May hummed in agreement.

The Oriental TV Tower was swamped with tourists. From a distance, it looked like a candy bar covered with ants. After squeezing through the crowd and fighting to get into the elevators, we reached the top of the tower.

I leaned against the railing and looked down at the city. Shanghai was under my feet. The wind blew my hair up. I wondered how seventeen million people could all fit into this small square and how everyone managed to find food and shelter. They must be different, more capable, or just fundamentally better than me, I thought.

Paul pointed out all the landmarks surrounding the tower and told me their names and histories. I nodded and once in a while tried my best to comment in my broken English. My eyes squinted in the sun and smiled at Paul, but deep down I felt at sea, like a person from the Qing Dynasty who had accidentally fallen through a time tunnel into the modern world. All these differently shaped skyscrapers were like UFOs to me.

I saw May walking gracefully in her blue denim skirt and high heels. I wished I could step forward and express my gratitude better, tell her how nice they had been to invite me, a country girl, into their home and how generous it was of them to show me around the city and even pay for the taxi and ticket into the tower. But as if there were a ring of dazzling light around her, I flinched and couldn't gather enough courage to face her educated, delicate eyes.

Paul and I gradually lost sight of each other in the flock of tourists. I moved along with the crowd, lost in contemplation. A few minutes later, I raised my head. Paul and May were walking in front of me. I saw Paul lean his head low, whispering, and then I spotted his hand on May's buttock. Quickly I averted my eyes. Foreigners were so different from Chinese people, and the city was so different from the countryside. How could a man grab a woman's butt in daylight and in public? It was unthinkable in the town in which I was living, where the public security officer might arrest a couple who kissed in public. I gazed at their backs as they moved forward. It felt strange, to see something so new and sweet and yet know it didn't belong to me.

Half an hour later, we were at TGI Friday's. A waiter in a bow tie greeted us in English more fluent than mine, and I became even more nervous. I sat with a stiff back and both hands in my lap, feeling my palms grow sweaty. The French windows with voile curtains and the soft country music didn't bring out the pleasant feelings that I imagined I should have had in such a classy Western restaurant. Why had I worn this washed-out dress and put my hair up in such a countrified ponytail? I peeked around and saw many city girls in the restaurant. They proudly displayed their milky skin in their strapless dresses and tittered to the men surrounding them. Cigarettes dangled between their fingers with polished nails. I curled my fingertips to hide my dirty nails and chastised myself for not even buying lipstick before I came to Shanghai. Teachers were not allowed to wear lipstick, but I should have known that city women wore it every day. I felt totally out of place, like a collier who had accidentally walked into a completely white room.

When the waiter brought the food Paul had ordered for me,

I froze. I stared at the rack of ribs decorated with asparagus and flowers carved out of vegetables on a big ceramic plate, the spotless white napkin, and finally the fork and the knife. I had no idea what to do with them. Everybody in the restaurant must be laughing, I thought, and I felt their eyes judging me. May looked at me quietly from across the table. Paul saw my embarrassment and gently showed me how to use the utensils.

When we finished dinner and walked out of the restaurant, Shanghai was blazing with lights. I said a quick good-bye to Paul and May and took a cab back to the bus station, pleased yet overwhelmed by my new experiences.

Shanghai became a sweet dream of mine. I knew I could never be one of the girls in TGI Friday's. My skin could never be so creamy, and I could never laugh that softly and enticingly. Yet I couldn't help but wonder: could I at least linger on the streets of Shanghai and watch those pretty girls clinking wine glasses through the windows? I would be happier to be a real beggar in Shanghai than a backroom beggar in Ba Jin. Confucius once said "Contentment brings happiness." But how could a person know when it was time to feel content? If someone had brought Confucius to Shanghai, showed him the air-conditioned buildings, and fed him delicious ribs at TGI Friday's, would he ever have been content with his old life?

Three weeks passed, and my mind still dwelled on the city. It was the end of the month, and Big Shen reminded me to go to the payroll department and draw my salary. Thinking of the little money I was about to get this month and every other month for the rest of my life, I was knocked back to reality. I couldn't go to Shanghai. I was destined to be a teacher forever. The government had paid for my education, and it was my duty to serve the people my entire life. They would never allow me to leave. Who would want to throw away an iron rice bowl, anyway? This is what secure government jobs were called. An iron rice bowl was unbreakable. You'll always have food with an iron bowl, my mother reminded me every time I went home. The rest of the family had only paper bowls that could disintegrate at any moment. She said I must have burned many cases of incense in my past life to get such a job, which would ensure me food and shelter as long as I lived.

I dragged my feet to the payroll department. Old Liu, the kindly accountant, sensed my low mood. "What's wrong, Little Shen?" he asked while counting out my stack of money on the table.

"Oh, nothing," I straightened my neck and said with a smile. Then I bent over the table and signed my signature next to my printed name in the book.

I glanced over the names on the list and noticed one I didn't recognize. Signatures were absent next to this name every month, which meant he had never picked up his salary. Curious, I asked Old Liu who this was.

"Oh, Chang? He is a teacher here, but on leave."

"What do you mean by 'on leave'? Isn't he a teacher at the school? How can he not teach?"

"He belongs to the school, but he doesn't have to teach. He can do whatever he wants, but he has to give the school a lot of money every year to keep his position. He can come back any time he wants. After all, nobody would want to give up a teaching job."

"You can do that? You can not teach but you can still come back?" I exclaimed excitedly. I could leave but still keep my iron bowl.

Old Liu threw me a knowing look and immediately started to lecture. "Little Shen, do you know who Chang is? He is the son of the richest man in this town. His father donates tons of money to the school. That's why Chang can do this. Do you see any other teacher acting like this? Nobody, not even the boldest male teacher who's been at the school for many years. Don't you even think about it, little girl. How are you going to make all this money every year? Besides, the leaders will never ever let you go." With him rattling on at my back that I should be content with what I had, I walked out of the payroll department despondently.

But I craved Shanghai like a drug. For weeks, I couldn't get it out of my mind. Everything—the smell of dust and gasoline, the car horns, the overlapping faces on the streets, and the feeling of being an ant on a vast plain—drew me to it like a magnet.

When July came, I found myself on the bus to Shanghai again.

I didn't know where I was going, so after getting off the bus I roamed the streets. With construction sites all over, the city was like a sick person in the process of a long surgery, riddled with gaping wounds. Giant cranes digging the ground grumbled day and night, and the mantles of dust they produced hung above the city like a big gray wok. People with frowning eyebrows walked by me in a hurry, but I felt happy. I raised my head and inhaled the dirty air, enjoying the brief freedom of being a total stranger in a city.

At a turn in a seemingly endless flagstone street lined with ivy-covered buildings, I stumbled upon a group of magnificent Western-style villas behind a tall Victoria arch. On the open ground near the arch, I saw two middle-aged country women chatting and four white children playing at their feet. The children looked adorable, like the dolls in movies from the West. Standing outside the guardrails, I stared curiously at them for a long time. This must be a foreigners' residence, and these two women must be nannies, I realized. I watched the two women enviously at the same time as I felt my chest expanding with excitement at seeing a light at the end of the tunnel. If these two peasant women could work here as nannies, maybe I could too. I didn't care how little money I'd make. As long as I could get out of Ba Jin, I would be happy. Besides, more doors would open to me in the city, and eventually maybe I would make enough money to keep my teaching post in case I needed to come back to it, I thought.

The next Sunday, despite the scalding sun, I went back to Shanghai, with a stack of handwritten seeking-nanny-job letters in my bag. I waltzed through the arch when the security guard was looking the other way, and I started to knock on the doors of the villas.

A tidy middle-aged white man with a thick moustache came to the first door. Facing his interrogative eyes, I held out my letter and stuttered that I was looking to be a nanny. Holding the door edge, he politely told me that he didn't have any children. Undiscouraged, I kept going. Nobody answered the second door. Then there was a polite rejection. Doors slammed before I could open my mouth. People pressed their eyes against the peephole and didn't even open up.

Two hours later, I had gone through all the villas, but nobody was interested in talking to me. Between a wall and some lush roses, I dropped down on the cement ground and buried my face between my knees, holding back my tears. The broiling heat of the sun was melting my limbs and cracking my lips, but I knew that the weakness I was feeling right then came from within. There was a desert in my heart, and I was the only traveler in it, and now I had lost my direction. I had never felt so desperate before.

Soon it got dark. I left the villas and started to walk on the street. I didn't know how far I went. I just kept going, not feeling tired. Finally I stopped at a small bridge and leaned against the stone railing. The sewage ditch under the bridge gave off a smell of rotten meat after the day's heat, but it didn't bother me too much. I stood there for a while, ignoring the looks from passersby.

A man in shorts and flip-flops stopped about a yard away from me and then leaned against the railing, glancing over at me once in a while. After five minutes, he had shown no sign of leaving, so I decided to go. As I walked away from the bridge, I heard him following me. I started to get nervous and walked faster.

After a few minutes, the man quickened his steps and was soon at my side. He was middle-aged and balding. He looked at me with drooling lust and smiled. "How much, Miss?"

He thought I was a hooker. I gave him an angry look and walked off in a huff.

What on earth made him think I was a hooker? How could he? Was it written on my forehead? Maybe I had been born a hooker. I chuckled to myself. I spread my legs quicker than a hooker. At least hookers got something in return. They were probably happier than me, too. Maybe I should become a hooker, I thought. Why not? It wasn't as if I couldn't use the money.

I wheeled around and made eye contact with the man. "How much can you pay?"

He pointed to a building across the street. "There's a café over there. We can go there and talk."

I followed him to the café, which was hidden in a basement. The only light came from a few candles flickering against the wall. A quiet, mysterious woman led us to one of the love seats behind the thick red curtains. As soon as we sat down and the curtains were shut behind us, the man grabbed me, and his hand started to rove my body. I sat still, closing my mouth tightly to avoid the man's wet lips, which were searching for mine.

When his hand unzipped my shorts and dug beneath my panties, I felt empty and anxious. When he inserted his middle finger inside me, an immense feeling of invasion came over me.

The cuticle around his fingernail scratched me. I suddenly felt so miserable that I wanted to die.

I pulled his finger out with a jerk, and then I started to sob. "I'm sorry," I said. "I can't do this. I'm a teacher, not a hooker. I just want to find a job here."

He seemed confused, but he just shrugged and didn't try anything else. We walked out of the café in silence. He took out a piece of paper, jotted down a number, and handed it to me along with a fifty-yuan bill. "Give me a call if you come here to stay," he said and walked away.

The evening lights were lit on the street, and a popular Cantonese song was playing in the distance. A crowd of people stood in front of a ditch left by construction on the street, sticking their heads over the edge and all talking at once. Beside it, a bicycle was lying upside down with its wheel still turning. Someone asked anxiously, "Is he dead?"

I rolled the piece of paper into a ball and tossed it into the ditch.

MY SHANGHAI DREAM broke easily, like a beautiful but fragile vase. I continued to live my life in the small town of Ba Jin, believing I would be there the rest of my life. I felt as miserable as before—the only difference was that now I had stopped dreaming. I resigned myself to my teaching life and resolved at least to try to fix what I could, since I was stuck in this small town.

I ended things with Gold Hill. Nights, I still went out to the club. Calm as lake water, my heart didn't ripple at all when I saw him with other girls. I had run out of feelings for men.

To ensure that Gold Hill never knocked on my door again, I requested yet another move. I was transferred to the attic on the third floor of the teacher's compound.

In the hot August of 1995, the tiny attic felt like a steamer. The water I fetched from the public faucet downstairs ran out constantly—I had to splash it all over my body every few minutes in order to bear the scorching heat. By the end of the first day in my new room, I was lying prone on the cement floor, dog-tired and stark naked.

I watched the sky in the west gradually flush pink through the window as the insufferable heat crept away. Downstairs, people's chatting and children's boisterous yelling continued as darkness filled my attic. I laid my cheek on the cement. It felt cool. I closed my eyes. The floor echoed with my strong, rhythmic heartbeat. I felt safe. Now nobody, neither Gold Hill nor Hao nor any other hooligan, would know where I lived.

It was not too late. Everything could be put in a jar, sealed up, and then thrown into the river. I could start over.

"When are you going to get a boyfriend, Little Shen?" an older teacher had bluntly asked me earlier in the day, when I had joined my colleagues downstairs.

I had smiled and shrugged my shoulders. "Nobody wants me," I said jokingly.

"Come on, Little Shen. You are young, pretty, and an English teacher. You're a dream girlfriend for men in this town," she had responded, comforting me.

Remembering that moment, I felt good for the first time in a long time. Being surrounded by colleagues and watching children play in the lively compound made me feel as if I had climbed out of a tomb and come back to life.

Maybe I should get a real boyfriend now, I thought as I dozed off.

A few days later, the new semester began, and the school was overrun with students again. After finishing my duty of giving out textbooks on the first day, I biked back to my attic. It was my third year in the town. It was also the final year of middle school for the students I'd been teaching since they had started at the school. Soon they would graduate and disperse to many different places, some to senior high schools in Suzhou, some to cheaper high schools in other towns, and some back to the rice fields.

I stopped at the grocery store at the corner, rested on the bench in front of it, and quietly watched the teenagers on the street laughing and chasing each other. I was jealous of them. I felt as though I had never really lived a single day of my life, and as though I never would.

A young man in a light brown suit appeared in the corner of my eye. I turned and studied him as he walked into the store. His leather shoes were shiny, and he was tidy and clean all over, like a newly washed and ironed white shirt. I saw him glancing around the store as he waited for his bag of salt. His skin was fair and delicate like wax. I saw anxiety flickering in his fine eyes, and I couldn't help but pipe up: "You must be the new teacher, Wang."

"How do you know?" He turned to me, surprised.

"Everybody in town knows." He looked so brand-new. No one here had such long and slender fingers. At first glance, they reminded me of piano keys.

Wang was a new math teacher at the local vocational school, which offered continuing education for students who had failed to enter any senior high schools. At first, since the school was located in a different part of town, we seldom saw each other. When we met on the street, we simply nodded our heads. But he was soon assigned to live in the teacher's compound, and we became acquaintances. When our paths crossed, we would stop our bikes for short conversations.

"Man, what a shitty place. What a shitty school. When they recruited me in my province, they painted it as a paradise. It's a shithole," he would say. He had an innocent smile, and his eyes were bright. He was like a shy boy. He spoke so softly when he was complaining that it didn't seem like he meant it at all.

I would nod my head and agree with him and then say

good-bye, jump on my bike, and leave quickly. I wanted to stay and look at his handsome face longer, but I had to keep moving. If we were seen together on the street more than three times, I was sure everyone would say we were dating.

But then, what would be wrong with dating him? It was common for a teacher to grab another teacher and rush to the marriage registration office. Sooner or later you needed to marry someone and have children, so why not do it quickly and conveniently? Then you would be set, entitled to a bigger room, a condo, or even a house from the school. Plus, you'd always have someone to look after you.

The thought of Teacher Wang being my boyfriend made my cheeks burn. What would it be like? I wondered. It had been so long since I'd had a real boyfriend.

But as soon as I opened my tattered door with its flaking red paint and saw my tiny attic, which was as ratty as a dump, I sobered. That sight drove away the thought of becoming a teacher's wife. I had suffered so much as part of a poor family. For a poor, lowly couple, everything in this world would be sorrowful. You couldn't be merry if you spent all day worrying about your next meal. Would you be in the mood for love when the mosquitoes were biting you like crazy just because you couldn't afford a bottle of bug repellent?

No, I couldn't marry a teacher. It would take us three years to buy a refrigerator and maybe five years to get a Sony television for the living room—if we had a living room. No, I definitely couldn't marry Teacher Wang, who also came from a peasant family and had no connections in this town. I didn't want to relive my parents' life.

I began to avoid Teacher Wang as much as I could and was reserved when I ran into him on the street. But when loneliness drilled into me, my heart wanted to go against my mind. I longed to have someone I could talk to, someone who had graduated from college and could speak Mandarin instead of the raspy local dialect that came out of the mouths of everyone in this town. So when one day after work Teacher Wang ran up the stairs to my attic and asked if I wanted to join him and his friend in his room for dinner, I looked into his tender eyes and said yes.

He asked if I could cook the chicken he had bought at the market, like a boyfriend would expect his girlfriend to do. His friend asked if I wanted a beer. I said yes to both, smiling, happy in his crude but warm room. Then I sat quietly at the table and listened to him and his friend complaining about their schools. He turned to tell me that he liked the chicken. When our eyes met, he quickly looked away. In the dim light, I saw his cheeks turning red. His friend chuckled. I lowered my head.

His friend left to catch the last bus to the town where he lived. I cleaned the pots and dishes, and then I sat down on the edge of his bed. He had been sitting in his only chair and watching me. The light from the bulb in the middle of the room seemed extremely bright through my tipsy eyes. There was a nervousness in the air. Faintly, I heard him speaking and my own voice talking back to him. I leaned against the folded sheet on the bed, wondering why I was suddenly so giggly. Then I saw his handsome face moving close to me, and, the next thing I realized, his lips were on mine.

The alcohol emboldened his hands. He stripped off my coat and then unbuttoned my blouse. He was breathing quickly. He seemed shy but glad. I realized that he liked me. He liked me in the way a normal man liked a woman. He got on top of me. He smelled fresh and clean, like bamboo leaves after a spring rain. He was trying to be my boyfriend, and then he would become my husband, and then—I couldn't think. I couldn't let him become my boyfriend. I liked him, but I didn't love him. I pushed him and leaped up from the bed before he got too far. I stood indecisively on the bare floor. He looked like an injured deer.

"I can't. . . ." I tried to explain but couldn't articulate the reason. It would hurt him like hell if I told him that I couldn't be with him because he was as poor and lowly as I was.

I turned around and ran.

Later that night, a couple of light taps on my door woke me. I got up, opened the door slightly, and peered out. Hao, who had discarded me like a cigarette stub a year earlier and left for Shanghai, was outside my door. How had he found me here? Fear started to rise inside me.

"How are you?" With his chin lifted, he slowly pronounced each word to me. Grinning, he unhurriedly exhaled whiffs of smoke through his nostrils.

He pushed the door all the way open and strode into my attic. He sat down on my bed and put his feet up on the chair, as if he had just entered his own home.

"I thought you were in Shanghai." I forced a grin.

"I come back here once in a while." With a cigarette dangling from the corner of his mouth, he looked as haughty as ever. Cold, I went back to the bed and wrapped myself in my blanket. It was autumn already.

"So, did you miss me?" he asked jokingly.

I giggled nervously and pulled the cover around my waist. "How is Shanghai?" I said, trying to make conversation.

"Oh, Shanghai is fucking awesome." Engaged by my question, he leaned forward and told me excitedly, "Hey, you know, you should really leave this fucking stupid town and go to Shanghai. You can speak English, right? Go wait in the airport. So many rich foreigners get off planes every day. Talk to them and take them to hotels. Do you know how much you can make sleeping with foreigners?"

I looked at his puffy face, the result of a lifetime of debauchery, as he prattled on about Shanghai, and I couldn't help but laugh at his absurd idea. A few months ago I had been willing to sell my body on the streets of Shanghai, but right now I just wanted to tell him to shut up.

He yanked the corner of the cover toward him and tried to sneak under.

"I'm cold," he said.

"No," I refused, but it was useless. He pushed me back and squeezed himself closer to me.

"I have a boyfriend now. Please leave," I begged, irritated. Teacher Wang's face flashed across in my mind.

Hao chuckled at my pleas and kept pulling the quilt toward himself. Then he wrapped his arms around my waist. I twisted myself away forcefully and got off the bed.

"If you don't leave, I will," I announced. I knew this time my heart wanted him to go, as well as my senses.

"Come on. Didn't you miss me?" He sat wrapped in the cover, an expectant look in his eyes.

I realized that it would be impossible to get him out of my attic without waking up the entire compound. I grabbed my coat and ran out of my own home. He could do whatever he wanted while I was gone. I knew he wouldn't follow me. I was never that important to him.

Outside, I stopped in front of Teacher Wang's room. I stood below his windowsill for a while. The moonlight reflected off the thin layer of frost on the cement ground. The world was bathed in silvery white. I pulled my coat tightly around me, raised my head, and looked at the full moon hanging in the sky.

I felt confused. I didn't know what I really wanted. Wang was so poor, but maybe he was the best I would ever find. After all, he was pure and fresh, while I was beaten and incomplete. I didn't feel love for him, but then, I told myself, I wasn't a woman who deserved to love.

I thought of what the great poet Li Bai had written two thousand years ago:

The luminous moonlight before my bed—
I thought it might be the frost fallen on the ground.
I lift my head to gaze at the cliff moon
And then bow down to muse on my distant home.

Suddenly an overwhelming desire to have a home hit me. I had a home in the Shen Hamlet, but that had never felt like a real home. Was a home really too much to ask?

I STARTED TO date Teacher Wang, whose full name was Wang Hui. Fate wanted me to, I thought, so I succumbed to it.

We rarely saw each other in the daytime. He got off work earlier and always waited for me at his rear window, through which he could see me standing on the top of the stairs to my attic. When I turned toward him, he would wave to me, smiling shyly. When I went to his room, he didn't speak much, but he would lift the lid of his rice cooker and show me the dinner he had made. With the door shut and curtains down, it was easy for me to start dreaming. Was this what I had been looking for all my life: a bowl of rice, a few bok choy leaves, flickering candles, and a hand on my shoulder?

But the next morning, the warmth would disappear. I avoided being seen with him on the street. The thought of being his girlfriend in public made every inch of my skin itch. His body felt real and warm, but when I lay next to him my mind rarely had a moment of peace. I was torn. I could not bear to think of a dismal future with him in this deserted town. I didn't want people to think I had chosen such a poor man.

"How do you picture your future?" I asked Wang one day when I saw him flipping the pages of a book titled *Introduction to Programming*.

"I don't know. It sucks here, but what can I do?" He shrugged.

"Why are you reading that book, then?" I asked curiously, some hope rising in my mind. Perhaps he wanted to get out of this town too.

"My cousin is working in a joint venture in southern China. He sent me this book and told me to study English. He says computers and English are really hot down there right now."

My body tingled with excitement. His cousin was in southern China, one of the few economic special zones in the country, where foreign investors flooded in with money to build factories, where the boldest Chinese headed for brand-new futures. If Wang Hui and I were going to stay together, I knew both of us couldn't be teachers all our lives. Maybe it would be better if Wang Hui joined the gold rush. Maybe his cousin could help.

"Are you thinking of going there someday?" I sounded him out nervously, praying to hear a positive answer. I hoped my boyfriend was an ambitious man who didn't want to waste his life in this small town.

"I don't know. Give up teaching?" He shrugged again. "I don't know if I can find a job there."

I replied tentatively. "No, maybe you should go. A man shouldn't be stuck here forever."

He scratched his head and didn't say anything.

We didn't talk about it again for weeks, but I couldn't get southern China out of my mind. All I could think about was "jumping in the ocean," a phrase newly coined to describe people giving up governmental jobs and joining the free market. Since 1949, when New China was founded, every governmental worker had been guaranteed an unbreakable iron bowl into which the government put just enough food to keep your stomach full. Most people chose to stay on the dry land, with their bowls. You might find gold and silver in the ocean; but if you couldn't swim, you would be lost. But the more I thought about it, the more certain I was that I would rather drown in the roaring waves of the South than let time slowly and painfully suck the life out of me in this town.

A few weeks later, I shared my thoughts with Wang Hui.

"Go to the South. I'll join you later," I said confidently.

He sounded doubtful. "Are you sure you'll come? Teaching is a pretty good job for a girl. Besides, will the school let you go? I am different. I'm a man, and my school is much more flexible."

"Yes, I promise I'll join you later. I am not going to stay here forever. Go and see if your cousin can get you a job at his company. I'll meet you there, and we'll build a future together," I encouraged him. I believed every word I said. By conventional standards, Wang was the ideal husband, good-looking, poised, and easygoing, and if he could succeed financially, he would be perfect. I was thrilled by the possibilities.

Wang Hui took my words to heart and arranged to leave for the South. At the end of the fall semester in December, it was time for him to go. Unfortunately, my mother visited me on the very day of his departure. When he appeared on my threshold, my mother was sitting on my bed wagging her tongue as usual. He stayed at the door and said good-bye. My mother looked at him suspiciously. He waved his hand once and smiled weakly before turning around and going downstairs. I pushed all my sad feelings aside. I wanted to remain calm and normal in front of my mother. I instinctively hid every emotion from her.

"Who is he?" she asked, getting up to clean my gas stove.

"Just a teacher at the school," I answered nonchalantly.

"Are you dating him?"

"No!" I said.

She clearly didn't believe me. She continued to vigorously scrub the stove, but soon she couldn't keep quiet. "I know you're dating him," she said.

I didn't respond.

"A teacher," she scoffed. "What does he have besides his own penis?"

I couldn't believe my ears. "Mama! He is leaving for the South. Come on. I am not dating him. I wouldn't date a teacher."

"Learn a lesson from me, Juanjuan. Date any man, just not a poor and incompetent man like your father," my mother said.

"Mama, have some confidence in me. I won't," I replied impatiently. I had faith in Wang Hui. I was certain he would build a warm nest for us in the South.

Wang Hui had come into my life and left in just five short months. I was alone again. My attic no longer had any scandalous visitors. I had no friends and lived like a hermit. But I felt calmer, since I had a future to look forward to.

In February I received a postcard from Wang Hui, on which he had handwritten a poem to me:

Raindrops fall onto the banana leaves outside my window.
When I wake up, my tears are all over the pillow.

A rush of sweetness mixed with relief swept through me. He was safe, and I was sure he would have found a job by then. I knew nothing could stop me from going to the South. My imagination had already flown me there. In my mind, I'd already touched the green banana leaves. Now I just needed to find a way out of the school.

By then, Principal Chen had left the school, and a new principal from out of town had been in the role for a semester. In April, I volunteered to write a long glorification letter about the new principal, which I read aloud in the town's committee meeting on electing outstanding leaders. My actions scored major points for the principal's political career. At the end of the semester, bringing a couple of cases of nourishment drinks, I visited his house one night. After rounds of sincere begging, I finally got his nod.

The next day, I signed my name on the contract of Shen Juanjuan vs. Hope Middle School. I was given my freedom for three years, during which the school would not only take my paycheck issued by the government every month, but also expect me to pay an annual fee of five thousand yuan. If I chose to return within three years, my teaching position would still be available, as well as the benefits of a governmental worker.

Five thousand yuan was equivalent to my whole yearly salary and year-end bonus as a teacher. I would have to earn at least double this amount in order to survive. How? I had no idea, and I didn't care.

My last day of teaching ended with me flicking the chalk dust off my clothes and walking out of the classroom with nothing: not my teaching notes, not my lunch box, not my pointer. The cement walkway outside the school entrance was no longer narrow and dull; it was a colorful, wide rainbow to the world beyond the sky. I skipped down the walkway. I was free. I couldn't believe it—I was free! I was going to leave this town, this trap that I had been in for the last three years, and I was sure I would never miss anything about it.

I did very little packing. After purchasing an airline ticket and sending Wang Hui a telegram, I spent the rest of the day dancing excitedly about my room like a lunatic.

The next day, I caught a bus to the Shen Hamlet. I knew that it would be almost impossible, but I still wanted to try to step over another stumbling block—my family. I wanted their support.

"Are you out of your mind?" my mother said as soon as I told her that I had signed the contract. "What are you going to do now?" she questioned me sourly.

"I'm going to the South," I said.

"The South? Only businessmen and hookers go there! What are you going to do there?"

"I don't know yet."

"Did that son of a bitch ask you to go?" She meant Wang Hui.

"No, this has nothing to do with him," I said instantly.

My father looked like he wanted to eat me alive. "What's wrong with you?" he howled. "Are you sick of being a teacher? Go plant some rice with me tomorrow, then."

That evening, Honor and Small Uncle came to the house. Surrounded by my whole family, I sank into the wicker chair, telling myself to be strong.

"You know that every girl wants to be a teacher. It's the most stable position for a girl like you. Do you remember how tough it was for you to go to college and become a teacher? For so many generations, our ancestors have worked in the fields, have always been peasants, and now that you're a teacher, a government worker, you throw it all away. Why?" Small Uncle said patiently.

"There's no future as a teacher. I'll be poor forever. I want to fight. I want to try at least once in my life." I wasn't sure if he could understand, but I tried to explain.

"Well, the girl at least has courage and ambition," Honor said. "Maybe it's not a bad thing, you know. Women have advantages in the business world. There is a woman in my circle; she gets the best cocoon silk from the dealer every time."

My mother and father both glowered at him. "Stop it!" my mother shrieked. "If she doesn't sleep with those guys, can she get the best silk every time? A woman can't do anything in this society unless she whores herself." Then she started to weep. "Are you crazy?" she said to me. "What the hell are you thinking? The South is a dump. Go back to the school tomorrow. I'll go beg the principal to ignore the contract and take you back."

"It's too late. I already bought the ticket." I threw the words out as toughly as I could, to extinguish her last hope. Sure enough, she cried even louder.

"What about your residence? What about your dossier? Everybody has to have one to live. Your dossier will still be in Ba Jin. You'll have no identity in the South. You'll be a person with no history," Small Uncle warned me solemnly.

"I don't care." Deep down, I longed to be a person with no history.

The reasoning and arguing continued for another four hours, all the way until midnight. I curled myself into a ball in the wicker chair, feeling like a hedgehog, resistant to all its predators. The only person who didn't join in was Spring, who just sat and listened. Perhaps she was the only person who understood why I wanted to throw away my past.

Finally Small Uncle gave a deep sigh and left. My father, who had been sitting like a simmering volcano all night, gave me an ultimatum. "If you walk out of this house tomorrow, you are no longer a Shen. Don't ever come back."

I wanted to yell that I had never felt like a Shen in the first place. I wanted to cry to him, Dad, do you have any idea how much I suffered during my three years in that small town? Of course, I was as silent as a sculpture. I didn't want to come back to this hateful house anyway.

The next morning was drizzly. I walked downstairs and saw

my mother sitting on the stool behind the stove. Her eyes were puffy like two apricots. She must have been crying the entire night. I avoided looking at her. The last thing I wanted to do right then was get sentimental.

I lifted my bag off the ground and walked toward the door. "Are you still going?"

I kept walking without turning around.

"Wait," she pleaded, weeping. "At least have a bowl of congee before you go."

I told myself not to look back. She followed me out the door.

The path from the front of the house to the main road was muddy. I put the bag on my shoulder and walked quickly in the rain. My mother ran behind me.

"Please, Juanjuan, don't go." Her broken sobs floated to me over the sound of the rain. "Don't go!"

I told myself to hold back my tears. I ran faster. I jumped onto a passing bus as soon as I reached the asphalt road. I looked out of the window as we pulled away and saw my crying mother limping on the muddy countryside road in the rain, waving her hand to me.

Three hours later, I boarded a Shanghai Eastern Airlines plane in Hongqiao Airport. The destination was the city of Guangzhou, the hub of southern China. It was my first time on an airplane. I sat on the plush chair next to the window, feeling numb. The sweet, soft voice of the flight attendant coming over the intercom was mere background noise.

The plane started to move slowly and then cruised down the runway. Then it accelerated. My eardrums popped, and I woke up from my trance. I looked out of the window and realized that the plane was taking off.

From now on, I told myself, I would no longer mourn my past. I would not loathe, degrade, or abuse myself any more.

Like the Monkey King from the epic *Journey to the West*, I was born from a crack in a rock, and with sunshine, rain, and dew it was I who had brought myself up. Now I was a person without family, history, or identity.

PART

III

IN JULY 1996, when I left the middle school and then the hamlet, all I wanted was to chop off the past. I didn't expect the process to be so painful. I didn't know that your past was as vital as your blood. But the bravest soldier swallows his pain. The fiercest shark only cares about going forward. A one-way ticket, a duffel bag, and Wang Hui's address were all I needed as I headed for the South.

Once I stepped out of the lobby of Guangzhou Baiyun Airport, I realized that I hadn't just come to a different part of China; Guangzhou seemed like another country entirely. The clouds hung higher in a sky that was bluer and crisper than the one over the hamlet, and the sun shone more ardently. People were smaller and darker, spoke louder and ran faster, and they took up almost every inch of earth. There were cars everywhere, small cars, like toys, and the entire road was jammed up like a pile of tangled linen. All sorts of noises converged into a dome of echoes droning continuously above the city.

Flustered, I didn't know how to melt myself into this pile of heat and noise, find my way to the bus station, and eventually get to a suburb called Gao Ming, where Wang Hui lived. At first I just stood near the airport entrance, not daring to step out into the city. But then, remembering my experience in Shanghai, I took a deep breath and held my arm out for a cab.

"Could you please take me to Gao Ming?" I asked the driver after I had squeezed myself into the car. He was lean and dark, reminding me of the image of a man working on a Malaysian rubber plantation that I had once seen on television.

He talked in a strange language, as if he had a twist in his tongue. I had no idea what he was saying. People in the South spoke Cantonese. Unlike most of the rest of the country, they didn't speak Mandarin, our national language. The pronunciation of the two languages is completely different, although they have the same characters.

I repeated myself. He repeated himself in Mandarin, but his accent was so heavy that his words didn't make any sense to me. Finally I gave up trying to understand him and let him take me wherever he had said he would, praying that I had run into a nice person. After many struggles with the snarled traffic, he stopped at the side of a road, at what appeared to be a gas station, and gestured for me to get out of the car. As soon as I got out he drove away. Full of misgivings, I stood and surveyed my surroundings. Before I could see clearly through the clouds of dust churning everywhere, a loud noise blared from a speaker a few feet away from me, giving me a start.

"Gaooooo-Minggg, Gaooooo-Minggg . . . going to Gao-Ming?" I saw a man shouting through a huge megaphone. I was stunned. I had never seen anyone crying out for customers with a megaphone as big as the one on top of the flagpole at the middle school, which was only used occasionally for broadcasting. Didn't he feel ashamed, displaying his desire to make money so out in the open?

"Yes. . . ," I answered uncertainly.

He grabbed my arm as he shouted to me in barely comprehensible Mandarin, "Gao-Minggg? Come with me, the bus is leaving." He led me to the gas station's parking lot, where several buses waited for customers. I was relieved to see the cardboard plates reading *Gao Ming* on their windshields and quickly got on one of them.

The air was hot and dry. I looked out the window. All the women I saw were petite, with brown skin, their hair put up at the backs of their heads with big plastic clips. Every man wore a suit, though most were crumpled, and the faces above the suits looked twitchy. The guy with the megaphone was still yelling for all he was worth. A man stood next to a gas pump with one hand on his hip, staring at the dust with a look of sheer boredom. In his other hand, I saw a small colorful cardboard box with the characters for waxberry juice printed on it. He was sipping the juice through a straw.

I was amazed that people in the South made juice out of waxberries and sold it for money. Even funnier, they put the juice in a cardboard box so that they could save money instead of using plastic or tin. I was fascinated. I'm really in the South now, I told myself.

Once it was full, the bus started to move. It maneuvered through traffic on the narrow, dirty streets of downtown Guangzhou and soon entered the suburbs, where rows and rows of factory buildings sat in front of small bare hills. About half an hour later, buildings became scarce and we were driving on a winding asphalt road among tall mountains covered in lush greens. I had grown up on a plain; having never seen mountains before, I gazed out the window and greedily enjoyed the breathtaking view.

Two hours later, we reached a small town. The bus driver shouted to me that this was my destination. I got off the bus, perplexed. I saw no sign of Wang Hui at the stop. A wave of disappointment hit me. Maybe my telegram hadn't reached him. Before I could think further, a group of motorcycles flew toward me and parked right at my feet. The drivers all stretched out their arms and tried to pull me onto their back seats, yelling in Mandarin with funny accents: "Only five yuan gets you anywhere in the city. Where are you goinggggg?" I gave one Wang Hui's address and hopped on.

Ten minutes later, I stood at the gate of a cement building. I looked at Wang Hui's postcard to make sure that this was where he lived. It was a shabby, dull apartment complex with clothes-lines or sticks protruding from every balcony, draped with clothes swaying in the wind. The alley next to the building was full of hollows and puddles. The air smelled like burning rapeseed oil. I heard two young women shouting to each other behind one of the windows with rusty bars. From their heavily accented Mandarin, I could tell that they were from northern China. They must be migrant workers, I thought, those who had left home and come to the South for jobs. From that day on, I would be one of them, I told myself, a grain of sand surfing on the waves.

I didn't know which apartment Wang Hui lived in, and I prepared to ask someone for help. But before I could step into the complex, he appeared. With his head lowered, he walked listlessly in shorts and flip-flops toward the gate. He was thinner and darker, and he looked like he had a load on his mind. A spell of tender affection came over me. I was happy to see him. I wondered how he had been doing during the six months we had been apart, whether he had missed me. I sure had missed him. Seeing him made me relax. There would be nothing to keep me away from him now. This was the man I had come to for shelter, the man with whom I was going to build a future.

When he was a few feet away, he looked up and spotted me. I saw his eyes open wide.

"I thought you were picking me up at the bus station." Though I knew I couldn't hide the happiness in my eyes, I still made my tone grouchy. I had pictured him opening his arms and embracing me at the station after we had been apart for so long.

"Y-yeah, I was on my way there," he stuttered.

I glanced at his casual shorts and flip-flops suspiciously. "You would have been so late. Didn't you get the telegram?" I whined as we entered the complex.

"I left work late."

I stopped walking and confronted him. "Did you know I was coming?"

I saw him blush. "I got the telegram, but I didn't believe that you were really coming," he confessed.

"You didn't believe? This is what we have been planning all along!" Shocked by his words, I was almost shouting.

He came up with an awkward, guilty smile as a response. All of a sudden, everything I had done—leaving the school, abandoning my running mother in the rain, and traveling hundreds of miles to this man—seemed meaningless. He had never even believed in me. I felt betrayed and angry. We walked up to his apartment in silence.

We stopped at an iron anti-theft door on the third floor. He reached into his pocket for the key, telling me that his older cousin rented this apartment with his girlfriend and let him stay with them. Knowing that migrant workers often crammed together in apartments, I wasn't surprised that he lived with his relatives, but I still couldn't help feeling a little disappointed. I had thought we would have a place of our own.

He told me that his cousin, a manager at a local joint venture, had gotten him a programmer job at the same company.

"Eight hundred yuan a month, less than I thought, but not bad. Three times what I was making as a teacher." He carried my bag through the door. I felt relieved. At least one of us had a job, though the pay was not as much as I had expected.

He took me to a small room and told me that I was going to share a bed with Rong, another cousin of his who had left her husband and children back home and come here to work on an assembly line at the same company.

"Where's your room?" I asked, puzzled and displeased by this arrangement.

He pointed to a small room next to mine. "Older Brother doesn't like young people living together before they get married," he told me helplessly.

"Why is he living with his girlfriend, then?" What a hypocrite this Older Brother was.

Wang's face still looked quite pleasant, and his eyebrows were still dashing, but he also looked cowardly. "He's the oldest cousin in the family. Older Brother is just like your father. You have to obey him."

So, after years of fighting for my freedom and traveling hundreds of miles, I had just walked into an apartment still ruled by a patriarchal family system.

Dissatisfied, I lay down on the single bed in the room I would share with Rong and told Wang that I was exhausted and wanted to take a nap. He left the room quietly, but just as I was about to doze off he came back and sat next to me. I kept my eyes closed. He bent down and started to take off my clothes. I heard his breathing getting heavier, and when I felt a sharp pain in my groin, disappointment washed over me. It was so different from the romantic lovemaking that I had imagined for our reunion. He was so impatient and hurried that he didn't even know he was hurting me. As he moved on top of me, I started to have doubts: had he ever loved me? Had we ended up together just because we were so lonely in that small town? I guessed that this was what he had wanted from me all along—sex. But there was nothing I could do now but accept it. I had no way back. Perhaps things would get better.

As the sky slowly turned dark outside the windows, we grew nervous, anticipating his family's return. We sat on the tiled floor in the living room side by side, absentmindedly watching the tiny 21-inch television and glancing at the doorknob once in a while.

Several times, Wang looked at the black dress I was wearing.

"What's wrong?" I asked.

"It may be a little too transparent. Older Brother doesn't like that," he told me hurriedly.

I ran back to my room and changed into the gray suit and skirt I had brought. I had brought little with me to the South: a dress, a suit, a skirt, my toiletries, and my college diploma were all I had.

As soon as I returned to the living room floor, the door opened and Older Brother and his girlfriend walked in. Of medium build with a pair of plain glasses, Older Brother was an ordinary-looking man, the kind you would forget instantly the moment you turned away from him.

"Older Brother!" I called respectfully, standing up.

He nodded his head to me slightly and kept walking toward the kitchen. The tall, thin woman behind him smiled to me like a blossoming flower and said, "This must be Hui's girlfriend. Hello. Welcome."

"Older Sister!" I followed Wang and greeted her tensely.

Meeting Wang's cousin and his girlfriend felt as scary as making a pilgrimage to see the emperor.

Rong soon came home, and we were ready for dinner. Wang Hui whispered to me to go to the kitchen and get rice for everybody. Rong followed me. She looked like an ordinary weatherbeaten middle-aged woman from the countryside who was always worried about something. As soon as I had lifted the rice cooker lid and put it on the counter, she rushed over, looking scared, and turned the lid over.

"Don't forget to put the lid upside down in the future. She'll get upset if you put it like that." She whispered, "She thinks it's bad luck. She is a typical superstitious woman from Shanghai."

"I thought Older Brother ruled here. And she seems so friendly," I said, confused.

Rong shook her head and lowered her voice even more. "Don't be fooled by her fake laugh. True, Older Brother makes the most money here, but he's divorced, and it's not easy for a divorced guy to find a girlfriend. She's really the one who wears the pants around here."

Rong and I carried the bowls of rice out to the table in the living room. I walked carefully, holding my breath and feeling like I was in Old China, where a woman had to be approved by a man's elders before being allowed into his family.

Rong put down a bowl of rice before Older Brother, who sat at the table waiting soberly. Then she placed a pair of chopsticks next to the bowl and said respectfully, "Older Brother, please enjoy your dinner."

It seemed the only thing the women in the Wang family didn't have to do was place the food directly into the men's mouths. While eating, I wondered if they also had to bring their men buckets of water to wash their feet in before bed, an old custom I had read about in books. Later, when Older Brother was ready for bed, Rong proved to me that indeed they did.

I sat at the table and ate, careful not to make too much noise. Wang Hui was sitting next to me, and I could sense his nervous fidgeting. This was ridiculous. Why should I be so afraid of

Older Brother? I asked myself angrily, but I remained respectful and quiet. It was my first day in the South, and this group of strangers was all I had.

Older Brother cleared his throat and lifted his chin in my direction. "Ah-Juan, what's your plan?"

I realized that in the South people usually called each other Ah-something. I guessed that from then on I would be Ah-Juan.

"I want to find a job, of course." I paused and then gathered all my courage and asked, "Older Brother, could you please see if I can get a job at your company? I heard it's a big company, and they may need people who can speak English."

He kept whisking rice into his mouth, and after a moment he said, "I'll see what I can do."

I was relieved and gratified by his words. Now I had hope. Maybe this was why Older Brother was treated like a ruler in this apartment—because he got jobs for everyone: Wang Hui, Rong, and his girlfriend.

Next came the endless and agonizing waiting. Every day at dusk when Older Brother came home, I fixed my eyes on him and hoped that he would mention a job opening, but every night I went to bed disappointed.

I waited and waited for the entire month of July. The days became longer and more unbearable as I tore more pages off the calendar. While everybody else went to work, I stayed in the apartment alone and learned to cook better and wash everyone's clothes so that Older Brother would like me more. I often sat in front of the window, lost in my thoughts with soap bubbles all over my hands. Sometimes I took a walk around the building.

"It's not easy for him to talk to his boss; he's just a low-level manager. Believe me, he always helps family," Wang Hui would explain to me as I stared sullenly out the window.

I didn't want to talk to him. I didn't know what to do. I

didn't even know where to go to find a job. I wasn't even sure Wang Hui was my boyfriend any more. The only time I could see him was in the evenings when everybody sat on the floor watching Hong Kong soap operas in Cantonese, which I could barely understand. He and I always sat stiff and still, holding our knees with our arms and avoiding touching each other in front of Older Brother and his girlfriend. Occasionally, when it became really unbearable, we would go out for a walk on the streets of Gao Ming. Only at those times would we talk freely.

That was when I'd see the real South, where there seemed to be a galaxy of migrant workers from everywhere else in China. Along the streets, there were endless rows of factory buildings with awkward English names like "Gao Ming Grand CMOS Chips Joint Venture Co., Ltd" carved at the top of them. Flocks of migrant workers were always making a ruckus and chasing each other in front of them. The guys all wore tank tops, shorts, and slippers and had such messy hair that you would think they hadn't combed it for at least a week. Some of them parked their grubby bikes against the curb and squatted on the seats like birds, whistling and yelling to the female workers passing by. The female workers all wore plain white shirts and loose dark-colored pants with their hair in two braids behind their ears.

In such a place, where there seemed to be only factories sitting on dirt roads, there was not much for these young men and women to do. Their most popular gathering sites were just some crude pool tables sitting in disorder in the open air. There were a few small restaurants with television sets hung on their back walls, blasting Hong Kong soap operas. The air inside them smelled like cabbage with garlic and stir-fried snails, the cheapest and most popular dishes. Bored workers sat in knots on plastic chairs outside the restaurants, sucking snails like woodpeckers, glancing at the television, and whistling to girls. If there was really nothing left to do, they would sneak to the back rooms of restaurants, which had been secretly converted to small theaters, and goof the night away with some pornography movies.

"These people are the real migrant workers. They have very little education. Left home and the fields to work their asses off here for the big bosses and still only make a few hundred yuan a month." Wang Hui sighed with sympathy as we walked hurriedly to dodge the groups of workers on the street.

"Still better than starving at home, though," he continued. "I'm pretty lucky. Got a job not long after I came here, and a good job too, not on the assembly lines."

I felt uncomfortable with Wang's self-satisfaction. After traveling hundreds of miles to the South, how could he be content being only a little better off than the "real" migrant workers, who were fresh from the fields? It was becoming clear to me that Wang had no ambition. I looked at him and wondered whether I had really found the right man for myself. Maybe I was just asking for too much.

Disappointed, I stayed silent and kept walking. A crowd of migrant girls passed by, laughing and joking and pretending to hit each other on the shoulder with their fists. They were so young. Their lily-white faces were babyish and innocent, yet they looked content, as if they had found what they had been searching for their entire lives. Looking at their identical backs, I asked myself whether I could possibly become one of them. No. I wanted to be different, because I felt I had a bigger dream. What was that dream, exactly? I wasn't sure. I only knew that I wanted to make more than eight hundred yuan a month. I felt like a rocket just out of its launcher, full of energy. I wanted more. I wanted a lot.

A MONTH AFTER I had arrived in the South, Wang Hui finally rented a place of our own, as I had secretly urged him to do many times. I was ecstatic. The rental house was cheap and small, but it was clean and made of concrete with two big iron front doors. It was completely empty inside. Except for a bamboo mat and some clothes, we had no possessions of our own, but we were young and cheerful. On our first night there, we spread the mat on the cement floor and cuddled together in the dark. There was a Chinese rose plant outside the window waving in the night breeze. I watched the dark shadows of the leaves moving on the wall while Wang Hui made love to me like crazy. That night in an alien land felt so serene.

The second day, Wang and I sat on the floor and drew up a list of things we needed for our new home, such as a bed, a mosquito net, a few chairs, a table, a stove, dishes, pots, and so forth. The more we wrote down, the quieter we became. Everything cost money, the very thing we needed the most.

We stepped out the door with the complete list. I locked up and turned around, and I saw Wang Hui looking at me oddly. "I don't have any money," he said, clearly embarrassed.

"Didn't you save any after you came here?" I asked, incredulous. He shook his head. "No."

"You made three times more than I did, and you knew I was coming." I found it hard to believe him, so I pressed on. I thought we had planned our future together, but once more it seemed that he had never believed I would really come.

"I spent it all here and there. I don't know." With free rent and food from his cousin, what other expenses had he had? All sorts of questions flew into my mind, but I swallowed them all and unlocked the door. Out of my duffel bag, I took the bonus I had received from the school before I left. I locked the door again and followed him to the market.

After Wang Hui left for work the next morning, I sat on our new small plastic stool and looked around the house. Even with all the furniture we had just bought, it still looked almost empty. We'd picked the cheapest stuff, yet it had cost all my savings—fifteen hundred yuan. I told myself that I now had a home, but strangely I didn't feel any joy. I felt as empty as the house. Not only did I have no job, I now had no money either, and as soon as I let this reality creep into my mind, it burned me like a match. I heard my mother's voice in my head: don't date a poor man like your father. I smiled to myself bitterly. My mother may have been illiterate, but she had taught me a lesson with her own life. For some reason, fate had arranged for me to run into Wang Hui, a man who was poorer than I was. But I wouldn't give in to fate, I told myself. I would not allow us to be poor all our lives.

Every day, Wang Hui left for work in the morning and got back as the six o'clock news was starting on the Hong Kong Pearl TV station on a neighbor's television. We would put the table and chairs under the eaves and start dinner. As the warm evening breeze blew into his relaxed, content face, I wanted to ask him whether the rice was too dry or moist or whether the chicken soup was too salty or just right, but the questions never made their way out of my mouth. It felt as if there was a gulf between us and it was growing by the day. After dinner, he would sit on the threshold, facing the mulberry bush, and read some junk magazines until it got dark. At night he always slept peacefully after he had used up all his energy on me. He never snored.

Two weeks flashed by. One day after Wang Hui left for work at eight o'clock, I picked up a magazine and sat under the eaves as usual. The sound of the neighbor's television became distant. Soon I found myself staring blankly into the air, the magazine lying at my feet. I was becoming a zombie. Suddenly, I felt the impulse to go somewhere. I stood up and locked the door hurriedly. I went to the bus station and soon found myself on a bus to Guangzhou.

Back in Guangzhou—a forest of steel and an ocean of noise—I started to walk aimlessly, just as I had in Shanghai a year earlier. Every face passing by was a stranger's. Every word I heard was in loud Cantonese. The sun in the South was relentless, so that every girl had a few zits on her flat face and every man had swarthy skin. The southerners loved durian and made the whole city smell like spoiled food. There were many old square cement buildings with air conditioners sticking out of every window, blasting heat into the streets. The air tasted like metal. There were no plants in sight. Girls in shorts and heavy makeup stood on the sidewalks, which were scattered with vegetable leaves and melon peels, pulling the sleeves of passing men boldly. Popular Cantonese music was playing at the maximum volume in every store.

For hours I walked in this strange city, thinking about how different it was from Shanghai. They were similar in size, but if Shanghai was a sophisticated Japanese geisha, Guangzhou made me think of the Times Square strippers I'd read about in magazines.

My mother used to yell at me when I hadn't opened my mouth for days. "What's that thing under your nose?" she would say. "You don't just use it to eat!" I had never been bold enough to just stop a stranger on the street and ask for directions. I would end up standing still with my face red, letting everyone walk by me, and then get lost for hours. But that day I knew I had to toughen up, because nobody was going to stop and help me if I didn't ask. So with some new force inside me, I approached a middle-aged man in a suit and asked him where the labor market was. I kept asking, changing buses, and walking, and eventually I was standing in front of the Guangzhou Labor and Talent Intercommunication Center.

I froze on the stone steps leading to the door, panicked. I just couldn't make my feet take me inside. I saw people walking quickly in and out of the revolving glass door in suits or skirts, carrying briefcases and looking confident, and I wondered if I should go inside at all. I only had an associate degree, and I was an ugly girl who smelled like the countryside. I had no charm and always blushed and stuttered when I was nervous.

I paced in front of the entrance, feeling cowardly. My knees were weak and my mind was like mush. It looked so easy for everyone else to go through the glass door without thinking, but I felt like there was a thick invisible wall blocking my way.

After struggling with myself for a while, I looked at the clock on a church tower not far away and realized it was time for me to get back to Gao Ming. I started to walk toward the bus station. I'll come back; I'll give myself more time, I told myself.

A few blocks away, I spotted a small tailor shop. I would

need some decent clothes for myself if I was going to look for a job, so I walked in. I chose some white cloth and told the needlewoman there that I wanted to have a blazer and a pair of pants made and that I would pick them up a few days later. I had never dared to wear white before, afraid that it would expose all my flaws. But in this foreign land, I didn't have a mother who would yell that white made me looked fatter. I didn't have any school leaders to warn me that, for the sake of our future generations' mental health, I had better not dress so flashily. Nobody at the school wore white, but those people were out of my life now.

I got home in time to make dinner for Wang Hui, and I didn't mention anything about my trip to Guangzhou. I wasn't sure what I was doing or whether I should let him know that I was looking for jobs on my own instead of waiting for one to fall into my lap. Though we were in the South, he was still a conservative man from Inner China who would get upset if he knew I had gone to Guangzhou without discussing it with him first. He didn't want his woman acting in such an independent way. Trust Older Brother, he had told me all along.

A few days later, I left for Guangzhou again. In a small copy shop near the Labor and Talent Center, I made thirty copies of my résumé. Then I picked up my new clothes and changed in a public bathroom. Armed with a sudden confidence, I strode into the center, the plastic folder that contained my résumés held tightly in my arms.

People who were hiring sat leisurely behind rows of tables, examining every person walking by. Behind them stood large boards with big posters glued on them containing brush-painted descriptions and requirements for the open positions. As my eyes scanned the posters, I grew discouraged. Phrases like "bachelor's degree" and "well-proportioned features" appeared on almost every poster. After circling around the tables a few times, I found myself back at one whose poster read "Secretary for Director wanted. Associate degree and regular features required." I stood sideways far away from the table and looked at the poster again and again, debating whether I should step forward.

Behind the table sat a tall man in a blue suit. He looked like he was in his early thirties, and he seemed to be in charge of the booth. Casually leaning back in his chair, he was looking at me, a thin smile on his fine-featured face. He seemed interested—playful, even—and suddenly I wanted to run away. It was like he saw the fear inside me as clearly as a blazing fire.

"Miss." His voice rang out before I could turn around. "Please come here."

I forced myself to walk up to him.

"Are you looking for a job?" He was obviously Cantonese, and his Mandarin was so bad that it hurt my teeth, but I understood him.

I nodded and slid a copy of my résumé out of the folder and put it on the table in front of him. He read it carefully.

"Are you interested in any of the positions we offer?" His eyes locked on mine. Something in them rattled me. I shifted my eyes away from him to the poster.

"Yes," I said with a smile. "I want to apply for the secretary job." After a moment I added hastily, "I think I can do it."

I waited tensely while he and his companions looked over my résumé and my college diploma and whispered in each other's ears. Then he handed everything back to me and said, "Come to our company next week for an interview. I am Manager Huang, head of Human Resources. Find me when you come."

I thanked him, grabbed the documents, and rushed out of the center. I stood outside on the steps and took a deep breath. The hot air tasted sweet in my mouth. I couldn't believe that I had just gotten an interview.

Back home, I decided to tell Wang Hui everything. He stood with his hands on his hips and listened to me quietly.

"Where is this company?"

"In the town of Long Jiang, about an hour and half's bus ride away," I said carefully.

"If you get the job, what are we going to do with this apartment and all the furniture we just bought?"

I didn't know how to answer. And what would happen between him and me? That was the bigger question hovering in the air. I didn't want to think about it further, though, so I just changed the subject.

The following week, I left for Long Jiang for the interview. I got off the bus at the main road. Through the heavy dust, I saw lots of furniture shops and office parks with low buildings behind them. Furniture manufacturing was the town's main industry. In the distance I saw several buildings with signs reading *LongJiang Enterprises Group* on the top, the name of the company I was looking for. I strolled down one of the paved walkways lined with trees and flowers for a few minutes. Before I could find the entrance to the company, I caught sight of Manager Huang approaching me, his leather bag tucked under one arm while the other swung back and forth like a pendulum. I narrowed my eyes and took a good look at him. He was very tall, over six feet. He had a noticeably small head, a straight stature, exquisite facial features, and dark but smooth skin. In my eyes, he shone in the sun like Apollo.

"Manager Huang!" I called out respectfully. A faint smile floated to his face.

He began filling me in on the company as we walked. "LongJiang is a very large entity. We have thirty subsidiary companies all over town. You can imagine how important the secretary to the director is."

I followed him closely. His long legs took big steps.

An hour later, I met Director Yip, the head of LongJiang Enterprises, in his large, empty office. Tall and well-built, but with a beer belly, Director Yip sat behind a huge oak table and glared at me with round dark angry eyes. He looked like a ferocious leopard, ready to bite at any minute. It was as if he was trying his hardest to appear terrifying. I understood now why it had seemed like everyone within a ten-foot range of his office was on tiptoes.

"You studied English?" He put his elbows on the table heavily and interlaced his fingers. His voice was a little hoarse. His thick eyebrows were raised, and he looked extremely irritated.

I put my sweaty palms in my lap and nodded.

"A teacher before?"

"Yes."

He threw his arms onto the table. "I'll give you a three-month tryout period at nine hundred yuan a month. Go work for Manager Huang first."

Then he stood up and walked toward the door, taking vigorous strides, leaving his black leather chair swiveling. I watched him leave the office. With both arms bent and swinging, he resembled a crab.

I sat there perplexed. Had I gotten the job?

After waiting a few minutes with no sign of Director Yip's returning, I decided to get up and go to the lobby. I saw Manager Huang sitting in one of the sliding chairs there. He sprang to his feet.

"You got the job! Congratulations!" he said in his horrible Mandarin. "Come on. Let me show you where you're going to live."

On the way, we stopped at his office, a real estate salesroom where I would work for three months before being considered for the position of Director Yip's secretary. In addition to being the head of Human Resources, Huang was also the sales manager of LongJiang's real estate company, which meant I would be working with him every day. I was pleased to hear this.

We climbed the cement stairs of a building that was one of the real estate company's projects but was temporarily being used to accommodate the employees. "I'll show you your room," he told me.

We stopped in front of a white-painted fiberboard door on the sixth floor. He fished a key out of his leather bag and unlocked it. Inside the room I saw a bed, a desk, a television, a table, a few chairs, and some clothes. Apparently someone was already living here. I stood at the door, confused.

He threw his leather bag onto the bed. "Sit," he ordered.

I looked at him, bewildered. He smiled mysteriously and then he sat down on the bed. He took out some pliers from one of the desk drawers and turned the television around and started to fix a broken wire.

"I thought you were going to show me my place," I worked up the nerve to say. He tilted his head sideways and looked at me again. I started to hate that smile on his face. He was a cat and I was a mouse. He was playing with me and enjoying it.

"This is where *I* live," he said.

"Oh." I chuckled nervously.

"You're going to live here too," he added in an assertive tone.

My forehead started to sweat. Was he serious or just testing me? What should I do? Should I tell him to go to hell and throw away the job I'd just gotten?

I laughed dryly, spread my palms, and chirped, "Sure, sounds nice, maybe in the future, but I don't think that's appropriate now."

He burst out laughing, still playing with the wire in his hands. When he was done fixing it, he picked up his bag from the bed, unzipped it, took out a key, and tossed it to me. "Your room is upstairs on the seventh floor. I was just joking with you."

What a bizarre experience, I thought to myself on the way back to Gao Ming. Everything I had seen so far in LongJiang was out of the ordinary. But hey, it didn't matter: I had gotten the job.

Upon hearing my news, Wang Hui was grouchy and unresponsive. That night he made love to me wordlessly and passionately, as if he wanted to get the most out of me before I left. I tried my best to cater to him. We would see each other on the weekends, I consoled him, and finally he seemed to consent to this arrangement.

The next day, I reported to Manager Huang. He put me at a desk adjacent to his in the real estate sales office. Then he brought me a bunch of real estate brochures and told me to get familiar with the real estate market and sales techniques. "Also, go buy a book and start learning Cantonese."

Manager Huang was so busy that I rarely saw him. Every morning he would show up in the office for a little while and then leave for all sorts of gatherings. He didn't appear to be paying special attention to me, but when he yelled at the other two salesgirls in the office for not wearing lipstick and then turned around and spoke to me like a gentle brother would, I felt pleased. I was still a little scared of him, but he fascinated me. Why did he seem so happy that I had gotten the job? Why was he so nice to me? As time passed, I felt thrilled whenever his tall figure appeared outside the heavy glass door. It became the highlight of my day.

Occasionally he took me to the evening dinner party, where all the important people in the company clinked liquor bottles and buried their faces in delicacies of every kind. Southerners rarely cooked at home and loved to drink and eat in restaurants. At the table, he introduced me to everyone as Director Yip's secretary-to-be and told them to treat me like a little sister. He would whisper in my ear when important people showed up at the table: "That's the assistant director, a bookworm. Talk to him honestly. That's Director Zhang, an easygoing big guy. Show some charm to him and he will be your slave. That's Director Jia, a slimy son of a bitch who uses the company's Mercedes 600 as his own. Be careful when talking to him."

He was always right. Director Jia's eyes remained on my face for only a second. He must be wondering why Manager Huang picked such an ordinary-looking girl to be the big boss's secretary, I thought. In the South, the most important prerequisite for becoming a secretary was to be beautiful. She primarily functioned like a decorative flower vase that her boss liked to show clients. "If you want to be Director Yip's secretary, you have to speak Cantonese. I give you three months," Jia said to me.

His tiny eyes paused on mine and then flicked away quickly behind his gilt-framed glasses. He was the type of person who could make you feel so uncomfortable that you wanted to punch him in the face.

I straightened my back and answered him calmly. "Thank you, Director Jia. I think I'll only need two months."

I started learning Cantonese. I couldn't afford a tape recorder, so every day I begged the two girls who worked in the same office to keep talking to me in Cantonese. I wanted to prove to Director Jia that Manager Huang hadn't made a mistake in recruiting me.

Manager Huang and I became closer as time went by. One night, after having a lot to drink, we walked together back to his room, and he told me about his personal life for the first time. "Long Jiang is my home town, you know, but I don't want to be here. My family is in Shenzhen." Shenzhen was the newest and most modern city in the South.

He leaned against his chair. "Director Yip and I grew up together, but he's the big boss now. He's the emperor, and it's almost like serving a tiger, working for him. If it wasn't for the money, I wouldn't be here." He sighed wistfully. "Life is so tough. I only have a high school degree, and it's hard to find a good job in Shenzhen."

"Do you miss your wife?" I asked cautiously. The girls in the office had told me that Manager Huang had been married for many years.

He shook his head. "No, I don't miss her. I wouldn't miss her no matter where I was. But I miss my son terribly." He sighed and mourned to himself, "Son, dad is so sorry. Dad cannot be with you."

I saw tears at the corners of his eyes, and my heart ached for him. I would never have thought that a seemingly high-spirited man like him could carry such a secret anguish. I wanted to hold him and wipe away his tears.

My heart was betraying Wang Hui. I felt guilty, but I wasn't going to stop it. In contrast to Wang's cowardice and incompetence, Huang was mature and masterful socially, yet he was also tender and complicated on the inside. More importantly, he looked after me at every occasion and protected me from the harshness of the South like a big umbrella.

Three weeks after I had started my new job, Wang Hui came to Long Jiang to see me. As I stood on the main road watching him get off the bus, I sadly realized that his once familiar and intimate face was no longer able to stir me. Still, I walked up to him and put my hands in his.

On the same day as Wang's visit, a girl my age came to our office. She had thick black rings around her eyes; pale, loose skin; and a distressed look. She walked around the office freely, as if she belonged, and everyone tolerated her, behaving as if nothing odd was happening. She took a tape out of her purse and put it into the VCR next to Manager Huang's desk. She said that she was working for a TV station in Guangzhou and this was a documentary she had made for our company, which, she emphasized, would really give us excellent publicity. The VCR squeaked as she pressed the buttons of the remote control impatiently. She grew frustrated.

"Take it easy. Let it go." Huang spoke to her in a soothing tone and took away the remote. I sat on the big leather couch at the window and watched this scene curiously. Was Manager Huang involved with her? I felt a little jealous.

Abruptly, the glass doors swung open and Director Yip stormed into the room. The two salesgirls lowered their heads, pretending they had been working hard all day. I saw fear in everyone's eyes. I stayed still on the couch, having no idea how to greet the big boss properly. There was only one person in the room who seemed not to mind the presence of Director Yip. It was that girl. She was sitting with her back to him.

At the sight of her, he paused and then turned around and sat heavily on the couch. I scooted a few inches away from him. Huang came up to him right away.

"Why is she here?" Director Yip asked him in a low angry voice.

"Ah, you know. She can't forget. She made this documentary tape for us," Huang explained, sounding like a parent trying to calm a child.

"Hmm. She was just a fucking secretary," Director Yip snorted. "Why did she want to be so ambitious and greedy, wanting to be a manager? It's a good thing that she's gone."

"Well, she is a girl, and the abortion wasn't easy," Huang said patiently.

"Damn her for threatening to call my wife. Who the hell does she think she is?" Director Yip stared at the girl's back furiously. "Give her ten thousand and tell her never to show up here again," he ordered, then heaved his big body off the couch and left.

Huang sighed. He turned to the girl. "Now you should feel better," he said.

She sat with a bent back and didn't budge.

I was astounded by what I had just seen. So this odd girl was Yip's former secretary, and he'd gotten her pregnant and was now trying to get rid of her with ten thousand yuan. Was Huang Director Yip's personal disposer? I frowned. Was he planning to get rid of me in a similar way one day?

Seeing my displeasure, Huang shook his head. He moved close and told me quietly, "Now you see why I brought you to my room on the interview day. I was testing you. She was Director Yip's Number 6 secretary, and she slept with him."

The girl turned her face to me. I couldn't bear to see the sadness and jealousy in her eyes. Was she thinking that I wanted to be like her, the mistress of the big boss? I would rather have died than sleep with the monstrous Director Yip and get money in such a pathetic way. I felt sympathy for this girl, but I knew it was stupid and self-destructive of her to have taken this path.

"She is staying with you tonight, Ah-Juan," Huang said.

"What? But my boyfriend just got here," I objected.

"Oh, please. He can have a break," he insisted, throwing his arm up dismissively.

He must be doing this on purpose, I thought. She could easily have stayed with another female employee. I opened my mouth, wanting to object more, but no words came. Strangely, I felt a little relieved. I knew Wang Hui had come to see me for sex. I had never refused him before, but that night I had no desire to be intimate with him.

I took the girl to my room. Wang Hui was sitting on the mattress on the cement floor, the only thing in the room besides the desk, reading a magazine. He looked up curiously as we entered. With a sad and solemn face, the girl went straight to the desk, sat down, took out a cassette player, and started to listen to music as if there was nobody else in the room.

I sat down on the mattress next to Wang Hui and told him that he would have to stay with one of the male employees for the night, since the sixth secretary was staying with me.

Looking angry, Wang Hui fell back on the mattress and stared at the ceiling with his hands behind his head.

"Why is it like this? I traveled an hour and a half on the bus to see you, and this is how you greet me?"

His response infuriated me. I had hoped he would be tolerant and understanding. Perhaps we could salvage our relationship at the last minute, I had thought. But finally I saw the truth—all he cared about was sex. That was what he had wanted from me all along; not love, not the promise of a life together.

I stood up. "Is this all you want from me? Sex?" I screamed with tears in my eyes. He didn't answer; instead, he punched the mattress. I left the room and went outside to walk off my anger.

When I came back, it was clear that Wang regretted having reacted in such a way. His face was relaxed, and we didn't argue any more that night. Together with two male employees of LongJiang, we had dinner at a small Cantonese restaurant in the local market downstairs. I looked at Wang Hui across the table and realized regretfully that we couldn't go forward any more. I knew that sooner or later I would tell him this, but I just couldn't bring it up right then. After all, I had feelings for him, had dreamed of a future with him. My feelings were changing, though, and every day my thoughts turned more and more to Huang. Wang had never been perfect, but he had been good enough in dinky little Ba Jin. Yet, like a grinding machine, the South had quickly crushed my old dreams and changed my feelings.

The next morning, Wang Hui went back to Gao Ming upset, like a debt collector who had just made an unsuccessful trip.

The following weekend, I returned to Gao Ming. That night, with the moon shining through the window, we sat against the wall on the cement floor of the house we had rented together. Facing each other, we both knew it was coming to an end.

"So you come here, stay for two months, and now you're just going to dump me?" He remained outwardly calm, but his voice shook. His eyes glittered in the moonlight.

There was nothing I could say. I was at fault in this relationship because I liked another man.

Wang Hui gritted his teeth. "Do you really think you were the only person I liked before?" he snorted. "When I was teaching math, a girl wrote a love letter to me and put it in her homework."

"Please, please. Don't ruin everything we had," I begged him.

He laughed exaltedly and ignored me. "So I opened the letter and I saw a heart made of red paper. And then there was another girl. . . ."

He spoke faster and louder as he told me these victory stories. I covered my ears as tightly as I could. I wanted to scream to him: Why? Why do you want to ruin the few good memories we had together?

The next day, with dried tears on my face and my duffel bag in my arms, I left everything behind—Wang Hui, the home we had once had, all the furniture I had bought with my savings, and Gao Ming, my first stop in the South—forever.

I LAY SLEEPLESS on the bare mattress in my room. Wang Hui, the man who I had followed here, whom I had planned to build a castle of a life with, was gone. I was alone in the tumultuous South, like a canoe in the roaring Pacific Ocean.

The heavy cloth curtains kept out the light and noise from the streets. I got out of bed and went to a window in the hall. I looked out. The lights of a moving airplane blinked in the bed of stars. Motorcycles zoomed by on the street. I tiptoed down the stairs and stopped at Huang's door.

I leaned against the washed-out white door. I imagined Huang lying underneath his thin cotton quilt. His blue suit must have been hanging on the back of his tall wooden chair and his leather shoes probably had been kicked onto the tiled floor. The smell of his room—linen mixed with dust—seemed to seep out into the hall like an aromatic poison, drawing me to it.

I knocked on the door shyly. I heard the sound of footsteps

in slippers. The door creaked opened. Huang's tall figure appeared. He gave me a sleepy look and then went back inside and clambered onto the bed, as if I wasn't even there.

I followed him and stood at the end of his bed uneasily, my hands clenching the bottom of my pajama top.

His impatient voice came from the bed. "What are you doing here?"

"Can I stay with you?" I mumbled. "I can't get to sleep."

"Go, go, go," he shouted brutally.

I bit my lower lip, feeling hurt. I didn't understand how this man who took care of me like a big brother could be so cruel.

I heard him sighing. He patted the edge of the bed and beckoned softly, "Come here."

I walked to the side of the bed and crawled in under the quilt next to him like the meekest lamb. I shrank myself down to the smallest volume I could so that I wouldn't disturb him during the night by taking up too much space. It grew cold, and I shivered. As I pulled the corner of the quilt gingerly, he turned, and his arm fell across my chest heavily. I didn't move and lay still for the entire night with a smile on my face, feeling like I had discovered a big diamond.

"Go. Leave right now," he ordered as soon as he woke up the next morning.

I jumped out of the bed.

"What did you come here for?" he kept yelling. "Why are you so foolish? Do you think you can become Director Yip's secretary if someone sees you coming out of my room in pajamas early in the morning?"

Under his bellows, I scurried out of his room like a rabbit on the run.

Two months after joining LongJiang Enterprise Group, I had learned to understand and speak Cantonese fluently, as I had promised Director Jia. By that time, Manager Huang and

I had slept in the same bed for a month. We cuddled together innocently like two schoolkids. We just held each other; there was nothing more to it than that.

I lived for these nights, as if sleeping next to him was my only chance of waking up the next morning. Every day, I longed for the sky to turn dark; every evening, I waited for the people in his room to leave. When he and his friends played mah-jongg until dawn, I sat to the side, half-dozing, and waited patiently. When he was in a bad mood and yelled at me to leave, I took it quietly, waiting for the next minute, when he would talk to me as gently as an angel. When he kept his distance from me on the bed or turned his back to me, as if I was filthy, I told myself that he had just had a bad day. I wanted nothing more than to be in his arms, touching his skin. Sometimes I wished I could feel his hands under my pajamas, but, as time went by, all my wishes were filtered down to just one—for life to go on just like it was, to be in his arms and feel safe and protected. For the first time since I had been with Chi, sex wasn't the only string that tied me to a man. I felt warmth, gratitude, adoration, and much more for him.

One night after coming back from a dinner with Director Yip, he threw himself onto the bed and swept me into his arms. "Ah-Juan, speak some Cantonese to me." His voice sounded a little raspy from drinking.

"Manager Huang, my name is Ah-Juan. I am so glad to know you, and I really like you," I said to him slowly in Cantonese, enunciating every word.

He pulled me closer and looked at me with blurred eyes, and then he sighed. "I knew you were different the minute I saw you," he said. "You're special."

I twined my arms around his neck and sighed contentedly.

After a while, he cleared his throat and said, "Director Yip praised my work at the board dinner tonight." His face was glowing with pride. "He said I did well, in front of all the other important people in the company. You don't know how hard it is to please him."

Knowing how insecure he felt about the approval of his childhood friend who was now his boss, I smiled happily. He was jubilant and hugged me tighter. He put his mouth close to my ear and whispered, "Let's do it tonight."

I chuckled, thinking that he must really be in a good mood if he was willing to joke about sex. I was sure he would never have the guts to actually do it. After all, I was the future secretary of his boss.

As if he wanted to prove me wrong, he quickly undressed me, like an unexpected typhoon hitting a town. A few seconds later, we were no longer just two people who slept in the same bed. Soon after we became one, I reached the heights of physical pleasure for the first time in my life. Then, before it died down, he finished with a loud moan. He rolled off me and immediately started to snore loudly.

I closed my eyes, enjoying the wonderful feeling of having reached the crest of joy. He was like the other men in my life, who had liked it quick, but he felt so different. He was the first one to have brought the most primitive desire out of my body. I had had no idea that it could be so wonderful. A funny feeling was growing in my chest, like how I felt watching the sun slowly rise above the horizon, and I grinned to myself. Finally he was mine. I took a deep, happy breath and then fell asleep easily.

—

The end of the three-month tryout came quickly. On the last day, I sat at my desk, skimming the real estate brochures absent-mindedly and wondering if Huang had talked to Director Yip about my formally becoming his secretary. At noon, Huang's tall figure appeared behind the glass door. I lowered my head and tried to appear professional and respectful. In everybody else's eyes, he was no more than just my manager and perhaps my mentor.

He walked directly to my desk. "Grab your things and follow me." We walked quietly up the stairs of the Group's newly finished headquarters building. The elevator was not yet operational, so we hiked all the way up to the eighth floor. The entire floor belonged to Director Yip.

The two leather-covered wooden doors to his office were closed. Their brass handles were shaped like lions. Huang pointed to the desk a few feet outside the doors, motioning for me to sit there, and then left quickly.

I sat in the Italian leather sliding chair at my brand-new wooden desk, at a loss as to what to do as the secretary of the boss of thirty companies. The entire floor was so deathly quiet that I didn't dare even to breathe loudly. I sat around waiting for someone to show up and direct me; but after half an hour had passed without even a bird flying by the windows, I decided to go downstairs to the main office, where all the other employees were located.

After collecting a stack of stationery and a few pens to decorate my empty desk, I asked the office manager what my job responsibilities were. He spread his palms in the air, shrugged, and made a face. "How the hell would I know? You're Director Yip's secretary. You do whatever he tells you to do."

So I went back to my secluded territory, to more waiting in boredom. After examining everything in the room, including the drawers, the wine racks, and the trophy table, and staring outside the window at the dusty streets for a while, I approached Director Yip's office doors. It was quiet on the other side. I summoned up my courage and pushed one of the doors with my fingertips. It opened.

Director Yip's new office was magnificent. It was really more like a show room. Well over a thousand square feet, there was nothing office-like in it except a giant oak boss table squatting in the center of the gleaming wood floor. It took up almost a quarter of the space and was empty except for a golden tissue box sitting on its corner. Along the wall behind the table, there were tall shelves on which stood nothing but the trophies I'd seen in his old office. There was a set of splendid-looking brown and gold leather furniture next to the table, on a giant oriental rug. The chairs were the kind that had golden rivets along the edges, the kind you only saw in European mansions shown on television.

I took a few steps forward, and I heard the echoes of my footsteps. Though there was no one else inside the magnificent room, I turned around and fled.

I spent the rest of my day sitting at my desk, feeling happy for myself that I had gotten the position I had applied for and at the same time wishing that my clothes were nicer and my nails were cleaner and blaming myself for not being a little taller, thinner, and prettier so that I could better match the office.

Just as I was lamenting my appearance, Director Yip stormed in. I stood up hurriedly and greeted him in Cantonese. He gave me a glance and continued swinging his arms, walking to his office like a crab, as if I were only a mannequin that came with the desk.

I sat back down in my chair, but before I could compose myself, Director Yip crab-walked out of his office and left the floor. It was now time to go home. I took a deep breath and started to lock the doors. It was dark outside, and some karaoke music was playing in the distance, the kind of noise that you heard every night in the South. Just when I was ready to leave, Xiao Ma, Director Yip's driver, came to tell me that Director Yip wanted me to accompany him and his guests to dinner.

Apprehensive, I nonetheless followed him down the stairs to the black Mercedes S600 parked outside the building. Two men were already sitting in the back seat. In the dark, I got in next to them. My heart started to race as soon as I realized that I was sitting next to Director Yip and that our arms and legs were touching. I recognized his two friends, one of whom was sitting in the front seat: both were the heads of local banks.

The men joked and laughed boisterously as the Mercedes glided quietly down the well-lit road. I couldn't believe how different the Director Yip in the car was from the Director Yip who showed himself to his employees. In the car, he shouted curses to his friends, clapped his hands, and cheered wildly like a teenager, as if a tube of excitant had been injected in his body to save him from the suffocating daily work of pretending to be a terrifying person. I guessed that he was only himself with his most important friends, such as these two heads of banks, whose continuous loans were undoubtedly the backbone of Yip's family business. I was sure that his two friends were feeling just as happy. They slumped back leisurely into the leather seats and their faces had a dreamy look, as if they were drunk already. How could they not be happy? I thought to myself. Not only did they get secret commissions from the loans, which came out of the Communist Party's pocket anyway, but they also got to go out for nights of dinners, parties, and girls.

I heard Director Yip say my name. Before I could turn my head to him, I felt a hand sneaking down to my crotch. Determined as the hand of an experienced thief, it started to rub my most private spot. I looked up and saw Yip's smiling eyes and twitching mouth.

I spoke as calmly as I could, trying to control my anger. "Director Yip, please." I brushed his arm off my lap.

His hand reached down again. It felt like a cold eel wandering on my skin.

"Come on," he said jokingly. "You fuck my manager, why not me?"

His words were like a bucket of cold water poured over my head. He knew what was going on between Huang and me?

"Director Yip, please!" I chuckled nervously and lightly moved his hand away again.

He tried again, and once again I moved his hand. Finally he muttered, "Fuck your mother!" and gave up. I leaned against the door, as far away from him as possible, my mind in turmoil.

Dinner was completely tasteless, given my upset state, though the meal went smoothly, with wild cheers and toasts as usual. I toasted with Director Yip's friends in rounds and bottomed up each time. Glasses of rice wine washed down my throat continuously. My stomach burned like the oven in a crematorium. Everyone was excited to have a girl so capable of drinking—except Director Yip, who didn't drink with me at all. I surreptitiously glanced at his face, afraid that my unsatisfied new boss might abruptly rise, point his finger at me, and tell me to get the hell out of the resplendent restaurant and his company.

Buoyant with drunken elation, the men cheered "More, more, more!" as the Mercedes pulled into the marbled archway of the Money-Locker Karaoke club. The three men tumbled out of the car and into a dark VIP room. One by one, they fell onto the low couches along the wall like sacks of potatoes. I sat quietly at the end of a couch and started to play with the remote control for the TV screen directly in front of the us. Should I go and sit next to Yip and put my hand on his arm, a common courtesy from a secretary to a boss in a dark and smoky karaoke room? I struggled with myself. He was not a bad-looking man: tall and sturdy with some fine features, especially his big eyes; but I just couldn't find enough courage or desire to approach him.

My inner debate ended as soon as a bunch of girls entered

the room and lined up in front of us. They were all tall and slender and wore short skirts with leather boots or dresses through which you could catch a glimpse of lacy bras and panties. Each boss pointed his finger at two of the girls, and the two selected walked to the couch and sat with the boss in between them. Director Yip chose two girls quickly and then ordered another for his driver, Xiao Ma. The girls, all of whom had sweet, charming voices, began to skillfully nudge the men's arms or lean themselves over their chests, feeding them orange wedges or pouring beer into their mouths.

The room started to boil with laughter, and the atmosphere became giddy as in a brothel. I sat alone, staring intently at the screen and pretending that I didn't feel awkward at all. Once in a while, one of the girls would get up to take the microphone and would give me a curious look. I would smile. So I was finally in the same room as those girls in the South who were cutely nicknamed "miss at the table" or, not so cutely, "whore." Their delicate skin, tall figures, red lips, and thickly powdered faces made men love them and women jealous; but once they opened their mouths, nothing could cover their lousy, heavily accented Mandarin.

I wondered whether I should talk to them or just do my best to ignore them. Most good girls would turn away at the sight of such a girl, perhaps even spit on the ground. But had I ever been one of the good girls? I remembered the time when I had roamed the streets of Shanghai and almost sold my body for cash. Although I had an associate's degree and could read those Western letters, I wasn't better than them. After all, we were all migrant workers. We all had flung away our past, left our home towns, and come to the South with the same dream—to have a better life.

At last the men called it a night. Yip stood in the middle of the room, holding a stack of hundred-yuan bills in his hand.

Each girl giggled as she took hers. After he was done, he scanned the room, making sure he hadn't missed anyone. His glance flickered over me for a second. I couldn't help but be mesmerized by the stack of bills in his hand. Maybe it was better to be one of those girls. I had come to the South to make money, and here they were getting so much of it.

With difficulty I forced my eyes to move away from Yip's hand. With one arm around his waist, one of girls he had picked for the night suddenly snapped another bill from his hand and hid it behind her back, giggling. "Fuck your mother!" Yip pinched her cheek, clearly teasing. He let her get away with it. Convulsing with laughter, the rowdy party moved to the door.

I shook my head firmly, trying to drive these thoughts from my mind. I would never, ever sleep with Yip, for money or anything else, not because I didn't want money, but because I already had a man in my life, a man who didn't have much money, a man who sometimes yelled at me but who also gave me warmth and care.

The next day I was alone again on the eighth floor. After taking a good look at Yip's office, I went back to my desk and idled my morning away. I felt like a bird sitting on a branch above a graveyard. Soon the boredom overtook me. It was so hard to fight off my sleepiness.

Just as I was ready to give up and let my head drop to the desk, Yip stomped out of the elevator, which was now in operation. My drowsiness flew away. I sprang to my feet and studied his face, trying to see if he was angry with me because of the previous night. He went right into his office and slammed the door behind him.

A minute late, he strode out and shouted, "Ah-Juan! Why is there dust on the table in my office? And did you mop and wax the floor?"

I stammered and stuttered. I'd had no idea that my job responsibilities included dusting the table and waxing the floor. I quickly shook my head. I was scared to death that he might yell more, and my legs were shaking. When Yip was extremely annoyed, I got the feeling that he could just eat me alive.

The moment he stormed out, I grabbed the mop and feather duster in the closet and started to do my work. As I knelt and poured wax onto the wood floor, I groaned to myself: Did I have to mop and wax this entire floor of over a thousand square feet every day? Was this what Bill Gates's secretary did, clean and dust, instead of copying, faxing, and translating? Well, maybe I shouldn't compare LongJiang with Microsoft, I thought to myself. After all, LongJiang was built entirely on bank loans and my boss showed up for work for only fifteen minutes a day.

I sat on that floor of the finest wood and sighed heavily. Then I rolled up my sleeves and started to clean like crazy. Three hours later, the entire floor shone with wax; I had not missed even one corner. My second day as secretary had ended, and I was exhausted.

Day three, day four, and then day five continued in the same way. Gradually, I decided that although I was called by the fine-sounding title "secretary of the director," in reality I was just his cleaning lady. The only difference between an ordinary cleaning lady and me was that I dressed up a little bit; I had an associate's degree in English; and occasionally I could become his drinking companion. I imagined that Yip wouldn't want an illiterate woman wearing ragged clothes in his fine new office, or in the deluxe room of his excellent Cantonese restaurant.

As long as I did my job well and behaved cautiously, I thought some day my boss would learn to respect and appreciate me. Though I lived like a mouse that trembled at the sight of a cat, my life as Director Yip's secretary was, after all, better than planting rice in the fields or eating chalk dust in front of a blackboard.

The days stumbled along. By thinking carefully before speaking or acting, I had survived as Director Yip's secretary for two months. Every day, my boss came to the office for only a short period of time, and once in a while he would give me an easy order, such as pouring a cup of tea for him or calling someone to his office.

One day I found a letter on his desk written in English. Out of sheer boredom, I translated it into Chinese for him. It was in fact a very simple invitation, but I was sure that Director Yip couldn't understand it since he had only reached junior high. Afterward, I heard through the grapevine that he had praised my translation in front of other heads of the company. I was happy and thought that I had finally attained his approval. As time went by, maybe he would give me more responsibility, I hoped.

"YOU ARE A devil!" Huang shouted through clenched teeth
as he moved on top of me. "Why don't you go to hell? I can't
even be a man to my wife any more." Every time he came back
from visiting his wife and son, he wouldn't talk to me for days,
and then he would let out his anger by making love to me like
a madman.

I kept quiet, as usual, with my eyes focused on his twisted
face. I was sorry that I made him feel guilty. But I couldn't
imagine not having him in my life in this strange land. He was
a brick wall, and I was the ivy. He was married, but I loved
him. He was the first man I had loved since Chi, although the
love was much different. My feelings for Chi had been innocent, but my love for Huang was consuming and heavy, like
loving a brother, a father, and a lover all at once. He had a wife
in another city, but in the small town of Long Jiang, Huang, I
thought, only belonged to me.

"Don't ever leave me alone here, please," I would murmur to him at night when he held me tight.

"Don't worry, Ah-Juan. No woman would want me except silly you! I am married and have no money," he'd tell me jokingly, and I would cup his face in my hands. I believed him completely, even when I overheard him talking on the phone with a girl.

"It's Ah Min, a friend," he explained. "We used to work together back in Shenzhen. She's very smart, just like you. She's from Inner China and also learned Cantonese from scratch."

One Sunday evening when Huang had gone to visit his family for the weekend, I was sitting in my room, flipping through a magazine, when I heard a loud noise coming from downstairs:

"Manager Huang, open the fucking door!" Someone was pounding on Huang's door. I ran downstairs and saw it was a mah-jongg friend of his.

"Has he come back from Shenzhen?" I asked. I wasn't expecting him until the next day.

"He should've. Before he left, he told us that he would come back and play mah-jongg with us tonight." He kept pounding the door for a couple of minutes. "Manager Huang, I know you are inside. Open the fucking door!" No one answered. "I guess he's not back yet." Disappointed, he left.

Why had Huang told his mah-jongg friends he would return Sunday night but told me Monday morning? I ran up a few stairs and looked at Huang's windows. The curtains were all drawn, and I couldn't see inside. They had been up on Friday morning when he left. He was in there. I could feel it.

I knocked on the door. No answer.

I stood outside, feeling my knees getting weaker. Why was he hiding? Was he with another girl? I couldn't think any further.

The next morning, I went to work early. Around ten o'clock, I called Huang's office. "Ah-Xia, is Manager Huang in the office yet?" I asked the salesgirl who answered the phone. "Director Yip might want to see him today."

"Yeah, he just came in ten minutes ago," she said.

I put down the phone and slipped out of the office. I ran all the way from the headquarters building to the dorm and then up the stairs to Huang's room.

I knocked on the door and waited. My nervous heart was twisting inside me. A minute later, the door opened, and a girl appeared, a small girl in a blue daisy-patterned dress with delicate skin and slanted eyes like two crescents.

"Are you Ah-Min?" I asked, lifting my chin.

"Yes. Who are you?" she answered in perfect Cantonese with a small, piercing voice.

So Ah-Min was his girlfriend, not just his former co-worker.

I walked past her into the room. She followed and sat on the bed. I took the chair across from her. We faced one another, reading the fear and pain in each other's eyes.

I cleared my throat and introduced myself. "My name is Ah-Juan. I'm his girlfriend." I stared at her provocatively.

Her shoulders were trembling, and her pale face was rigid. She looked so small and delicate, like a gust of wind would just blow her away. Jealousy spread through my heart. I felt as though someone had grabbed me by the waist and was breaking me in two.

"Has he been seeing you all this time when he goes back to Shenzhen?" No answer. I continued: "You know, our relationship isn't ordinary. We have deep feelings for each other." After a short pause, I told her coldly, "I had an abortion for him."

I started toward the door. I realized that I had just lied without flinching. The white clothes I was wearing suddenly felt dusty and heavy. The four lime walls were shrinking, closing in, trapping me. I turned and I saw tears flowing down her cheeks. Good, I had hurt her, just like he had hurt me.

I raised my head and left the room with a straight back.

When I went back to Huang's room that evening, he was sitting on the bed, sighing. I looked around. Ah-Min was gone.

The fire of jealousy that burned inside me earlier had died down a little. I waited for his explosion. "Why did you lie to her?" I wanted him to yell at me. But he just looked gloomy.

"Why did you do that?" He sighed. "It's meaningless."

"I thought I was your only girlfriend." I sat next to him gingerly. He was not as angry as I'd thought he'd be.

"But you've seen her. She isn't like you. She's not the kind of girl you can easily leave behind in a strange city. After I left Shenzhen, she called me all the time and cried on the phone. She's fragile and needs someone to take care of her," he explained patiently.

So because I was strong, I was doomed to be hurt?

"She cried and cried, wanted to follow me here. What could I do?" Then he smiled. "Ah-Juan, you're like a fierce tiger. I do like that."

I wanted to tell him that I too was fragile and soft, that I wanted love more desperately than anyone else in the world, but I was silent. As long as he didn't tell me to get lost, I could sacrifice my pride and hold back my tears.

He took me in his arms. We lay in bed silently and never mentioned Ah-Min again, but her desolate face and slender figure had permanently cast a shadow on our relationship. It shook my love for this man, who I had thought was my warrior but who turned out to belong to more than one young girl in need of love.

Why was love in the South so flimsy and easily changed?

I realized that my affection for Huang was a tree that would never blossom.

—

It had been three months since I'd become Director Yip's secretary when, one day, two girls, both of them tall and pretty, followed Huang into the office.

Huang introduced them to me. "This is Mei, and this is Chen. They are Director Yip's new secretaries. They just came from Harbin." I remembered that Director Jia recently had gone up north and had hired seven pretty girls to become secretaries for the directors in the company. This was one of the tricks of the business world, to decorate the façade of the company, the deputy director had claimed.

I stood up and shook their hands. They were so tall that my head only reached to their shoulders. I arranged for them to sit next to me. Now I would have help with mopping and waxing the floor and perhaps people to talk to during these boring days, I thought happily.

"What? Wax the floor? I'm a college graduate. I didn't come all the way here to wax his damn floor," Mei snorted as soon as I told them that this was part of the job. Then she took out a cosmetic bag from her purse and started to pluck her eyebrows, holding up a tiny mirror in her hand. The other girl, Chen, shrugged and walked away.

Shocked, I looked at their powdered faces and pursed red lips and wished I had the strength to stand up to them. "You were here first, so you should tell them what to do," Huang had counseled me earlier, but I realized that there was no way I could order these two city girls around. They were ten times better looking than me and as proud as two peacocks with their tails spread.

Chen eventually agreed to help me sweep the floor and take care of the tea service for Director Yip and his guests. But Mei, who completely detested the place, spent most of her time putting stuff on her face and then taking it off and complaining that the company had lied to them at recruiting. She fiddled with her cosmetic tools constantly, plucking, shaving, or smoothing, and at the end of the day her face always looked like a shelled whole egg just rolled out of an oily pan.

After she'd been there a couple of days, I couldn't restrain my curiosity any longer and asked her how she got her face to be so smooth. She held her mirror up higher and told me contemptuously, "You shave it!" She then turned her head and looked at it sideways in the mirror. "My sister brought this shaver for me from Japan, the best ever made."

I was embarrassed by my ignorance and rustic background. I had only one red lipstick and no relatives in Japan who could bring me goodies like a shaver. No wonder Director Yip always smiled at them but never at me.

Mei abruptly tossed her mirror on her desk and grumbled, "What a lousy job." She turned toward my desk, which was behind hers. "One of my friends who came to the South earlier goes to the Garden Hotel in Guangzhou and meets foreigners there, and do you know how much she makes every night?"

I shook my head.

"Five hundred American dollars! That's four thousand yuan, five times my salary!" she exclaimed. She dropped her elbows on her desk and whined, "What the hell am I doing here?"

I had a feeling that she wouldn't last long. Sure enough, a couple of mornings later she didn't show up. Just one week after the company had flown her all the way from the North to the South, she had vanished.

That left only Chen and me on the eighth floor, and we didn't talk much. Sometimes I sat at my desk, scribbling bits of poems or popular songs on a pad, and wondered how Mei was doing now. Was she working the lobby of the Garden Hotel and making five hundred dollars a night? Was she happy now?

I couldn't help but wonder: Were those girls out there who slept with men for money just being realistic? Did I, who was stuck with a monstrous boss, a low-paying job, and a married boyfriend, belong to the group of stupid and stubborn girls? I started to doubt whether it was worth it, whether some day Director Yip would ever tell me to stop mopping his floor or whether Huang would ever be able to give me a home.

During the dull days on the eighth floor, I contemplated my future. My life wasn't going forward, and I felt lost. Was my mother right that only businessmen and whores came to the South? Couldn't an educated woman succeed without sleeping around?

I remembered the story of a successful businesswoman I had heard from a friendly young man I had met on the bus from Gao Ming to Guangzhou.

"You have the courage to pursue your own dreams. Don't get discouraged by setbacks in life," the young man had encouraged me after hearing about my jobless situation at the time. "You know, I have a friend just like you. She studied a foreign language in college and was assigned to a travel agency after graduation, but she didn't like the job, so she resigned, and she's doing business on her own now. I'll introduce you to her if you come to Guangzhou again."

So once more I visited Guangzhou to try to change my life. When I got into the city, I picked up the public phone at a newspaper stand on the sidewalk and dialed the young man's pager number. The lady at the page station asked for my name and number. I shouted the information to her over the noise of the dense traffic and then I waited nervously. I wasn't sure he would remember me. He had looked urbane, affluent, and out of my league.

He called back right away. "Of course I remember you. Who could forget such a pretty girl?"

His solid, pleasant voice was like a ray of sunshine penetrating through the thick layer of gray air above the city. Southerners liked to tell every girl that she was pretty, but such a word from him, a sophisticated and good-looking man, stirred me like a pebble thrown into a river.

Half an hour later, a Harley-Davidson, the newest model, shiny as a mirror and wide as a canoe, stopped in front of the newsstand. The rider took off his helmet and I saw his lean, dark face. I had never believed in stories of knights on white horses, but seeing a city man on a Harley-Davidson smiling at me with white teeth made me think they might be true after all.

"Call me Brother Yong," he said. As the bike maneuvered in the traffic, he shouted, "Hold my waist!"

I did as I was told. "Do you remember the girl I told you about on the train, the one who left her governmental job?" he asked in the wind.

"Yes, of course," I shouted back to him. "She's my role model."

"Do you want to meet her? She's giving a speech tonight."

After making a big half-circle through the city, we came to an old cement building. I followed him to the second floor, and we stopped at a closed door. He gestured for me to be quiet and then pushed the door open a crack. A blast of warm air mixed with sweat escaped. I peered in and saw that the room was packed. People stood pressed up against the door with hunched shoulders and flattened stomachs.

Brother Yong carefully squeezed into the crowd, found a free spot, and waved to me. I sneaked in and stood a few inches from him. I looked through the gaps between the shoulders surrounding me. Everybody was gazing at the front of the room with their heads raised, listening with rapt attention, men and women, old and young.

A forceful, cadent female voice came to my ears. "Brothers and sisters, this is a golden opportunity you are offering to your friends and family, because you're saving them from many misfortunes and you're giving them the chance of a lifetime."

She was in her late twenties; she stood in front of a blackboard, clutching the microphone with both her hands and speaking to her audience with wholehearted sincerity. She wore a dark green wool skirt-suit and high heels, with a small colorful silk scarf around her neck.

"Ouch!" the man next to me cried out in a low voice.

I realized that I had just stepped on his foot.

"Sorry, sorry," I apologized hastily. To my surprise, instead of glowering or cursing, he smiled and said it was no problem. What kind of people were these, and why were they so nice?

I turned and caught Brother Yong's eye. His high-cheekboned face smiled at me gently. I wondered if he had been watching me the whole time.

He moved closer to me. "The woman speaking is the one I told you about," he whispered. "Her name is Grace, and we all call her Sister Grace. Listen to her carefully. She's incredible."

His warm breath tickled my neck. Why was handsome Brother Yong so nice to me? After the speech, would he take me somewhere quiet to sit and talk, like a café or a teahouse, like how normal young city people got together: like . . . a date?

I didn't hear much of what Sister Grace was saying with such utter sincerity. I only woke up from my own fantasies when she said, "Now it's time for self-reflection."

Everyone quickly and efficiently pulled chairs into circles, as if this were a military training camp. Before I even found out what the circles were for, someone had seated me on a square stool next to Brother Yong in a circle with a dozen strangers, all of whom seemed extraordinarily friendly.

"My name is Bo. I met Brother Yong eight months ago, and I have been following him ever since. I was so moved by Sister Grace's speech tonight. She was so determined to become successful, and now she is, and I know I want to be like her," a young man declared passionately. The others followed his lead, all smiling and making similar statements.

It seemed that everyone had to speak. Having no idea what to say, I glanced at Brother Yong anxiously. Wholly absorbed by everyone's individual speeches, he didn't notice me.

Then everyone's eyes fell on me.

"Hi, my name is Juanjuan," I said softly. My mind drew a blank. I was too nervous to go on.

"Who did you come here with?" a middle-aged woman asked me with a smile.

"I came with Brother Yong." I turned to Brother Yong, who smiled at me with encouraging eyes.

"Hey, I wonder why Brother Yong always meets pretty girls," Bo quipped, and everyone laughed.

"You know, Brother Yong has obtained Diamond rank, and he's one of the hottest bachelors in the city, so we call him the Diamond Bachelor. You're lucky he brought you here," the middle-aged woman said, and everyone nodded and looked at me admiringly. I did feel lucky to have met Brother Yong, who seemed to like me and had introduced me to these friendly people.

"I like being here, and I want to learn from everybody," I said bashfully, stealing another glance at Brother Yong, who was still smiling at me.

People's focus moved on to the person next to me. I listened to the rest of the group carefully, and gradually I felt like I was becoming one of them.

After the meeting, Brother Yong drove me to the bus station. I hopped on the last bus to Long Jiang in a hurry, and when I got home it was already past midnight. I went to my own room and fell asleep, thinking happily of Brother Yong and his friends.

A few days later, Brother Yong called to tell me that a very successful man was giving a motivational speech that night and that I should attend. So I went after work. Once again, I was in the same room with Brother Yong and all the friendly people.

The speaker, a tall man in a fine suit with a tidy haircut, was Sister Grace's husband. As he was delivering his passionate and stirring speech, Brother Yong said to me, "He's the boss of a major bank in Guangzhou, but he believes in Amway so much that he devotes part of his time to it. He is very highly ranked in the Amway system. He and his wife are quite well off now."

It was the first time I had heard the word "Amway."

"What's Amway?" I asked.

"Amway is an American company that manufactures home cleaning goods, such as soap, shampoo, and detergent. Their stuff is just amazing, but the best thing about Amway is its pyramid sales system. You can start your own Amway business very easily and then build your own network. Doing Amway, you don't just sell detergent; you build a career for yourself," Brother Yong explained in a low but excited voice.

"Have you ever dreamed of having a meaningful life, becoming a millionaire, and at the same time helping your friends and family become millionaires?" Grace's husband was saying. "Well, if you ever have, 'do' Amway, because you only need 721 yuan to start this career. Because Amway teaches you and supports you along the way. Because you will find so many friends in Amway. Amway is for ordinary people, for everybody who wants to succeed!"

His enthusiasm was infectious. Applause rocked the room as the crowd went crazy.

"Let's all hold hands and sing the 'Song of Success'!" the speaker cried out.

Everyone quickly grasped each other's hands as catchy music filled the room. As the speaker clapped his hands rhythmically, the crowd rocked slightly from side to side to the rhythm and started to sing:

> *I once had a dream in my heart,*
> *I wanted to become a real hero in my dream.*
> *Never give up!*
> *Never say I failed. . . .*

The room resounded with impassioned, lusty singing. Everyone beamed. I even saw some tears. With one hand in Brother Yong's, I gazed at him with glistening eyes. I was such a lucky girl to have met him, the Diamond Bachelor, and to have been brought into the promising and exciting world of Amway, I told myself.

From then on, five times a week, I took a two-hour bus ride to Guangzhou right after work. I would rush to the Amway gathering place, listen to the speech, and then, as soon as the gathering was over, I would hop on the bus back to Long Jiang and fall asleep around midnight. Rain or shine, I never missed a speech Brother Yong wanted me to go to. The eighth floor of LongJiang Group became even duller. Brother Yong—and the success I was sure he was leading me to—was the new brightest star in my sky.

Huang didn't say much about the changes in my life. "You are busy as a bee," he would sometimes remark. "Just be careful with whatever you are doing," he told me once. "Don't let people in LongJiang know about it."

"I met a man, and I'm learning Amway from him." I sat down on the bed next to him.

"I've heard of Amway. It all sounds marvelous but not necessary practical," he said.

I jumped up and shouted, "No, you don't understand. Amway is a career, the greatest career ever."

Unaffected by my fervor, he shook his head.

"Do you like that man?" He sounded casual, but I could tell that he was anxious to know.

I smiled at him, unsure of what to say. Eventually I nodded.

With a knowing look, he sighed. "I know you're not going to stay here forever." He looked at me with such gentle eyes that my heart melted. "You are young and should think of your own future."

I put my head on his shoulder.

"Do you think you'll ever want to get divorced for me?" I murmured.

He chuckled softly in the dark. "You know I could never do that to my son."

We both knew that it was naïve to think we might have a future together. Fate was like a strong wind, and we were just grains of sand that it lifted up and took with it. We kicked and struggled, but we had no choice but to go along with it because we were so small and insignificant.

While Huang slowly faded from my life, Amway and Brother Yong gradually were taking his place. I had great admiration for Brother Yong. The words of my favorite modern writer, Eileen Chang, described my feelings perfectly: "When I see him, I become low and low, so low that I sink to the dirt, but I like it in my heart, like it so much that it grows a flower from the dirt." I longed to go to Guangzhou and do Amway things with him every day.

Without letting Brother Yong know, I crafted a beautiful dream. I knew the Guangzhou natives looked down on people born in hamlets. I knew the people living in big cities separated themselves from drifting outlanders. I knew that a man driving the newest Harley-Davidson model would not marry a girl who couldn't afford a second pair of shoes. I knew a Diamond Bachelor like him wouldn't normally talk to a clodhopper like me; but what if the story of Cinderella and Prince Charming was true? Maybe Brother Yong was a man who didn't care about social norms and status.

I was tired of drifting from place to place, from man to man. I desperately wanted a home. The house in the Shen Hamlet had never been a home to me. In the South, I rarely thought of it and had only mailed my family one letter with my address. The only person from the hamlet whom I had talked to was Honor, who had told me that my mother had spent a lot of money to have a telephone installed so I could call them. I never did, unwilling and unable to deal with the past.

ON A CHILLY day in March 1997, two months after I'd started attending Amway lessons, I went to meet Brother Yong at the Amway headquarters in the Tianhe business district in Guangzhou. The building stood on high ground, and people gathered in groups on the plaza below, most carrying cardboard boxes or plastic bags with the Amway logo on them.

After spotting him at the top of the marble staircase leading to the building's entrance, I ran up the steps. I had just received my monthly salary. I proudly handed him 721 yuan. In return, Brother Yong handed me an Amway cardboard box and said joyfully, "Congratulations! Now you are officially an Amway businesswoman and my protégé!"

With all the detergent and cleanser inside, the box was heavy. I held it with both hands and gazed at Brother Yong. The flags behind him waved majestically, and his clean-cut face looked firm and determined. I promised myself that I would work very hard to become the protégé he was most proud of.

I started to imagine the day when I would have thousands of subordinates in my pyramid and be a millionaire, and I couldn't help but smile.

"You know, Ah-Juan, Sister Grace is holding a three-day seminar this weekend at a hotel. I think you should come. People learn tremendously from successful people just by being with them every minute," Brother Yong told me.

"Three days? That means I would have to skip work on Friday?" I stammered. "And . . . hmm . . . do you know how much the seminar costs?"

"Ah-Juan, this is very important to you. You need to look at it as your new career. Be prepared to invest, to suffer, to fight, and to work hard," he said emphatically. "Get a day off from work, and get the money you need. It's all worth it."

He spoke in such a decisive and encouraging tone that I couldn't help doing what he said.

I skipped work on Friday, hoping that Director Yip, who might not even come to the office, wouldn't notice my absence and that the other secretary, Chen, would not tell anyone. During the three-day seminar at a Guangzhou hotel, I listened to numerous speeches given by successful Amway businessmen. I introduced myself to thousands of strangers, who came from every corner of China and who all clutched small tape recorders to record every single speech. We shook hands wildly and called each other brother and sister. At night, we sat on the beds and shared our life stories. I listened to other members telling each other excitedly how many subordinates they had developed, how many Amway products they had sold, and how promising the Amway market was. I felt like part of a big family composed of all kinds of people—professors with gray hair, peasants from Inner China, young nurses, retired street cleaners—who all shared the same dream: success with Amway.

"Brothers and sisters, let me tell you, my vision has been

widened a thousand times since I joined Amway. Our business is everywhere. Think about it: if everyone in China gives
you one yuan, you have 1.2 billion yuan already! Go talk to
the old man cleaning the street. Go talk to the woman serving you noodles. They may buy your products. They may join
Amway and become your subordinates! Because, brothers and
sisters, remember this, you are bringing a brand-new future to
them, and you are helping them and at the same time helping
yourself!"

Roomfuls of passion, roomfuls of ambition, and roomfuls of
responses and applause! I was falling in love with Amway. By
the time the seminar had ended, I had become a member of the
dare-to-die Amway squad.

At the end of the seminar, I left the hotel alongside Brother
Yong and a few others, feeling overwhelmingly happy about
my experience. The chilly wind blew into my face. I shivered
in my thin clothes. I reached into my pocket and found that I
had a hundred yuan left. It was Sunday. I was cold and hungry,
and I should have headed back to Long Jiang to work the next
day. But no, I told myself. Sister Grace was holding another
seminar in Hangzhou, a city that was twenty-five hours away
by train in the Yangtze River Delta, my own "home" territory,
and I had to keep following her in order to become successful
like she was.

"Go. You should definitely go. Follow her. Be her protégé.
This is the exactly the kind of passion you need to succeed in
Amway." Brother Yong gave me an approving smile.

"Yeah, you should go. I've been following Sister Grace for
two months, and so far I have developed two subordinates,"
someone else chimed in.

I decided that I should go directly to Hangzhou. Let Director
Yip go to hell. Let everything else go to hell, I cursed loudly
into the evening wind as I marched toward the train station.

Huang would be worried about my disappearance, I realized; but, filled with passion for Amway, I quickly put the thought behind me.

Before boarding the train, I went to a public phone and called Spring, who now sold clothes in Zhenze for a living. I told her to meet me in Hangzhou, three hours away from the hamlet by bus, and to bring me a jacket and not say anything to our mother. Without giving her time to ask questions, I hung up.

I took out my list of potential subordinates and called one of my old college classmates, Wu. She and I hadn't been good friends in college, but, after she was assigned to a middle school in the town next to Ba Jin, we had started talking on the phone once in a while. I knew she wasn't satisfied with her teaching job.

As soon as she picked up the phone, I asked, "Do you want to succeed in life?"

"Yeah, of course. Where are you?" Wu sounded confused but curious.

"Don't ask. I have an incredible career opportunity for you. Take the next train to Hangzhou, and meet me at the Community Center on Jinling Road."

"Right now? That's four hours away by bus! What—"

"Don't ask. I promise you, you won't regret it. Just come here." I hung up.

Next I called Fish, my best friend from college. I repeated the conversation I'd had with Wu. I had done exactly what Amway instructed—get your friends to a lesson first and then tell them what a life-changing opportunity Amway was. I had just tricked my friends into traveling hundreds of miles, but I didn't feel guilty at all. I was giving them Amway, and I truly believed I was helping them change their lives.

The train stopped in Hangzhou just as it started to get dark.

After standing in the crowded cabin for most of the ride, I was exhausted. March in Hangzhou was much colder than in tropical Guangzhou. Wearing an unlined dress, I rubbed my arms and rushed to People's Square, where Spring was waiting for me.

The square was bigger and more crowded than I'd expected. The circular fountain in the center, which was as tall as two people, sprinkled water into a pond at its base surrounded by colorful flowers. Children were chasing each other, and adults were strolling on the vast cement plaza. I ran around a few times and at first was unable to find Spring. I became worried. In my mind, Spring was a quiet and timid young country girl, and I chastised myself for asking her to take a three-hour bus ride to this strange city to meet me.

Finally, I saw her standing next to some flowering shrubs, carrying a plastic bag and looking around anxiously. I ran to her.

"Meimei!" I called, using the term for younger sister.

She turned at the sound of my voice. I saw her face, still puffy from the motorcycle accident, in the setting sun. I was grateful to see her but saddened by all the heart-breaking memories brought back by her appearance. I hadn't thought of her face in a long time.

"Why are you so late? I've been here for a couple of hours," she complained mildly, taking a jacket out from the plastic bag. I quickly put it on.

She scrutinized me for a few seconds. I saw tenderness and worry in her eyes. Exhausted and thin from all the rushing about, I knew I didn't look good for someone who had left home determined to pursue her dreams. She pursed her lips as if she was going to say something important, but only said, "I have to leave now." She turned around.

"Meimei!" I called to her. She paused and turned back to me.

"Do you have any money with you?" I asked her after a short hesitation.

She searched her pocket and took out ninety yuan. "This is all I got."

I took the money. Then I stood in the crowd watching her figure getting smaller and smaller and eventually disappearing. Family would always be there for you, I realized, no matter how much you wanted to distance yourself from them. Spring would never expect me to pay back the money. I felt ashamed that I had had to ask her for help.

On the train to Hangzhou, I had schemed to bring Spring to the Amway seminar, but now, standing on the street with phoenix tree leaves strewn about, I doubted if she belonged to any of my worlds. I knew little about my only sister. She must have had a complicated inner world just like I did, but she never let anyone in. We were like two trains running on parallel tracks: watching each other, yet never getting closer. What we shared—our childhoods, our parents—were the very things that created the distance between us.

I quickly shook away my sad feelings and rushed to the Amway seminar. I had much more important things to worry about: I had two friends waiting for me to change their miserable and boring teaching lives.

Wu and Fish were just as responsive to Amway's message as I had been—after two days at the conference, they joined right away. Thus I became a superior of two subordinates. They went back to their teaching jobs and promised to carry out Amway business in their small towns.

How happy and proud Brother Yong would be when he heard my news. Despite my disheveled hair and dirty face, I was bubbling with joy on the train back to Guangzhou. What I was wearing, whether my face was clean, and when I had last eaten were the farthest things from my mind. I was occupied with one mission—to spread Amway to every corner of the world.

I surveyed the packed train car. My eyes scanned each

person's face—they were all my potential subordinates. Amway was a business you could do anywhere and at any time. Yes, I was a cheetah, and anyone in the car could be my next meal.

I took the Amway showering gel out of the Amway bag, which never left my shoulder. I put the gel on the small table in front of the benches, and then, under everyone's inquisitive gaze, I took out a bottle of Lux with the name covered with a sticker because of the anti-competition policy that Amway preached.

I cleared my throat and spoke loudly to the people around me. "Folks, have you all heard of Amway products?" Once I had their attention I started to talk about the gel in my hand. Different passengers had different responses to my speech. Some leaned forward and listened carefully; some sat there indifferently; and some even closed their eyes. I knew people were wary of scams, but I told myself that I shouldn't feel guilty because I wasn't spreading a scam—I was introducing a career.

"Friends, do you know that a very good way to tell whether a showering gel is good is to see if the mixture is pure?" I poured a drop of Lux into a clean tube, added some water, and then shook the tube wildly. Immediately the water in the tube became cloudy with drops of white secretion floating around. Then I did the same thing with the Amway gel.

I placed the two tubes side by side in front of everybody and said proudly, "Folks, do you see how crystal-clean the Amway solution in this tube is? And do you see the white drops bobbing in the other tube, which I cannot tell you the brand name of, but I am sure everyone has seen enough of their commercials. Can you imagine putting these on your body every day? You can easily see that the Amway gel is much better."

"I don't believe you. If Amway products are so good, why aren't they selling in stores?" a sturdy man sitting across the aisle asked.

"Well, Amway is smart. It costs a lot of money to set up stores and hire staff, so Amway does a pyramid sales system. Instead of giving the money to second-hand wholesalers, Amway decided to skip them and sell directly to consumers. What's even better is that ordinary people, people like you and me, can become successful by selling Amway products and also introducing Amway to people we know—or even to strangers. Everyone needs showering gel. Everyone needs shampoo and detergent, right?" I flourished the Amway brochures, putting the techniques Amway had taught me to good use. "Take a look at the brochures. Go ahead and take a look. Believe me. I used to be a middle school teacher. I am not a swindler."

While I was busy explaining, a man suddenly threw the brochure in his hand down on the table and said with a contemptuous sneer, "Save your breath! These are fraudulent practices. The government should forbid them all."

I looked at him and wanted to scream: Why don't you believe me? I'm doing a good thing! I'm helping you!

—

I returned to Long Jiang on Friday afternoon. It was a windy and dusty day. I went back to the eighth floor of LongJiang headquarters and sat at my desk. I looked around the still-magnificent office and felt as if I had been away for a lifetime. I prayed that Chen had been enjoying her solo reign over the eighth floor so much that she hadn't drawn undue attention to my absence.

Director Yip appeared behind the glass door. I stood up and held my breath.

"Where the hell have you been?" He glowered and continued into his office.

I thanked God that that was all he had said. For Director Yip, it was a mild response. I shot a look at Chen, who was pouring water into a teacup with her back to me. She must have kept Director Yip happy. He had rarely been so easy on me before.

That night, I went to Huang's room. He was sitting on the bed watching TV. At the sight of me, he shook his head and scolded me mildly: "Ah-Juan, where have you been?"

I sat next to him and put my arms around him. His image rarely entered my mind when I was in my frenetic Amway world. I still loved him, but we weren't close any more. I had emerged from under his wing and taken on my own mission.

I continued to work at LongJiang as one of Director Yip's secretaries. I realized it was best to keep my job while doing Amway business. After all, I hadn't made any money from Amway yet. But one month later, Assistant Director Li called me in for a serious talk.

"I heard you're selling Amway products around the town. Do you know how bad this sounds? The secretary of Director Yip of the LongJiang Group, the biggest boss in town, is selling shampoo and detergent to people on the street?" The scholar-like Assistant Director Li spoke softly but sternly.

"I want to make some money," I mumbled, feeling a little scared and embarrassed.

"I know LongJiang is not paying you a lot right now, but you need to think about the consequences of your own action, and always have Director Yip's reputation in mind," he cautioned. "Ah-Juan, you need to think about your future. LongJiang is a big company, and you're so close to Director Yip that maybe some day he'll promote you. You'll have a much better future here than with Amway."

I nodded but inwardly rolled my eyes. I didn't really look forward to a promotion at LongJiang, where I had to tiptoe around to avoid being yelled at by my boss.

One week later, Director Yip stuck his head out of his office and yelled to Chen and me, "What the hell is going on with the floor? Why is it so dirty?"

Chen and I exchanged looks, and then, to my surprise, she pointed her finger at me and said, "I don't know. It's her day to clean the floor."

I looked at her in disbelief. It was, in fact, her day.

Upon hearing her words, Yip glared at me and exploded, "What the fuck do you think you are doing lately? You can't even do this one little thing?"

I felt a mixture of anger and disgust toward both of them—toward Chen for pushing her blame off on me, and toward Director Yip for scolding me before bothering to hear my side of the story. As soon as he finished his diatribe and returned to his office, I sat down at my desk and started writing my resignation letter. I knew Yip would never like me, and I would never be calculating enough to compete with Chen, so it was time for me to leave, to march on toward my bright and promising Amway future.

Later that afternoon, as I was packing up my things in my room, Huang came in with a sad look on his face.

"I heard what happened and that you wrote a letter." He sat on the edge of the bed and sighed. I kept throwing things into my duffel bag and didn't say anything.

"Yip told me that in the letter, you said that he heeded and trusted only one side. You shouldn't have said that. After all, he is the big boss," Huang said.

"I hate people not believing me," I told him angrily.

"Come on, you shouldn't have made such a big deal of it. Everybody, including Yip, knows that you're very honest, and he's realized now that perhaps he shouldn't have yelled at you like that."

"Too bad honest people aren't popular." I chuckled. Nothing could change my mind. Amway was calling me.

"Well, it happened, and there's nothing we can do about it. Yip is the big boss. He can't apologize to you. But guess what. I just talked to him. He says if you don't leave, he'll consider promoting you to the position of departmental manager." His tone had turned cheerful, and he looked at me expectantly.

A little surprised, I raised my head and stopped packing. I felt so sad at that moment, seeing Huang's efforts to keep me there. I didn't understand why Yip had treated me like a slave if he had expected to promote me one day.

"Too late. My heart is not here any more," I said. I cringed at the look of disappointment in his eyes.

"Are you going to your Amway friends?" he asked me carefully.

I nodded.

"I knew you would leave me some day," he murmured.

His distressed tone affected me, but it was time for me to move on to the next phase in my life, and he didn't belong in it. It was heartbreaking to leave him, but I knew I had to.

I forced a smile. "I'll come back and see you as long as I am in Guangzhou."

"Be really careful out there," he counseled.

—

I called Brother Yong and told him that I had quit my job and that I would come to the meeting that night in Guangzhou.

"Brother Yong, do you know any place I can stay for tonight?" I asked.

"Let me see what I can do."

I had my long hair cut to my ears, bought a new dress for myself, and left for Guangzhou that evening. I wanted a new start, to appear as a new person in front of Brother Yong.

"Wow, you look even prettier now!" Brother Yong exclaimed as soon as I came up to him after the Amway meeting.

"Everyone!" He clapped his hands. "Ah-Juan followed in Sister Grace's footsteps and had her hair cut short. And what is even more exciting is that she has quit her job to do Amway. Now she is a full-time Amway doer. Congratulations!"

People applauded my devotion to Amway. I stood in the middle of the circle with my hands clutched together, turning red and glancing bashfully at Brother Yong. Now that I had cut my hair for him, now that I had given up my job for Amway, now that I was willing to follow him everywhere, would he want me, a country girl?

After the meeting, we went to his motorcycle together. Quietly I glanced at him walking steadily next to me, hands deep in his pockets.

We had been alone many times this late at night, but I had never felt so romantic before. Stars were shining in the sky; my dress rippled gently in the wind; and I had quit everything to come to Brother Yong, a city man I desperately admired.

I stopped and clasped his sleeve. "Brother Yong, I have left everything for Amway. Now I can follow you everywhere."

"Good!" he said.

I looked up at him. "Brother Yong," I said timidly. "You know I like you, don't you?"

"I know," he answered, cracking a thin smile.

Ah, he knew. I smiled happily. I dared not ask if he liked me too, afraid of breaking my big dream. I blindly followed him.

We traveled on his motorcycle to the northern edge of the city. He led me down a dark lane and into a small room through a back door. The rolling steel front door was shut and the room was crude and dusty, containing only a desk and a chair. "A friend is going to open a store here," he explained. "He let me use it tonight."

AISLING JUANJUAN SHEN

We stood in the middle of the room in the dark, listening to the sound of rats running around and feeling awkward.

"I guess this is my bed tonight." I walked over to the desk and lay down on it. "Brother Yong, do you want to lie down too?"

"No, I just want to look at you." He chuckled nervously.

"'Look at me'? What do you mean?"

"You know, just look at you. I have never looked at a woman so closely before."

I sat up. "You mean . . . you've never slept with a woman before?"

"Yes."

I was astonished. He was a thirty-three-year-old good-looking city man who rode a Harley and yet *still* a virgin. I felt more tenderly toward him, having discovered this secret.

"Brother Yong, I'll let you look if you want."

I took off my clothes and lay down in the dark. I heard him approaching the desk carefully and then felt him putting his hands on my knees. He touched and examined me cautiously, like a curious child with a glass ball. The Diamond Bachelor everyone looked up to, the man who gave such stimulating speeches in front of everybody, was a virgin. I wasn't sure if I felt closer to him now or if I was even further away from him since I was not a virgin.

"Do you want to try it, Brother Yong?" His touch aroused my desire. I closed my eyes. I could hear him taking off his pants. He moved closer to me and then knelt on the desk, and I felt the warmth of his legs as they touched mine. He felt so soft.

After a while, I heard him getting off the desk and getting dressed. I opened my eyes and sat up. "I don't think I can do it," he said softly. And then the confident, sunny look reappeared on his face, as if nothing had just happened. I tried to hide my disappointment. He liked me, otherwise he wouldn't have touched me, I told myself. Some day he would be moved by my persistence.

The next day I moved into an apartment that Brother Yong helped me find. It was hidden in an alley deep in a dirty neighborhood. Butchers, street cleaners, hookers, and Guangzhou's poorest working classes lived there. The alley was littered with beer cans, coal cinders, and vegetable leaves and was seldom swept. The smell of rotten meat and urine was ever-present.

I shared a bedroom, a living room, a bathroom, and a kitchen with eleven other penniless and frustrated Amway adherents. Six females shared the bed in the bedroom, and the men just crashed in the living room, like dogs that could lie down and fall asleep anywhere. The apartment was moist and humid and smelled like a rat house. The bathroom, which was merely a squat toilet and a showerhead above, was covered with layers and layers of filth. I pinched my nose in the kitchen and the bathroom, telling myself that there were people in this world living in worse conditions and that I could take this.

Brother Yong never talked about what had happened that night. I still looked at him admiringly and believed that some day he would look into my eyes and tell me that he liked me.

—

A few weeks later, I followed Brother Yong on a trip to Guangxi Province, where one of his subordinates needed help developing his local network. You are a seed; you can take root and blossom anywhere and grow into a towering big tree, Amway taught. Everyone in Amway is your brother or sister, your arm; you should never hesitate to help, Brother Yong told me. So I grabbed all the money I had left, put on my jacket, picked up my backpack, and hopped on the train.

We arrived at a small city called Bingyang, and when Brother Yong told me that we were right next to the border between China and Vietnam, I was surprised that somehow I had gotten myself all the way to the border of my country. I knew little about Vietnam except that my country had helped the Northern Vietnamese fight off the Americans in the 1960s.

"This is what's so cool about doing Amway: you get to travel to so many places," he told me as we dodged the locals squatting on the sidewalks. They stared at us strangely, as if we were aliens. All the stories that I had ever heard about drug dealers came to mind. Brother Yong had told me that this region was close to the Golden Triangle, the notorious area where the borders of Laos, Myanmar, and Thailand converge, where opium is grown, turned into heroin, and smuggled out. The Golden Triangle was the source of half the world's heroin. Heroin was the only illegal drug people could get in China and was considered a great scourge, and anyone who touched one drop of it was seen as a dead person or destined to become a life prisoner in a rehab center. I had never heard of anyone using drugs except in vague stories, let alone met an addict.

We stayed in a mountain village. Life was simple there. Brother Yong and I worked well as a team; when he gave me looks of approval, I felt content and happy. Our audience shook our hands after lectures, thanking us for bringing such a great opportunity to such a backward place; at moments like that, I felt fulfilled. I imagined that this was how Chairman Mao had felt after liberating the peasants from the oppression of the capitalists in the olden days. How simple and frank the people here were!

I slept on a wooden bed in a small room; and every night after the village went dark at around eight o'clock, I thought of Brother Yong's daytime praises, recited Amway's mission statement once, and fell asleep peacefully. I stopped worrying about my future, for the first time since I had come to the South.

Before we returned to Guangzhou, Brother Yong suggested visiting the checkpoint where General Chen Yi had fought off the Southern Vietnamese in the Vietnam War.

We strolled through the fruit stands along the path leading to the gun turret. In every fruit stand, golden mangos were spread on the square bottoms of the hand-woven wicker baskets.

"The best thing about this place is the local mango, so sweet and soft. Oh, I can never resist it." Brother Yong sighed with contentment.

Rays of afternoon sunlight shone on his face, making it look extra bold and vigorous. I smiled leisurely and nodded my head.

"There is something I've been meaning to tell you," he said to me slowly.

I heard my heart thumping heavily. It felt like it was being hit by a hammer. The moment I had been waiting for had finally arrived.

"I hope you are not going to be offended. I want to tell you because, as your superior, I think it is important for you to do Amway well," he continued.

I held my breath, waiting, a wait of a thousand years.

"You have this smell that comes from your body. I think you should find a way to get rid of it."

I froze where I was, mortified, and watched him continuing to stroll ahead. I wished I could find a place to bury myself right then. I gazed at his back and wanted to run and tell him: I don't have body odor. In this rural village, I can only clean myself with a towel and a bucket of water every couple of days, and I couldn't even find any sanitary napkins. It's not my fault. It's these conditions.

But all I could do was run after him, force an awkward smile, and say, "I'm sorry."

"That's okay!" he answered cheerfully, and then he ran ahead to his other subordinate, who had spotted us and was waving from the foot of the turret.

I walked slowly up the steps to the top of the turret. I sat down on the stone surface and crossed my legs. It was secluded and quiet, except for the trees of the woods surrounding the turret murmuring in the breeze. Through the leaves I saw the checkpoint below, where women dressed in robes holding flat bamboo baskets on the tops of their heads walked stiffly in the clouds of dust and men whipped their oxen through the gate.

I looked around myself, almost in a trance, and suddenly wondered why I was here. Brother Yong had never liked me. Everything he did for me was because of Amway. I had left Huang and my job and chased him all the way to the end of the world only to find I was just chasing my own dream.

WHEN WE RETURNED to Guangzhou, I found that the halo around Brother Yong's head had vanished, and I was no longer intoxicated by his presence. I told myself to look at him strictly as my superior. After all, except at Amway meetings and seminars when everyone shared equally in the Amway dream, Brother Yong and I lived in two different worlds. After the gatherings, he got on his Harley and roared away to his apartment in downtown Guangzhou while I walked through the alleys, stepped over the puddles and the cabbage leaves, opened the rusty iron gate to the hallway, climbed the urine-stinking stairs to the seventh floor, and fell onto my bed in my slum home.

As the days went by, my mind came to have just one focus—Amway. Forget men; forget love; and forget the idea of a home, I told myself. In this turbulent world, I had to stand on my own two feet, and nobody could build a future for me except myself. Men were untrustworthy, and I didn't need

AISLING JUANJUAN SHEN

them to make me feel safe, to make me not worry, because I could do that on my own.

I threw myself into Amway and worked as if there was no tomorrow. It had completely taken over my mind and soul. I examined the carpets wherever I went and would frequently take out Amway detergent and demonstrate to everyone in the office how efficiently it removed stains and gum, ignoring the rolled eyes and mocking laughter. On the street, I would observe every person walking by me, then approach the street cleaner in her mask and ask if she wanted to do something better in life, though I knew that in the end she would probably brandish her broom and threaten to scream if I didn't leave her alone. In the hotels where I stayed for Amway seminars, I would knock on the next room's door; persuade the guests, who were busy playing mah-jongg, to take a look at my brochure; and eagerly tell them how the boss of a major bank had joined us. I wouldn't give up until I was pushed out of the room and the door was banged in my face. Then I would stand in the corridor, stare at the door for a long while, and finally tell myself to gather up my strength and move my feet because there were many people out there who were unaware of Amway and many people who were successful because of Amway.

Whenever I felt like I was at the end of my rope, when I despaired so much that I couldn't get myself out of the bed in the morning, I would go to Amway seminars to recharge. After rounds of inspiring speeches, I would be back to feeling ready to conquer the world.

In May 1997, I left the communal Amway apartment and lived a life of homelessness for weeks, following Sister Grace on a multi-city seminar tour. I usually couldn't afford a seat on the extremely crowded trains, so I would sleep on layers of newspaper on the floor under the seats at night as I rode between cities along the east coast. Daytime always went by quickly in seminars where thousands of Amway fanatics spoke and sang. When night fell, if I wasn't getting on a train, I would squeeze into any bed offered to me, usually with five or six Amway sisters. When I wasn't so lucky, I would spend the night curled up in a corner at the local train station.

My belief in Amway never wavered. Even when I hadn't eaten for the entire day, even when I was exhausted and collapsed on the street, I never questioned the philosophy of the Amway career. It was not Amway's fault; it was mine, I told myself every time I had doubts. It was because I didn't work hard enough or wasn't competent enough that I didn't succeed.

In June, I returned to hot and rainy Guangzhou. New transients occupied the apartment in the alley, but there was always space for one more. I moved back in. It was moldy and humid and felt like an oven. The bathroom reeked of mildew and looked so disgusting that I couldn't even bring myself to set foot in it. The air in the apartment felt rotten. On the days I wasn't out on the street doing Amway, I stayed in the only livable place—the bed. I would cover my head with the quilt and sleep like a log while the other Amway fanatics debated hotly with a Pacific Insurance salesman who had just moved into the apartment about which career was better and chalk made squeaking sounds on the tiny blackboard in the living room.

I didn't have much money left, and my strength was gone. I wasn't able to sell many Amway products and couldn't develop any more subordinates. There was a time when I had regularly called my two subordinates, Wu and Fish, my former classmates, and pretended to be optimistic, shouting that they should keep trying because they would be successful soon, but now I had no energy left even to lift the phone when someone called me. Phone calls used to get me so excited, because it could be someone interested in Amway who would become my next subordinate.

Even worse, I had lice all over my body. I wondered if everybody in the apartment had them, but I didn't even feel like investigating. I sat on the bed and madly scratched my skin with both hands until blood oozed out of the bites, but still the itch didn't stop. I fell back down on the bed, wrapped the quilt around myself tightly, and retreated into my cocoon. But the itching didn't stop, so I kept scratching, and seeing bloody spots constantly being added to my body, I eventually panicked: it struck me forcefully and clearly that I needed to get rid of the lice.

So one day when all the brothers and sisters were loudly singing the 'Song of Success' at a seminar, I let go of their hands and left. I didn't feel much. I crossed the lobby like a walking corpse and went out of the hotel door, past the fountain in the yard, and onto the sidewalk leading away from the hotel.

My hand reached into my pocket and took out the Bank of China checkbook Brother Yong had given me the day I joined Amway. I remembered how excited I'd been that the password Brother Yong had chosen for me was the same as my regular password. I had kept mentioning this to him until one day he impatiently told me that it was just a password. I had once ardently believed that Amway would be wiring lots of money to this account, but now in the wire column, the only number I saw was RMB310, and the account balance was 0. After all my effort and pain, I'd made only 310 yuan from my Amway career. Now not only was I penniless, I also had lice crawling all over my body.

You need to stop this, I thought. You need to cure the lice. You need to go home. I recalled the house in the Shen Hamlet.

I tried to picture my mother and father, but after the roller-coaster of life in the South, their faces seemed strangely hazy. I longed for a home like never before, and the Shen Hamlet suddenly appeared to be more of a home than anywhere in the South.

Brother Yong was displeased when I asked if he would lend me some money for a train ticket home. I knew borrowing money was taboo among Amway brothers and sisters. "I promise I'll pay you back very soon," I assured him. "I'm going to my home town to build a new Amway career there. I promise you I will have a network there soon."

"I'll see what I can do," he said unenthusiastically.

Feeling uncomfortable and hurt by his reaction, I decided not to bother him any further. Though I was poor, I still had my dignity. So the next day I made a quick trip to Long Jiang and borrowed some money from Huang. I left town right away, before he had a chance to persuade me stay in the South.

Before I boarded the train, I called Brother Yong and told him that there was no need for him to lend me money and that he should wait for good news from me.

So, in July 1997, I returned to the Shen Hamlet all covered with lice. As I walked along the ditch between the blossoming safflower fields, I wondered if I was in a dream, if I was a ghost drifting in this world of golden yellow flowers. The familiar smell of the soil, the sweet smell of the safflowers, and the humming of the bees brought tears to my eyes. It had been barely a year since I had last left the hamlet, but it felt like much, much longer.

The door to the central room of my parents' house was ajar. The sound of silkworms nibbling mulberry leaves came to my ears, a sound that had accompanied my entire childhood. Oh, home! I stood on the threshold observing the room. A layer of white silkworms wiggled on the dark green mulberry bush leaves that rested on top of straw beds spread on the floor. In the space between the beds, I saw my mother squatting on her heels, her back to me and her dark green scarf wrapped around her head. She was taking leaves out of the bamboo basket next to her feet.

"Mama," I said.

She turned. I couldn't believe what I saw. My mother, whose pretty, well-proportioned face used to make me feel secretly proud and jealous, looked like a different woman. Her face was twisted and pulled to the left; her lips were slanted; and her cheeks were swollen like two loafs of bread.

She just looked at me and turned back to her chore. I felt like I'd been stabbed with a needle. Her eyes, jammed in their swollen sockets, had been cold, as if she was looking at her worst enemy.

I stood where I was for a good while, shocked at what I had seen and hurt by my mother's reaction to my return. Then I went into the kitchen. I poured myself a big bucket of water and grabbed a towel.

In the dark storage room to the side of the house, with the blue plastic curtains drawn as usual, I sat in the big plastic tub, soaked the towel with clean water, and slowly rubbed myself. I saw the rotten spots from the lice on my body, the dirt under my long fingernails, and my ugly feet, swollen from the days of walking. My face was wet, but I couldn't tell whether it was water or tears.

Guilt attacked me. I had been such a bad daughter. I hadn't been here when my mother's face got damaged. I had been thousands of miles away, trying to forget her. I hated myself. I had only written once and had pretended to myself that my family was dead. And what had I done while I was in the South? What had I achieved?

When my father came home that night, he didn't say anything to me, as usual. When Spring discovered my presence, she responded with neither surprise nor happiness. "Oh, you're back," she said as she parked her bike in the front yard, and then she went straight upstairs to her room. I felt like a piece of furniture.

Like everyone else in the house, I stayed quiet. I ate and slept and spent the rest of my time helping my mother with the housework. For the first time in my life, I tried to be a good daughter to her.

A week later, after rubbing my body with soap and water every day, the lice were finally gone, and my mother started to talk to me. The swelling was leaving her face little by little, and when she was in a good mood—still rare—she explained that she'd had a stroke of apoplexy.

"Why?"

She puckered her still-slanted lips. "You know. Just life. Nobody listens to me. Nothing is ever good."

"Did you go and see a doctor?"

"I went there once, alone. Who cares about me in this family, anyway?"

I wished I knew how to comfort her. Until then, I'd never realized the effect of my behavior on my mother, how truly devastated she had been when I'd quit the teaching job and gone to the South. Spring wasn't the ideal daughter either. She'd rented a store in town and was barely scraping by selling clothes. Plus, she was hanging out with some bad guys, according to my mother. My father, who was busy working in the rice fields, still wouldn't talk much to my mother. What a poor woman she was and what a lonely life she led.

For two weeks I stayed at home, trying my best to help my ailing mother. At night I tossed and turned until daybreak, analyzing my failure with Amway. When the swellings and twists on my mother's face were almost gone, I took out my Amway bag, got on a bike, and rode toward the surrounding villages.

One of the many principles Amway had taught me was that you could do Amway anywhere, because Amway was good for everyone. After my merciless failure in Guangzhou, I decided to conquer the countryside.

It was close to the height of the summer. With the scorching sun above my head, I zigzagged over the dirt paths in the neighboring villages and visited a few of my high school classmates. I had high hopes. People in the countryside needed great opportunities like Amway more than the people living the city.

"This is what you are doing now? Selling American detergent? What happened? You were the only one in our class who went to college," one former classmate said, throwing the brochure back at me.

I was undaunted by this negative reaction. After all, I'd experienced worse in Guangzhou. The second day, I biked for an hour to visit another classmate, who shook his head and said that he was too busy for this kind of childish thing.

I kept shuttling back and forth between villages and was turned down by everyone. One classmate smiled modestly, saying he was too stupid to undertake such a complicated career. Another one told me sincerely that this Amway thing was just not good for the countryside folk. I wouldn't give up. I kept hopping on my bike every day, until I was thrown out by the mother of Peony, my old school friend. "You're a college graduate!" she yelled. "Whatever you're doing is not good for our Peony. She's just a country girl. Why don't you go somewhere else to put on your hoaxes?"

I stood in their courtyard, humiliated. It was the busy farming season, and everyone had just come back from the fields in straw hats, with sickles in their hands and cuts on their faces from the rice-shoot edges. I looked at Peony. She was dirty and dusty and busy soothing her wailing child, and I realized I was in the wrong place to preach Amway. I had forgotten that people in the countryside tended to stay where they were and never wanted much in life.

I hopped back on my bicycle. Pedaling listlessly in the high noon sun, I felt a new sense of despair. For the first time, I started to question: Did Amway really work? That day, my belief in Amway began to waver, and I considered that it might be the scam everyone said it was.

"You are completely out of your mind, going around the countryside like that," my mother nagged. "Look at you, as dark as a black monkey. Go back to the middle school, okay? It's not too late. I'll go with you and beg the principal to take you back. He won't cancel the contract you signed with the school, but I'll beg him to give you some time to pay them back." She coaxed and cajoled me as if I were a little girl.

I spoke to her as earnestly as I could. "Mama, I really hate teaching. Please understand. There's no future in teaching. I'll always be poor. Our family has always been so poor, and I don't want to be poor any more."

"I know teachers don't make much money, but even teaching is such an honor for our family. All the generations of our family have been bare-footed peasants. We eat and breathe dirt every day. Finally you become a teacher, but then you throw it away," my mother said bitterly.

I didn't know how to make her understand that there were many opportunities out there, many different occupations, and that not teaching wasn't the end of the world. I tried to imagine myself going back to Ba Jin, to the middle school, taking the pointer, and standing in front of the blackboard every day. The image frightened me. Though I had tried very hard to keep my teaching post open when I first left the school, now that I had seen the much bigger sky outside that town, I didn't ever want to go back to it.

"There's no need to talk about this any longer. I am not

going back to that school," I said with curt finality, despite my mother's angry glare. I wished her face would heal completely soon so that I could carry on with my life, the destiny I had chosen for myself, free of worries and guilt.

I continued preaching Amway. Often next to a manure pit or in a ditch in the rice fields, I explained the Amway career to somebody with a carrying pole on his shoulder or with pants rolled up to his knees and feet soaked in mud. Knowing how ridiculous I looked in people's eyes, I had to tell myself to forget my self-consciousness and concentrate on the extraordinary opportunities Amway was offering.

Yet a rock never blossoms, no matter how often you water it. By the end of July, I had given up all hope of succeeding with Amway. Sadly but calmly, I accepted the fact that, despite all the blood and tears, I had failed completely. But for the first time in my life, I didn't blame myself for this failure, because I knew I had tried my very best to make it work. The fact that it didn't must have been Amway's fault, not mine.

I put away all my Amway products and tore all the Amway posters off my wall. I took a deep breath and told myself, I am free of Amway. A huge weight was off my back. I could see through Amway and Brother Yong now. He was just a clown, good at manipulating people, and Amway was just a scheme played on thousands of Chinese who had ambitions but few opportunities to succeed.

The day after I quit Amway, I called Huang.

"Come back here, you silly girl. What are you doing in the countryside?" he shouted at me over the phone. "I just heard that a knitting company here is looking for an English translator. A good friend of mine knows the boss. You can go work there. They pay eighteen hundred yuan a month."

Eighteen hundred yuan a month, more than I had made in LongJiang as Director Yip's secretary!

I hung up the phone and went out to the asphalt road in front of the house for a walk. As I listened to the honking of the boats on the canal, I felt the high aspirations I'd had a year ago growing in my mind again. I had thought that I had been completely defeated, but as it turned out, the ambition was still there. I hadn't had enough sufferings in the South yet. Now after the weeks at home eating well and returning to health, I was reinvigorated, ready to go again.

The night before my departure, I packed two bags, left them downstairs, and then went upstairs to inform my mother of my decision to return to the South. She sat on the bed in her room and couldn't do or say anything except sob. Honor was sitting next to her, sighing. His face was yellower and skinnier. I had heard that his business was not doing well and he was now short of money himself. I prayed that he would continue to take care of my mother as he had done for the past ten years.

At my mother's temples I saw streaks of gray. She was growing old. Time had erased the hatred I had had for her. I didn't know when I had decided to forget the way she had treated me as a child, but at that moment I only wished she could get some love and care in her life, which had been so full of misery.

The next morning, I came downstairs feeling refreshed but a little reluctant to part from home. My mother was on the stool behind the stove, weeping just as she had when I had left the house a year earlier. I hardened my heart and turned to fetch my bags, but when I entered the side room I saw only one bag lying on the cement ground. The big bag with all the vital items such as clothes, shoes, toothbrush, and comb was missing.

I ran back to the kitchen. "Where's my other bag?"

"I don't know. Go ask your father," my mother replied.

I looked at her suspiciously. My father had been as cold as ice to me ever since I had come back. I didn't think he would bother to hide my bag.

I searched everywhere in the house, flustered and dismayed, but couldn't find it. "Where is he?" I said, returning to the kitchen, really annoyed.

"He's gone to the fields." She stared at the fire in the stove.

Fuming with anger, I stamped the floor with my foot, grabbed the small bag, and ran out of the house. Nothing would stop me. I would have to do without my other bag.

On the way to Shanghai, I visited Wu's town. Though the guilt of dragging her into joining Amway tormented me, I faced her and admitted that I had given it up and assured her that soon I would compensate her for the money she had lost, no matter what. Her face relaxed, and she took out the two thousand yuan I'd asked to borrow for my plane ticket. I promised her earnestly that I would soon pay her back.

She was the only person I could think of to ask for help. The idea of asking my parents never even occurred to me. Borrowing money from my parents and admitting my financial failure to them was the last thing I wanted to do.

Later that day, I boarded a plane from Shanghai to Guangzhou. Sitting on the plane, I felt a sense of déjà vu. It was July again, the same month I had flown to the South a year earlier. I had many new scars, and I was even poorer than I had been then, indebted to almost everyone I knew. But this time it was going to be different, I promised myself solemnly. This time I was going to find my piece of sky.

PART

IV

"THIS IS XIAO Yi. She's a translator here too. She'll teach you what to do." My new boss, Zhou, a bald man with an egg-shaped face and a round stomach spilling over his belt, pointed to the girl feeding a piece of paper into the fax machine.

She turned her head. I smiled. Her thin lips moved slightly sideways and a faint smile floated over her waxy face. She had dark circles under her eyes and a big head that looked dispro-portionate to her skinny body. This is a wary girl who trusts no one, I thought. Hopefully she would relax her vigilance when she realized that I was just in the South to make a living.

It was a spacious office. Two oak boss desks occupied the east side of the room. They faced a big television that sat on a shelf against the west wall. Against the south wall, a long leather couch stretched across the room. Xiao Yi's desk and her fax machine took up the north side of the rectangle, facing the win-dow. After being told I would share Xiao Yi's desk, I sat down in the chair next to her.

"Hi, Xiao Yi, could you give me something to read?" I asked politely after sitting awkwardly in silence for a while.

She took out a blue folder from a desk drawer and handed it to me. I opened it curiously. It was jammed with faxes, all of which had Xiao Yi's delicate, hasty handwriting on them in blue ballpoint pen. I read through the pages quickly, eager to learn more about my new job.

The first stack of faxes was a series of negotiations between Zhou and a couple of foreign suppliers.

03/12/97 8:58pm From: Paris To: GrandKnit China
Dear Mr. Zhou,
  My lowest price for the 45 sets of 1982 KOKETT machines
  is $17,000 each.
Best Regards,
Jacques :o)

*   *   *

03/12/97 9:00pm From: GrandKnit China To: South Carolina
Dear Carl,
  Your KOKETT are too expensive. Jacques offered $15,000
  each. Please give us your rock bottom price.
Best, Zhou

*   *   *

03/13/97 9:30pm From: South Carolina To: GrandKnit China
Dear Mr. Zhou,
  The best price I can offer is $15,000 each. They are in per-
  fect condition, still running in Russia. I can give you accesso-
  ries with them, beams and needles. I cannot do it any lower.
Best wishes,
Carl

*   *   *

03/13/97 9:40pm From: GrandKnit China To: Paris

Dear Jacques,

   Carl's price is much cheaper than yours, $12,000 each.

   But we prefer to buy them from you.

Best, Zhou

* * *

03/13/97 9:55pm From: Paris To: GrandKnit China

Dear Mr. Zhou,

   OK. I'll sell them at $12,000 each. :o(

Best regards,

Jacques

* * *

03/13/97 10:04pm From: GrandKnit China To: Paris

Dear Jacques,

   We'll buy the 30 KOKETT from you. 40' containers to
   Guangzhou Port. Deposit will be wired from HK tomorrow. Thanks. You are always our best partner!

Best,

Zhou

* * *

03/14/97 5:37pm From: GrandKnit China To: South Carolina

Dear Carl,

   The KOKETT are not popular lately. We decide not to buy
   them.

Best, Zhou

* * *

03/15/97 11:35pm From: South Carolina To: GrandKnit China
Dear Mr. Zhou,
    I heard you bought the 45 KOKETT from Jacques. Why
not from me? I can be cheaper.
Best wishes,
Carl

*   *   *

03/16/97 8:43am From: GrandKnit China To: South Carolina
Dear Carl,
    We didn't buy the KOKETT, must be somebody else. We
would of course buy from you if it were us. Don't worry.
You are always our best friend.
Best, Zhou.

*   *   *

Zhou's loud voice on the phone made me look up from my reading.

"Old Song, this is Old Zhou!" He was almost shouting. "How are you, Old Song? You've gotten yourself some pretty whores lately?"

He chuckled lasciviously and then, raising his voice even louder, said, "Listen, I just got in some KS3, 1991, beautiful condition, 350,000 yuan each, very good price, but only for you. Interested? Yeah, yeah, I'll be in the office this month. Fly over. But I have to warn you, you'd better hurry. I can't hold them too long, even for you, my best customer."

After hanging up the phone, he turned to his brother, who had been listening at the desk next to him. "I think for 350,000 each he would take them all. Let's fleece this sucker again." His brother, a bald man with a droopy, unhappy face and a pair of goldfish eyes, looked pleased to hear this news.

"What are KOKETT and KS3?" I whispered to Xiao Yi.

"Knitting machines made in East Germany." She spoke briefly and coldly, eyes remaining on the notebook in front of her.

"I thought GrandKnit produced warp-knitted fabric. Do they actually buy and sell used knitting machines? Is it legal?"

"It makes more money. Who cares whether or not it's legal?" she whispered. She pressed her index finger to her lips and gestured for me to stop talking, her thin eyebrows frowning.

Thus I started my second job in the South, as a translator for GrandKnit. It was a small company in Long Jiang a couple of miles away from LongJiang Enterprise's headquarters. It consisted of a few factory buildings, a warehouse, and a small office building and was enclosed by a tall cement wall with a big iron gate in the front. It was essentially closed off from the outside. There were roughly twenty employees, most of whom were migrant workers who spent their entire days in the factories and then at night jammed into the four dorm rooms on the second floor of the office building. I didn't understand how just one floor could accommodate all the workers until Xiao Yi took me inside. Each dorm room was as tiny as a chicken barn and had a very low ceiling, but they were further divided into six or even more sections with pieces of thin wood, and each section was only long enough for a single-size bed and wide enough for a person to turn around in.

My assigned sleeping spot was next to the window. Xiao Yi's was on the other side of a board, next to the squat toilet with a faucet above it, the bathroom for the six girls in the room. It was summer, and the toilet was so stinky that Xiao Yi and I spent most of the days and nights in the air-conditioned office upstairs. One of us always had to be in the office anyway, because the fax machine spat out quotes and counteroffers at all times. These faxes, Zhou emphasized, required *immediate* attention. He demanded that we contact him right away with any valuable information, no matter where he was at the time—at the drinking table, in a karaoke club, or even sleeping in his apartment upstairs. So Xiao Yi and I took turns napping on the couch, and whoever was on duty watched the fax machine while the television constantly showed the exchange rates of different currencies.

Soon I understood why Xiao Yi was thin as a stick and pale as a ghost—this was a job that required at least sixteen hours' work if you were the only one doing it. Work and sleep were really the only two activities in the place. You didn't need to worry about passing the interrogation of the guards at the iron gate to get out of the compound, because you didn't really have time to go out.

"I have always gotten sick frequently, even under normal conditions, but I have been sick every day since I came to this company. This work is just too exhausting. That's why I asked Zhou to hire another translator," Xiao Yi told me one day when we were sitting on the couch alone in the office. It had been two weeks since I had started work there, and Xiao Yi and I now chatted every once in a while. I looked at her sympathetically, understanding her pain at being far away from home and fighting for a life in the South.

Unlike Xiao Yi, I was happy with my job. Now I had enough food for every meal. The food in the company's cafeteria was cooked in cauldrons, placed on big, filthy bamboo plates, and sold through dirty windows in the cement wall. Every day it was the same dish—pork with green peppers swimming in oil—but I was content. When I was a child, we had never had enough meat.

At first, I didn't understand why the cook, a local man who threw spatulas and yelled at the outlanders who complained about the food, always smiled at me, refused my money, and even put extra food on my plate. So one day I asked Xiao Yi.

She seemed to secretly know about everything at this company and was never reluctant to teach me.

"He's currying favor with you. Don't you know how important your position is in this company? Without you or me, the Zhous can't do any business. They can't even write their own names decently in Chinese, let alone read English letters," Xiao Yi said scornfully.

She looked around the office, made sure that the door was shut, and then whispered, "Do you know how much money I have made for the Zhous these past two years? Millions and millions. When I first came here, GrandKnit was just one of the thousands of knitting companies in China competing for the domestic warp fabric market. Then one day I accidentally discovered that Chinese knitting companies were dying for used Western machines. These machines, they are trash in Europe and America, but they are gold in China. So I searched around for foreign dealers, and I found so many for the Zhous, and then we worked out all the other details such as shipping, customs, method of payment, et cetera. And since then, they have been rolling in dough.

"But these men are so cheap." Her tone turned sour. "I do all the work for them—negotiation, shipment arrangement, order of bills, everything—but they pay me only eighteen hundred yuan a month, not a penny more. They don't give me any days off during the year except Christmas time, when the foreigners are not working. I can't stand the food in the cafeteria, but they don't even allow an electric stove in my room, just to save that tiny bit of electricity. People here have secretly asked me so many times, why haven't I betrayed these two black-hearted Zhous? If I did, their business would collapse." Xiao Yi's cheeks flushed with anger and resentment.

"Have you thought of leaving?" I asked her sympathetically, feeling that we were two people crossing a river in the same boat.

"I'm planning on it."

"Have you found a new job?"

"No, not yet."

"Well, if you find a job, could you please let me know? Let's stay in touch." By then I considered Xiao Yi a close friend. We spent practically every waking moment with each other.

She hesitated a little and then said reluctantly, "Yeah, sure, I will let you know, but promise me you won't tell anyone. I will only give two days' notice before I leave, and I don't want the Zhous ever to be able to find me for the rest of my life."

"Xiao Yi, when did you come to the South?" I was curious about her. She appeared weak and frail but seemed to know how to take care of herself.

"About three years ago. I've lived in three different towns for jobs, but I can't find a good one. There's no stability in the South." She sighed.

One month after I started the job, Xiao Yi gave the Zhous notice three days before her actual leaving date. After making sure she had taught me everything and given me all the data, the Zhous happily let her go. Xiao Yi told everyone that she was going back to her home town in Jiangxi Province for a break before searching for a new job, but I knew she wasn't telling the truth.

"Good luck with your future. Call me. You know where I am," I said during the final long talk we had in the office the night before she left. I grinned. "I'll just be here, making fortunes for the Zhous."

She made a small laugh. Then after a short silence, she spoke. "You know, I've thought about importing machines myself before. It's so tempting. This business can make you rich overnight."

Her words caught my interest immediately, like a flame suddenly appearing in the dark and tearing apart the night before my eyes. To become rich. It was the universal dream of every outlander drifting through the South. If I became rich, I could give my parents lots of money so they would stop fighting, and I could finally have a happy family. I could buy a lot of cosmetics and clothes and become a city girl. More importantly, though, I could prove to everyone, my mother, my father, and all the villagers in the Shen Hamlet, that I could succeed, that I was different.

I held my breath and asked, "Do it yourself? How?"

"Well, I know all the suppliers' information and the procedure. We'd only need someone to put up the money."

"It's not *that* easy, is it?"

"The most difficult part is getting the machines through customs. It's very tough to import used machines into China, because the government protects domestic manufacturers, so there's a quota on them every year. Do you ever wonder why the Zhous unload their machines at night? They've bribed somebody working at Customs and figured out a way to bring the machines into the country under the category of 'parts' instead of as whole machines."

A strong desire to make money surged through me. If the Zhous could do it, why couldn't I?

I grasped Xiao Yi's arm. "Xiao Yi, let's do it ourselves. We can make it work. You must have thought it through already."

"We really need a millionaire. Every deal is at least half a million, and the turnover takes two months including the shipping, clearing, selling, et cetera." Xiao Yi thought for a few seconds and then lowered her voice even more. "The best person would be Song, the Zhous' biggest client."

"You mean the fat guy who loves hookers and doesn't close the bathroom door when he pees? The one Zhou's wife calls a country bumpkin?"

"Yes, the guy with the huge stomach. But you would be wrong to think he's just an illiterate peasant. He has a lot of money and buys at least half of the Zhous' machines and then sells them himself. I think he would be thrilled to be able to bypass Zhou and import himself."

"Why haven't you talked to him, then?"

"Well, it's not that easy." She sighed. "What if Song can't find a way through Customs? Would he really want to work with us? What if he tells the Zhous? They'd kill us. I'm not kidding. You and I are just two of the millions of migrant workers drifting here from Inner China, but the Zhous are powerful men in this town. Nobody would even know if we disappeared one day."

She was right about everything. We could get in big trouble with the Zhous. But the idea that we could become rich teased me like the tip of a goose feather. I just couldn't put it out of my mind. I knew it could be life-threatening to approach Song, but this was my chance, the opportunity I had longed for when I came to the South.

"Xiao Yi, Song should be in town soon again. Don't leave yet. Stay somewhere in the town, and we can find an opportunity to approach him."

She grinned. "No, Ah-Juan. Don't get too excited. It's just a beautiful dream. Who knows if it would ever work out? It's too risky. I am leaving, no matter what. Life is too tiring. I just want a peaceful job in some small town where I can work normal hours and stay healthy." She looked at me. "But why don't you go and talk to Song? You seem to be good with men."

I crossed my arms in front of my chest. I summoned up my courage and said resolutely, "I'll find a chance to go and talk to him, and I'll let you know how it goes."

Her eyes glinted. She didn't believe I'd do it. I would prove to her that I was serious. I was young and impatient, and I had nothing to lose.

—

The next day, Xiao Yi left the company and I became the only translator. I worked day and night and gradually became familiar with the two major suppliers, Jacques in Paris and Carl in South Carolina. I kept getting good deals for the Zhous, and they seemed pleased with my performance.

Finally, the day I had been waiting for arrived. Song, the rich country bumpkin who always had stacks of cash in his pockets, flew in to buy the KS machines. Sitting at my desk, I heard Zhou telling his driver to pick up Song at Guangzhou Airport.

After the driver left, Zhou turned to me and ordered, "Ah-Juan, lock all the drawers and don't let Song near the fax machine."

Song's oval stomach, wrapped up in a blue suit, was the first thing to appear at the door, and then came his flat, swarthy face with its two small eyes. After dropping his buttocks into a leather chair, he quickly surveyed the room. I smiled to him politely and then turned back to the faxes scattered on my desk. I could feel his eyes burning into my back.

"Old Zhou, I see you have a new translator. Damn, you change translators as often as you change hookers. That stick Xiao Yi is gone now, and you got yourself a round one. Good choice. I like meaty ones." He winked to Zhou and laughed lasciviously, swiveling his chair with his bottom like a naughty child.

I kept my eyes focused on the paper and fingers grasping the ballpoint pen.

"Of course! Hookers—you need to change them often, just like machines. You need to change them often too." Zhou cackled. "Old Song, I've told Ah-Juan that being a hooker is the best job for a girl, because not only do you make money, you also have fun. I told her that in my next life I want to be reincarnated as a hooker, and she scoffed. But don't you agree?"

Both of them roared with laughter. God, how could such sleazebags get so rich? But then I thought of what Chairman Deng Xiaoping once said—white cat or black cat, as long as it catches mice, it is a good cat. Moral character was not worth a penny. I shouldn't care how many hookers Song dealt with or how terribly he behaved, as long as he could help turn my destiny around. I had to like him, and I had to make him like me too. My chance came later that night when Zhou invited me to dinner with them.

I knew Song liked to drink and, like the LongJiang executives, would enjoy watching me drink. So at dinner I filled both our cups with the strongest rice wine the restaurant offered, proposed a toast, and then downed mine in one gulp. Sure enough, he became extremely interested in me and kept pestering me to have more.

"So, where are you staying tonight?" I asked as we clinked our glasses.

"The Golden Swan Hotel. It's not far from here," he answered quickly and then ordered me to finish my rice wine.

Soon his face turned red. He took off his blazer and loosened his belt. His belly was as big as an eight-months-pregnant woman's. He definitely could not see his own toes. After five or six glasses, the rice wine was burning all my internal organs, and I could hardly focus on his face. I saw Zhou stand up and go to the bathroom. I shook the tipsy feeling out of my head and gathered up my remaining sense.

"So, what room are you staying in?" I asked. I tilted my head flirtatiously.

"Why? Are you going to visit me tonight?" He squinted and

smiled cunningly. He was playing with a toothpick, sticking it in the gaps between his teeth.

"No, why would I visit you?" I said. Immediately, I realized my tone had been too harsh, and I said sweetly, "Oh, well, maybe, if I don't have to work too late."

"Two-oh-seven." He winked. "I'll be waiting."

When Zhou returned to the table, I told him I had had too much to drink and needed to go back to the office building. Zhou instructed his driver to take me home. I said a quick good-bye to Song. I didn't want to appear too friendly and arouse Zhou's suspicions.

I stayed next to the fax machine that night as usual, waiting anxiously for Zhou's return. At around eleven, I heard his Lexus pull up and park and then his footsteps going up the stairs to his bedroom. I waited another hour until I was certain he would be asleep, and then I locked the office door and tiptoed down to the iron gate.

"Miss Shen, going out so late?" the guard grunted.

"Yeah, a friend of mine is really sick, and I need to go and see her. I'm so sorry to wake you up," I apologized. He picked up the big chain of keys from the table and walked toward the small gate next to the big iron gate. I followed him closely. As soon as he opened the small gate, I stepped into the darkness and ran to the road.

The one-mile distance between the factory and the hotel seemed to take forever to travel in the pitch-dark night. I jogged on the empty asphalt road, looking behind me repeatedly. After ten minutes, I arrived at the entrance of the Golden Swan Hotel, carrying a gust of dust with me.

The receptionist was sleeping behind her desk in the dark lobby. I hid in the space beneath the elegant wooden staircase, which was ornately carved with dragons and phoenixes. After double-checking that the receptionist was still asleep and no one was watching, I ran up the stairs as fast as I could. The rooms on the second floor were located along the four sides of a square whose open center overlooked the lobby. I walked around the square as discreetly as possible, glancing quickly at the golden plates on the doors of the rooms.

I found number 207 and halted. I clutched my jacket with both hands and paused for a moment, waiting for my heart to slow down. I was poised to knock, but my hand dropped to my side. Maybe the cost would be too high. I didn't know if I was ready for this. But a voice inside of me thundered, Yes! Yes, you are. I knocked.

Song appeared, wearing an open robe, his eyes foggy from sleep. I said a soft hi to him and squeezed in. The funk of foot odor rose to my nose. He slipped back into the bed and leaned his back against the pillow, looking at me, a bit puzzled.

I sat down on the edge of the other bed in the room. He examined me from head to toe, and then I saw a sly smile emerging on his face. I started to get scared, and before he could develop wilder thoughts, I said, "Boss Song, don't misunderstand. Sorry that I came to visit you so late, but I have a very important matter to discuss."

"Oh, really?" he said skeptically. "What is it?"

Solemnly and slowly, I asked, "Would you like to bypass Zhou and import machines directly from overseas yourself?"

He was clearly taken aback. "Why do you ask?"

"Because I know everything, and I can help you make so much more money by bypassing Zhou. Right now, the money you are making is just a drop of dirt leaking out of the gaps between Zhou's toes."

"You're selling out your boss? How can you be so bold? Zhou will kill you." He chuckled a little, but his voice had an edge to it.

I grew frightened, wondering if I had miscalculated. Was

there a chance he'd tell Zhou? I stuffed down the fear. "You know the old saying: unless a man looks out for himself, Heaven and Earth will destroy him. I want to make money. I want to succeed. And I think you're too smart a businessman to let go of this opportunity."

"No, you're wrong. I am very happy working with Zhou. I'm content with the current arrangement."

I didn't understand how he could reject such a good opportunity. I struggled with the sudden disappointment, but I wasn't ready to give up. "You can double and triple your profit by importing them yourself. I can arrange for everything. I know the suppliers and how to get through Customs. All you need to supply are the funds."

"Nah, importing is too much trouble." Scratching his scalp covered with one-inch long hairs, he sighed contentedly. "I am happy now. All I have to do is to buy machines from Zhou and then sell them to my customers. Very easy, quick money."

In the mirror across the room, I saw my face losing its color. I couldn't move my lips. This was it. My grand plan, which I had spent so long concocting and had bet my future on, had turned into a disaster. Now I had to walk out of that door, go back to my fax machine, and pretend that this had never happened.

"All right, Boss Song. I thought I should offer you this chance. Since you're not interested, please forget what I said tonight." I forced a smile and drew myself up, acting as dignified as possible, and turned to the door.

"Hey! Where are you going?"

"I have to go back to the office now."

"Wait, wait, wait," he called. "Why are you rushing? Come back. Sit down and let's talk some more." He pointed at the bed. I sat back down and tried to figure out what kind of game he was playing.

He leaned back. "How can I know that you're not a spy Zhou sent to test me? You know, I don't want to offend him and lose my business. He's the only person importing machines to China right now."

He sounded half serious and half joking.

I tried to figure out what he wanted to hear, but I could only see daggers behind his genial smile. With my palms open, I said, "Boss Song, I don't know how to prove my sincerity to you. You'll just have to trust me."

"I barely know you. How can I trust you?" His small eyes were narrowed to slits, fixing on my face like a fox's. Now I could tell where he was going. I felt disgusted, but I controlled myself.

He moved over a little on his bed and patted the space next to him. "Come here," he said.

I hesitated.

"Come here," he repeated more emphatically.

I sat next to him. He put his arm around my shoulder and cupped my chin, snickering. "You little thing, coming to my room in the middle of the night! What do you want from me?"

I tore his hand off of my face. "Come on, Boss Song, I didn't come here for this."

"Look, how can I believe you if you don't prove yourself to me?" His voice became impatient and loud.

His words rang in my ears. I couldn't believe that this big, fat guy breathing heavily on me, whose body smelled like meat, controlled my fate. I felt trapped. I wanted to make my fortune, the fortune I'd dreamed of for so long, so badly. I had given him my word, and now I had nothing left except my body. I didn't know whether to push him away or embrace him. But I couldn't dally. I had to make a decision. I steeled myself. If this was what my fate had arranged, if this was the price I had to pay for my dream of getting rich, I'd just close my eyes and do it.

Pushing down the wrath and indignation boiling inside me, I stripped off my clothes quickly and lay on my back. I spread my arms above my head. He got on top of me clumsily. The pungent smell of alcohol mixed with deodorant wafted over my face as he lowered his head and tried to stick his tongue into my mouth. I closed my teeth tightly and raised my chin as high as I could.

"Oh motherfucker, it feels so damn good!" he cried with ecstasy. He collapsed like a dead pig on a butcher's chopping board. I just wanted to grab all my clothes and run away, but I stayed to explain to him what we would need to get the company started. I insisted that Xiao Yi and I be treated as equal partners, not just employees. He didn't talk much, just listened, and I couldn't tell if he was seriously interested.

"I'll think about your idea," he said in a perky voice as I stepped out into the corridor. I was too ashamed of what I had just done to press him, and I got out of that filthy hotel as quickly as possible. I didn't regret it, though. I had done what I had to do.

Two weeks later, Song called me from the city of Xiamen in Fujian Province, where he was from, and told me that he'd found an agency that could import the machines for us in the way I had described to him. He offered to pay Xiao Yi and me five thousand yuan a month each and ten percent of the profits. I wanted more, but he held all the cards.

"Fly over right away, and we'll find an office space together and set up a company here." He was in a rush to get me off the phone. I confirmed with him that he would still bring Xiao Yi in, and then I agreed to meet him the next day. I didn't know how I was going to get the money for the plane ticket, but then I remembered I had someone I could always count on.

I tore a piece of paper out of the notebook on my desk and grabbed a pen.

Boss Zhou, it was my honor to have worked for you for
the past two months. Now I have to leave. Please for-
give me. I am really sorry.

I ran to my dorm and grabbed my handbag. I didn't have
time to take more than just my ID and phone book. Everything
else—my clothes, shoes, toothbrush, bedding, and so forth—I
left behind.

I waited in the shadows by the corner of the office building
until the guard got up and stepped behind his booth to urinate.
Then I reached in and took the key off the table and unlocked
the small gate. I didn't stop running until I reached the main
road. I looked behind me, but I saw nothing but darkness. The
iron gate of GrandKnit was already out of my sight and out of
my life.

Late at night, I knocked at Manager Huang's door. Sitting
on his bed and catching my breath, I told him I was going to
Xiamen to set up a new company with Boss Zhou's biggest
client.

"Did you run away from them? God, don't you want your
poor little life any more?" Manager Huang said as he drew all
the curtains in his room.

He could see that I was ready to defy death. He sighed and
sat down next to me. "I just don't know how to deal with
you." He took out two thousand yuan.

"Go to Guangzhou airport and buy a ticket right now," he
urged me. "Leave as quickly as you can."

18

"JESUS FUCKING CHRIST, I thought you would never show up," Song yelled out in the capacious, marble-floored airport lobby, spreading his arms. "Welcome to Xiamen."

His huge stomach looked like it was about to drop to the ground and break open like a watermelon. I moved my eyes away from it. There was a giant Dell billboard on the wall. In its glass frame I saw the reflection of my ashen, gloomy face.

Yes, you've made it, I told myself. I had climbed one step up the ladder. I controlled my own life once more. But I was filled with trepidation. All I knew of this beautiful seaside city was the tiger in front of me. I quickened my steps and walked past his extended arms. The bright and beautiful sunshine embraced me as soon as I stepped out of the revolving glass doors. In the distance, mushrooms of white cloud offset by the deep blue sky floated leisurely behind a row of mountains.

Song snapped his fingers, and immediately a new green Volkswagen taxi pulled up in front of us.

"Why Xiamen?" I asked Song from the back seat. "I thought you lived in another town."

Song sat in the front passenger seat, his arm hanging out the window, his hand playing with the wind. "That's where I live, but it's better to trade in Xiamen. It's one of the largest ports in China. Besides, it's more discreet here. It's too noisy in my town."

"What do you mean by 'discreet'?" I lifted my head. "You are going to formally register the new company and pay taxes, right? We should do this right. I don't want to be involved in any more illegal business."

"Of course," he said flatly. "You don't have to worry about those things. I just meant that too many people in my town were in the knitting business. They'll get jealous, and I want to avoid trouble."

I reminded myself to stay alert. As long as Xiao Yi and I were in charge of accounting and sales at the new company, which I was sure we would be since Song was illiterate, we would know whether the business was legal and how much our share of the profit should be.

We drove for forty minutes until we reached a hotel downtown.

"Come meet Old Two, my buddy from Shanghai. Since I'll be spending the majority of my time in my town, he'll be the manager here in the Xiamen office. He'll do the accounting and deal with Customs. Be nice to him." With a laugh, Song pointed to a short man in his forties who was standing in the middle of the hotel room and gazing at me with a smile, his arms crossed on top of his stomach.

Old Two looked like a typical canny man from Shanghai. Gravity had not been kind to him. One word immediately sprang to mind when I saw him: *droopy*. With his pale, flabby skin and baggy eyes, he looked like he was made of flour.

I couldn't believe that Song had already found one of his

own people to boss us. It seemed he had never taken me seriously about us being equal partners and he was planning to treat Xiao Yi and me as just translators, the same as at GrandKnit.

As soon as Song led me to my room, I closed the door and questioned him sternly. "What is this Old Two doing here? I hope you will still honor our deal. We are partners, not just boss and employees."

"Relax. He'll just pay the bills, cook and clean for you, and he'll deal with customs. He is an old cunning fox, good at those kinds of things." Explaining slowly with a false smile on his face, Song settled into a chair by the window.

He didn't trust me at all, I realized. He wanted his own people to get the machines through Customs and keep Xiao Yi and me in the dark. No doubt he was worried that I would betray him, just as I had betrayed the Zhous. I had no plans to deceive him, though, and as long as he treated me fairly, I intended to be a faithful worker. All I had wanted was enough money for a stable life with enough food and clothing. I guessed that this was retribution—once you betray someone, no one will ever trust you again.

I bit my lip. I needed to swallow this bitter melon I had planted for myself. Even if I wasn't going to be a full partner, I still deserved more money than the Zhous had paid me. "Where is the five thousand you promised you'd give me once I arrived?"

"Fuck you. All you care about is money. Don't you care about me at all?" Song asked, exasperated.

"No," I said. "There is *nothing* between you and me. From now on, things are strictly business."

He walked toward me. "Come on. Wouldn't it be better if you and I were lovers? We'd work well together."

I cringed and backed away. Shoulders squared, I tried to

appear as menacing as possible and declared emphatically, "I don't want to sleep with you any more. And if you don't give me the five thousand, I'll leave *right now.*"

"All right, all right. I'll stop bothering you, damn it. Relax. Here's your five thousand. I am a man of my word." He took a stack of money out of his leather pouch, threw it on the bed, and then stormed out the door, cursing loudly.

I gripped the five thousand yuan tightly in my hands and fell to the bed. I could feel my body shaking, but I couldn't tell whether it was out of anger or excitement. For the first time in my life, I was holding a fortune in my hands, but strangely I didn't feel like jumping up and down for joy as I had imagined doing thousands of times. Instead, I felt like crying, as though this stack of cash had been hidden deep among prickly bushes and I had had to crawl in slowly and push aside the brambles with my bare hands so that by the time I had fished it out, my skin was cut and bloodied.

The next day, we signed a one-year lease for a spacious three-bedroom apartment on the nineteenth floor of a residential and commercial building called the Huicheng Commercial Center. That afternoon, the first two things we moved into the living room were a fax machine and a Compaq computer we bought from the city's electronics center.

At three in the afternoon—nine in the morning in Paris—I sat down at the desk and gazed at the fax machine nervously.

Fifteen minutes later, it started to squeak and slowly spit out a piece of paper. "Congratulations to the new China Knit Company!" I saw Jacques's handwriting on the smooth surface of the fax paper. I relaxed.

Song was jubilant. "You are right. I shouldn't have worried that they'd only sell machines to the Zhous. These foreign devils will do business with anyone as long as they can make money. Tell him that I'll buy many more machines from him than the Zhous."

I happily agreed and started writing. Turning to leave, Song cocked his head to Old Two. They were leaving together.

"Where are you going?" I demanded.

"Oh," he said, "we're going to the import-and-export agent. We also need to find a warehouse to store the machines once they are unloaded at the dock."

"Wait up. I want to go with you."

He waved me off. "No need. It is a men's occasion, not good for a woman to be there."

Old Two said, "Ah-Juan, I didn't think you'd be so eager to walk around outside. I heard the Zhous were hiring assassins to get rid of you and Xiao Yi." The door closed behind them. The red *Make a Fortune* banner attached to it swayed lightly.

I stopped writing and pondered my situation. I could feel fear slowly rising within me. I had just turned twenty-three. I wasn't ready to die. I pressed my hands to the edge of the desk. Outside the windows, a dark cloud had just blocked the sun and the room was in shadow. A feeling of depression and regret took control of me. What a tricky situation I was in. My old boss was out to get me, and my new boss was trying to control me.

Eventually, the cloud moved away and the sky turned crystal blue. The air coming into the room smelled clean and sweet and tasted like the ocean. Cars were honking leisurely on the street below, and once in a while I heard the whistle of a traffic cop. Xiamen is just across the strait from Taiwan. It's warm and breezy all year around. There is not a lot of traffic on its wide, clean streets lined with small palm trees. Most of the vehicles are red or green Volkswagens. People walk around in casual clothes and flip-flops, more relaxed than Cantonese. But they speak loudly and stiffly, as if they are trying to crack walnuts with their teeth as they talk. The sound of people shouting in the local dialect drifted to my ears, and I found that I couldn't understand a single word. I remembered the hot summer day when I had arrived at the Guangzhou airport a year earlier, when I couldn't understand a single word the Cantonese-speaking taxi driver said.

Yet I had survived, I thought, through LongJiang and through Amway. I still had problems, but now I was in a new city with five thousand yuan in my pocket. After everything else I'd been through, I knew I could get through this.

I grabbed the phone on the desk and called Xiao Yi. She was now working as a quality controller in a toy factory in a town near Long Jiang.

"Xiao Yi, please come here as soon as possible. I need you. The city is beautiful, and I got the five thousand from Song," I said.

"Is everything set up? Customs, wire transfers?" She sounded very skeptical.

"Not yet, but we are working on it. Why don't you come here and we can work out everything together?"

"No, I'm not coming now. I won't give up my job here until you have brought in the first shipment of machines. I'm happy here. It's a private company, but they're much better than GrandKnit. They even have medical insurance. I need to be safe in life." Her tone was so decisive that I could picture her shaking her head at the other end of the line.

I put down the phone, disappointed. I was alone, and I was nervous. I didn't know how to protect myself from Song and Old Two. But I told myself to sweep aside the worries and keep going forward. I had gotten this far, and I was not going to turn back now.

That day, I went to the post office on the first floor of the building and wired two thousand yuan to Huang. I left the *note to the recipient* page blank except for my signature at the bottom. Next to the post office was a beauty salon with a big garish sign flashing the words *Best in Xiamen*. I walked in, sat down on a chair, and told the young handsome barber in a suit that I wanted him to cut my hair very short, as short as possible.

"Jesus, are you a monk?" Song yelled unhappily at the sight of me, his eyebrows frowning. "I'll fire you if you have your hair cut so short next time. A secretary can't have inch-long hair like a man's."

"I am not your secretary, and it'll grow back." I glowered and stormed into my room.

The next day, we purchased $125,000 worth of KOKETT machines from Jacques. Song slowly scribbled his name down at the bottom of the purchase agreement Jacques had faxed over. A feeling of joy filled the room. Song put his arms behind his head, leaned back in his leather chair, and said loftily, "Now that you work for me, you can't dress yourself like a country bumpkin any more. Go to this store in the LianHua district, and get yourself some decent clothes. Talk to the owner, Ah Mei. She's my woman and will take care of you."

He reached into his bag, took out some cash, and shoved it in my hands. "Here is seven thousand yuan. Go buy yourself a cell phone, the newest Ericsson model. Don't tell Xiao Yi. It's a bonus for you only."

The Ericsson mobile phone was no bigger than my palm, and as I held it tightly in my hand and walked briskly in the enchanting afternoon sun, I felt like I had truly joined the ranks of the wealthy. In 1997, very few people could afford a mobile phone, especially the newest and smallest Ericsson model. It would have cost an ordinary person in China five or six months' salary.

But as soon as I walked into Ah Mei's store, my brief self-glorification was shattered by what greeted my eyes—rows of delicate lace bras, silk panties, and thongs displayed on wooden shelves and exquisite wool suits and pants hanging in open compartments as classical music flowed out of a central speaker system. Staring at my reflection in the shiny marble floor, I hoped nobody would notice my worn-out cotton blouse and linen skirt.

Ah Mei, a short, round thirtyish woman wearing heavy makeup, greeted me warmly. I realized that Song must have told her I'd be visiting. I chuckled nervously in response and then sat in a chair and watched her run around the store picking out things for me.

Following her instructions, I grabbed the pile of lingerie and clothes she had chosen and hurried into the fitting room. I shrugged off my clothes and looked at myself in the mirror. I couldn't bear to look at my ordinary face and rough skin for more than a few seconds, and I quickly moved my eyes away. Staring at the pile of lace and silk on the chair, I was at a loss for what to do. I almost felt that the blossoming lace at the edges of the bras, as delicate and thin as butterfly wings, would bite me.

"Are you all right?" Ah Mei's voice asked, and before I could reply, the door swung open and she was standing behind me.

"God! Are you still wearing your grandmother's panties?" Bending down to where I had left my clothes on the floor, she exclaimed, "Look at this. It's almost rotten."

She picked up my bra with the tips of her polished nails and hastily threw it into the garbage can in the corner. I wrapped my arms over my chest and moved to the shadowy part of the fitting room, extremely embarrassed.

"Come here. Try this on. It's called a push-up bra, the newest model. It makes your boobs look incredible. Every girl in the city has one of these." She grabbed a bra from the pile and dangled it in front of me. I was too shy to take it from her, so she pulled my arms apart herself and looped the straps over my shoulders.

"God. Your skin is rough like a chicken's. You need to go to a beauty salon. Look at mine, smooth like a baby's. Touch it, touch it." She chattered and scolded me interminably, all the while forcing me to try on different clothes. Occasionally she would grab my hand and make me rub the skin on her arm. I would giggle awkwardly in response.

An hour later, all my old clothes were in the garbage can, and, in addition to the new clothes I was wearing, Ah Mei threw in two suits, two skirts, and two bras.

"Here you go. Now you look like a city girl." She handed me the bag containing the clothes.

It was more than three thousand yuan for all this. I couldn't possibly afford it.

Ah Mei dismissed my worries. "Just take it. Song opened this store for me. This little money is just like a dinner to him."

I looked at Ah Mei's heavily made-up eyes and blood-red lips and simply smiled. I wasn't sure how I felt about this short, curvy woman who couldn't even speak good Mandarin—jealous, admiring, or hateful? She might not have even finished elementary school, but she was the boss of a fancy clothing store in downtown Xiamen, and she never had to worry about her next meal. All because she had agreed to be Song's mistress.

Her cell phone rang. "Come over here right now," I heard Song command. She closed the shop in a hurry, and we went back to the apartment together.

As soon as Ah Mei sat on the couch, Song pushed her down, stuck his hand under the V-neck collar of her silk blouse, and started to run it all over her skin. She rubbed his watermelon stomach, writhed in his arms, and giggled obscenely. "Oh, my dear Boss Song, I love your big stomach. It makes you look so mighty."

Song glanced at me with a victorious smile. He sucked her lips and said proudly, "Of course. Every girl loves a big boss stomach. The bigger your stomach is, the richer you are."

With arms entwined around each other, they tumbled into Song's bedroom and dropped to the bed with a thump. Without closing the door, they started to moan and groan loudly. I went to my room feeling disgusted, as if I had eaten too much lard.

Thank god, the new company had signed its first deal. At least I would be getting something in return for being around these ridiculous people. Song was a fool for showing off his wealth and his mistress. He was trying to goad me into sleeping with him again, but instead I was more repulsed than ever. I just wished the machines had been shipped already. Once the containers arrived at the dock and were cleared by Customs, I would get the upper hand. Song would realize how much he needed me to stay so he could keep making money, and I'd have Xiao Yi for company. I missed her, the only female friend I had made in the South.

It took the ship forever to arrive at the Xiamen Port. Finally, forty days after we had set up the new company, the first load of machines was cleared through Customs and brought to the warehouse, the location of which was still kept secret from me. Xiao Yi arrived the very next day, after I had assured her that everything had gone smoothly. I gave her a big hug at the airport. She was still skinny and pale and looked at everything suspiciously. Song kept his promise and gave her five thousand yuan.

The next day, Xiao Yi and I took a taxi to Zhong Shan, the famous shopping street downtown, which was crowded with department stores and brand-name boutiques. In the evening we returned home with many shopping bags. We shut our bedroom door and tried on every piece of clothing and all the cosmetics. When Xiao Yi shook her bony butt in her new

miniskirt in front of the mirror, I couldn't help but laugh. I felt
so happy, as if I were in a dream. Everything seemed unreal. I
pinched my leg with my fingers and told myself that yes, indeed,
we had made it, and things were only going to get better.

"Xiao Yi, go ask Song to buy an Ericsson mobile phone for
you. He bought one for me, and he should buy one for you
too." I knew Song would be upset that I had told Xiao Yi this,
but I was so glad to have a friend at my side. For me, that was
far more important than making Song happy.

I was right not to trust Song. Weeks went by after the
first load of KOKETT machines was transported to his home
town, from where he said they would be sold to the many
knitting companies there; but every time we asked him about
the sales, he waved his hand impatiently and told us that the
market was not doing well lately, and he hadn't sold the
machines yet. Xiao Yi and I had no way of tracking the sales
in his home town, which was a few hours away. Gradually
Song began spending most days there and only coming to the
Xiamen office once in a while, when there were good offers
from the foreign dealers. Xiao Yi and I began to realize that
he wasn't going to keep his promise of sharing ten percent of
the profits with us.

We didn't dare utter a word to Song about it, but we both
realized how naïve we had been to trust him in the first place.
After all, he was a cunning businessman, and we were just two
young girls wanting a step up in life. We knew nothing about
his sales network, and there was no way we could know how
much profit he was making or whether he had even sold the
machines.

Sure enough, one day Song told us casually that he had successfully sold the machines but at such a low price that he had
barely made any money, and of course there was no profit to
share with us. Xiao Yi and I looked at Song's lying face with

anger and disappointment filling our eyes, but in the end we merely lowered our heads.

We could have left, but at that point we couldn't summon up the will. Although we had been deceived by our boss, we were making five thousand yuan a month, living in a beautiful city near the ocean, and sharing a big, comfortable apartment where we enjoyed Old Two's daily Shanghai cooking. Life was good for us.

Besides, by that time Xiao Yi and I were hooked on one thing—the Internet.

"IN THE SOUTH I heard about this new World Wide Web thing, very cool. We should connect our computer to the Internet," Xiao Yi suggested to me one day.

So one slow afternoon, we went to China Telecom and registered for an account. The same day, a technician came to our apartment. He typed in "www.yahoo.com" and immediately text and pictures of all kinds popped up on the screen. "This is a very popular search site, created by a Chinese guy who went to Stanford. You girls should look at it."

Xiao Yi and I inspected the Web site from top to bottom, as if getting a load of a new neighbor. We had no idea what to do next. Xiao Yi tried moving around the mouse while clicking the button, and, boom, suddenly a new page came up with a big flashing headline: *Yahoo! Personals.*

"Look, you can post a personal ad here and become friends with the people in America," Xiao Yi said excitedly.

"Really?" I moved closer.

I ran my eyes over the words and pictures on the screen. "I would love to have an American friend to practice my English with," I told Xiao Yi. "My English professor in college told us that America is very rich, like a paradise. Even the moon in America is rounder than the one in China, and it's so clean there that you can walk for three days and your boots will still be so shiny that you can lick them with your tongue."

Enraptured by this new mysterious world we had just discovered, Xiao Yi and I crammed together in front of the screen for hours. We stayed up late at night to compose our personal ads. When Xiao Yi had finished hers, I took over the keyboard, and after rubbing my sleepy eyes and hitting the backspace key hundreds of times, I was finally satisfied with mine. After hitting the send key, I sat back, thinking of what I had come up with:

Hi, my name is Caroline, a twenty-three-year-old Chinese girl living in Xiamen, China. What am I looking for? I don't know. My birth animal is tiger in China, so I am a fierce tiger most time, but once a while I am a rabbit, only with the right person. I am active, optimistic, energetic and healthy. I used to be a teacher, now I am a translator in this beautiful seaside city, and if you ever have a chance to come here I would be glad to take you around. Thanks, looking forward to knowing you.

It had been surprisingly difficult to choose an English name for myself. As life had become more stable in Xiamen, I had started to read again, particularly books in English. Drawing inspiration from these books, I had contemplated the name Violetta for a while, as in Violetta in *La Traviata*, but in the end I had settled on Caroline, the name of the governess in Mary Martha Sherwood's novel *Caroline Mordaunt*. I told myself,

I shouldn't think of myself as a prostitute like Violetta any more. From then on, I would be a normal, decent girl, like a governess.

The next morning, after eating my usual bowl of congee, I sat at the computer and clicked open my mailbox. I couldn't believe my eyes. "Dear Caroline, you have 57 messages," it said. Xiao Yi and I were astonished. Yesterday we had just been two ordinary girls known by practically nobody, but today we were connected with dozens of people living in the faraway land of America.

"What should we do now?" Xiao Yi sounded excited.

"We should reply to everyone. Otherwise people would be disappointed." I felt like every single person who had replied to my ad had already become a friend who I ought to be as nice to as I could. But soon my head started to swim from the continuous responding, and the screen become blurry.

Two weeks later, my fingers ached from the typing, but the mail kept pouring into my inbox. The number of messages had reached 381. I pushed the keyboard away and turned to Xiao Yi. "I am dead. I can't write to everyone. I have to be selective."

She nodded feebly. "Yeah. Who knows if these people are sincere and expecting us to write back? Some of them might write to everyone on Yahoo."

I agreed and rested my head on my shoulder. Yet the smile on my face just wouldn't go away. I decided to share my secret with Xiao Yi.

I looked around the room, made sure Old Two wasn't nearby, and whispered, "I think I'm in love with this guy Steven."

Xiao Yi leaned in. "Who is he?"

With a face glowing with joy, I shyly told her about my new love. "He's a consultant living in California, an MBA. He's so sweet. He writes long letters to me every day. God, nobody has ever said such sweet words to me. When I read his letters and poems, I feel so sweet and lucky. And he's so handsome. He has a personal Web site, and I saw his picture. Blond hair, blue eyes. He looks so different from Chinese men, so noble, like the aristocrats in English novels."

Xiao Yi frowned. "You've only known him for two weeks. How could you be in love with him already?"

"I don't know. His long, sweet letters, his romantic poems, they make my heart beat faster. He's told me everything, his life, his children. In today's letter he even asked whether I thought getting married was a good idea. I know this sounds crazy, but why would he spend so much time writing such long letters—just to impress me? I'm just an ordinary, ugly girl half a world away."

"Get married? This sounds like a movie. He doesn't even know you." Xiao Yi rolled her eyes.

"He said he would come see me," I insisted. "He's leaving for a vacation in Singapore next month, and he said he would try to come to China."

"Are you serious?" Xiao Yi asked. "What are you going to do?"

"I don't know. I'm very attracted to him, I think."

"God, you're crazy. How old is he?"

"Uh . . . a little old. Forty-three. Divorced, with three daughters and a mean ex-wife. He said he had never met a girl as nice as me." I watched Xiao Yi intently, worried that she would shake her head and tell me that he was too old for me.

Xiao Yi just blinked her small eyes and looked at me as if I was from another planet. "I think you should be careful about him."

"His ex-wife cheated on him and then took away their daughters. He's innocent."

"How do you know he's telling the truth?"

"I believe him. He called me yesterday, from America! I can tell from his voice that he is a truthful person. It sounds so sincere, so soulful." Steven's deep, tender voice came to my mind as if he was still murmuring to me on the phone. "Oh, dear Caroline, I wish you were here right now. Then we could hold each other in front of the fireplace," he had whispered to me affectionately, and his words had coursed through me like a stream of hard liquor. American men were so bold in expressing their emotions. I found myself longing for a different kind of love, now that my life was different than it had been in the past.

The New Year of 1998 soon arrived. Winter in Xiamen was warm, with the temperature in the sixties almost every day. While enjoying the pleasant weather and my new life, I anxiously awaited Steven's arrival in China. He called me from the Sheraton Hotel in Singapore. "I wish you were here, lying by the pool in the sun with me. It would be so nice," he whispered gently. "Dear Caroline, I think I am in love with you." I thrilled at the sound of his crisp, virile voice. I imagined this dashing MBA graduate, who made so much money every year, standing right in front of me, his masculine body dripping with water from the pool, promising to take me to America and love me forever.

I had never met Steven, but I felt drunk with love for him. Steven made my dream of America grow wildly. Every Chinese wanted to go to America, a land of dreams where there were more opportunities and everyone could own his own car. So many Chinese had gone to America to study and never returned. So many Chinese girls worked in every possible way to get to America. If others could do it, I could too, I thought.

But Steven wasn't my knight in shining armor, as I bitterly concluded a week later when he called me from the Singapore airport and told me he couldn't find an opportunity to come to

China. Listening to him explaining apologetically, I began to see reality. "But dear Caroline, please don't be disappointed. I am planning a trip to Xiamen in March, and I want to take you with me. Could you please find out if you can come to America with me, my darling?" His voice was as enticing as ever, but it didn't work its usual magic. I took the Trésor perfume he had sent me from its translucent Lancôme box, drew the brown triangular bottle to my nose, and sniffled greedily. It smelled like vanilla and chocolate. I didn't understand why he would send such a beautiful gift all the way from America if he was just playing with me. Despite having gone through so many men in my life, I still felt like an impotent child when dealing with them and their inexplicable behavior.

With the daily exchange of E-mails with Steven, the days went by quickly, and soon it was February, the time for the Lunar Spring Festival, the Chinese Christmas when every family gathers together for lavish dinners and fireworks for days. Xiao Yi and I were granted a six-day vacation by Song, but we weren't allowed to leave until the day before the Lunar New Year since it was not a holiday for our foreign suppliers.

Since the company had been founded, we had purchased hundreds of machines from overseas, yet Xiao Yi and I had never seen them with our own eyes and had no idea whether or not they had actually been sold. Frustrated and anxious, we remained distant and cold with Song and Old Two.

Song showed up in the apartment two days before Xiao Yi and I were leaving for our own home towns. He sat in his leather chair, rubbed his stomach, and sighed deeply. "It's so difficult to make a living nowadays. The market is down right now. God damn it, I haven't made much money at all selling those machines." Xiao Yi and I didn't buy a word he was saying. Song continued, "Xiao Yi, Ah-Juan, to be honest, I am not even sure if we can continue this business next year. Old

Two and I will see how it is going once the holiday is over, and then we will call you and let you know whether you should come back."

I saw Xiao Yi's face become taut. She raised her head high and hissed, "Boss Song, you cannot just fire us like this. I gave up my good job in Zhongsan to come here."

Song took out two stacks of money from his bag and handed them to us. "I said we don't know yet. Possibly we will have you back. Here is ten thousand for each of you, as an end-of-the-year bonus."

Xiao Yi and I took the stacks and then retreated to our room.

"Don't worry, Xiao Yi. Song is lying. He's definitely made some money. We'll fight." Feeling responsible for Xiao Yi, who I had talked into coming here, I forced a brave smile and tried to comfort her, but it was just a show. I was deeply worried about our futures.

In the evening, while Xiao Yi was lounging in our bedroom, I went to fetch a glass of water from the kitchen. Old Two saw me and gestured for me to come with him to his room. Puzzled, I followed him. He closed the door behind us.

"Ah-Juan, listen to me. We haven't been on good terms since we started to work together, and I know you see me as an uneducated bad man, but that's all in the past," he whispered, trying to appear as honest as he could, but I still looked at his baggy eyes suspiciously.

"I know that you treat Xiao Yi like your own sister, but there are lots of things that you don't know about her. Over the past several months, someone from this office has been secretly talking to one of Song's biggest competitors, and we just found out that it was Xiao Yi."

His words hit me hard. I couldn't believe it. Xiao Yi was my best friend. We had shared the same room, same bed, and same computer for the past five months. We went shopping, ate fried tofu that we bought from street vendors, and went to the KK disco together. I had trusted her. I felt as if I had been bitten by a spider. "How did you find out it was her talking to Song's competitor?" I asked Old Two furiously.

"Song's home town is small, and it's hard to keep secrets. We know this guy is trying every possible way to import machines himself too, and I am sure he is willing to pay big bucks for information. Xiao Yi has been talking to him ever since she came to Xiamen. We checked phone records." Old Two lowered his voice. "Song and I decided to get rid of her and keep you. She is a snake. Besides, there is no need for two people to do one person's job. Song is not crazy like the Zhous who wanted you to work 24/7."

I stared at his wrinkled face, speechless, unable to accept the fact that Xiao Yi, my shadow, my best friend for the past several months, was going to be fired and gone from my life.

"Ah-Juan, Xiao Yi is much slimier than you think. Think about it. She didn't come until one month after the company was started. By that time, everything was running well, and we didn't need her. She didn't do anything. You did everything," Old Two said indignantly. I knew that what he was saying was true, but Xiao Yi was my only friend, and I had taken her from her job in Zhongsan. I had fought for her, and she had betrayed me.

"Ah-Juan, this world is not as simple as it looks from the outside. You need to protect yourself. I didn't have much schooling, but I know Darwin's survival of the fittest theory. I am letting you know Song's decision now so that you won't worry about this over the holiday, but don't tell Xiao Yi that she's not coming back."

I nodded, feeling like a wilted flower, and left his room.

On New Year's Eve I returned to the Shen Hamlet, distraught by the news about Xiao Yi. It was my first time going back to the hamlet since I had left for the South the second time. After I had settled down in Xiamen, I had called my mother and told her that I was making five thousand yuan a month. She simply didn't believe me.

Now on the plane from Xiamen to Shanghai, I touched my handbag, where I had thirty thousand yuan in stacks. It immediately cheered me up, and I smiled to myself. Finally I was returning to the hamlet with victory instead of lice, with joy instead of sorrow.

Instead of the crowded bus, I took a taxi from the Shanghai airport, and it pulled up to the curb in front of the house just in time for dinner. The cacophony of fireworks rising and exploding filled the air. My mother came to the passenger-side door. "You stupid girl, why take a taxi?" she said. "Instead of twenty yuan for the bus, you pay 360 yuan for the taxi."

I patted my handbag. "Mama, don't worry," I said proudly. "Look, I have money now."

Seeing her huge happy smile made me forget my troubles with Song and Xiao Yi. I was delighted to make Mama proud. Watching her from behind as we walked to the house, I vowed to try to forget the past and enjoy life in the Shen Hamlet. Here, now, this was what I had—my aging mother on New Year's Eve, who was finally happy to see my return. She ran around busily, getting me rice and chopsticks. It didn't matter, I told myself, that my father was icy-cold or that Spring acted as if I had just come back from running to the store for a bottle of soy sauce. I should just be appreciative that I was home and no longer a pauper.

I sat down at the table, on which there were so many dishes that they had to be stacked on top of each other. I saw all the familiar dishes that I used to long for year-round because they were only served on New Year's Eve. My parents always prepared them, no matter how little money we had, because a lavish dinner on New Year's Eve was symbolic of good luck and a good beginning to a new year. A whole young chicken, soaked in a creamy broth and stuffed with marinated sticky rice, lay in a big aluminum bowl with a few pieces of winter mushroom floating around it. In the middle of the table, a big smoked pork shoulder was steaming in a ceramic bowl. I knew it would be delicious, as my father always soaked it in soy sauce for at least a month before taking it out and drying it in the sunshine for another month.

I looked across the table at my father. I wanted to say something to him like, Dad, how are you? How is the end of the year treating you? Do you know that I made money in Xiamen? But my tongue flinched when my eyes met his, as cold as the frost outside. I watched him sip rice wine silently, and I shivered. Winter in the unheated house in the Shen Hamlet was as cold as it was in my memory.

WHEN THE VACATION was over, I returned to Xiamen with tangled emotions. The plane circled above the bay for a long time before it was granted permission to land. Looking down at the ocean, as deep-blue and pure as a sapphire, I almost wished that we could stay in the air forever.

The anti-theft door of the apartment was shut tightly, and Old Two didn't appear to be home. I opened both the anti-theft door and the wooden inside door and paused at the threshold. The apartment was empty and quiet. The Compaq computer sat on the desk in the corner; beside it, the bonsai Xiao Yi and I had bought together was as verdant as ever. Yet Xiao Yi, my former best friend, was not sitting in front of the screen. In fact, she would never be there again, and I had ultimately been part of the scheme to get rid of her. The guilt gnawed at me.

I put my luggage down on the floor and went to the computer. Besides Xiao Yi, there was one other person who I had thought of often when shivering in the much colder weather in the Shen Hamlet—Steven. It would have been so nice to hear a sweet word from him at that moment. But when I opened my mailbox, there was nothing from him or anyone else. Had the passionate American lost interest in me?

I heard a key jingling in the lock, and then Old Two entered, carrying two plastic bags of fresh vegetables and some seafood.

"Oh, Ah-Juan, you are back," he said.

"Yeah, I just got in."

"I bought some fresh crabs and jumbo shrimp for dinner. Do you want to help me cook?"

"Oh, no, Brother Two, you know I don't know how to cook. I'll burn down the kitchen." After a short hesitation, I said, "Brother Two, did you call Xiao Yi during Spring Festival?"

"Yes. I told her that she didn't need to come back to Xiamen. Oh my God, you would never guess that such a skinny girl could yell so loudly and curse with such dirty words, like a peasant woman. Even worse, her mother took over the phone and yelled at me even more." Old Two grinned and shook his head.

I turned my eyes back to the computer screen, to my empty inbox. Downstairs, the young boy from Shandong Province had already set up his barbecue stand on the sidewalk and lit the coal in the stomach of the sheet-iron stove. While fanning the fire with his tattered bamboo fan, he quickly sprinkled spices on the skewers and flipped them. Soon smoke filled the air, and the smell of marinated lamb strips rose all the way up to us on the nineteenth floor. Xiao Yi and I used to run downstairs at this time every day, get at least ten skewers of these strips, and then walk along the street in the evening breeze, enjoying the delicious meat.

I made the pain curl inward, like an injured snail. Everything was memory now. I told myself to let it go. I took a deep breath and grabbed the phone. I needed to talk to Steven. It was the first time I had called America. He was the only person I could think of talking to at that moment.

His melodious voice came to my ears: "James Bond."

"Hello, Steven. It's Caroline, from China." My mouth was dry.

"Oh, Caroline! Darling, what a surprise. I was just thinking about you and how nice it would be if you were here. We could lie in front of the fireplace and make love to each other."

I giggled at his words but didn't forget the reason I was calling.

"Steven, you haven't written to me for many days. You don't like me any more?"

"Oh, Caroline, of course I still like you." His voice still sounded like a spring breeze, but then he sighed wearily. "But I've become more realistic about our future together. You are so far away, and I'm still living in my sister's basement, and I need to support my three kids. I am not sure what we can do."

I stood at the desk, holding the phone to my ear and feeling disappointment lick me like a snake. But you said you would come to China and marry me and become my knight on a white horse, I thought. You said you had never met such a loving person as me. You said you would give me perfume and flowers every day. Millions of questions swirled in my mind, but I only said, curtly, "I understand." We hung up.

So all my feelings for Steven had been wasted? I sat down in the chair, feeling sad. Page after page of love letters and poems, boxes of chocolate and perfumes—what was this American man doing if he wasn't serious about the courtship?

A chime from the computer caught my attention.

A chat window popped up with a message from Ethan, one of the American men who had responded to my Yahoo ad and whom I had been talking to sporadically. "Hey, Caroline, how are you?"

"Not good, really. This guy I once told you about, Steven, who I am in love with, isn't coming to China."

"Oh, I'm sorry to hear that. Maybe he was never serious about it. After all, China is half a world away."

Ethan's words seemed light-hearted but made sense. "But why did he write so many letters and send perfume to me? Why did he talk to me almost every day?"

"I don't know. He is nuts perhaps. Some people talk the talk but never walk the walk."

"What do you mean?"

Before Ethan could answer, Old Two called my name. I turned my head, still enmeshed in my own doleful world. With his index finger, Old Two signaled me to follow him. In a haze, I stood up and walked into his room.

"Ah-Juan, now Xiao Yi is gone. It's just you and me. We ought to look after each other. You are from Suzhou, and I am from Shanghai. We are practically fellow townsmen," he said genially.

I knew this old fox didn't give a damn that we were from the same region. Like a typical person from Shanghai, he never even bothered to look straight into my eyes.

"Ah-Juan, I know you think I am just Song's watchdog, but there's more to me than that. I am doing so much for him, but that greedy son of a bitch is only giving me five thousand yuan a month."

Five thousand yuan a month, and he was still complaining? All that for the little work he was doing? This man had only completed elementary school. His greediness amazed me.

"Do you know how much Song has been making since we started this business? You have no idea, do you? He tells you he is not making anything, doesn't he?"

I kept quiet, trying to hide my enormous curiosity and waiting for him to continue his speech.

"He just ordered a Toyota SUV shipped directly from Japan, the newest model. Do you know how much it is worth? Seven hundred thousand yuan! How can he afford such an expensive thing if he hasn't made millions from this business?"

Fury flared up within me at this news. Son of a tortoise! I'd been sure he had been concealing his earnings, but I'd had no idea it was so much. He had lied to Xiao Yi and me. He had put all the profit into his own pocket, and I hadn't gotten a penny. I was too angry to keep pretending I didn't care.

"Bastard!" I said, enraged. "He's been lying to me all this time! Brother Two, do you know that in our original agreement he was supposed to share ten percent of the profit with me?"

"I am well aware of that," Brother Two said, exuding sympathy.

"I am not going to let him keep doing this. He's got to give me all the money I deserve. Otherwise I'll leave." I pounded my fist on Old Two's desk.

"Ah-Juan, you are so silly. Think about it. Do you think Song will give you the money if you go and fight with him? Not only may he not do it, he would also become suspicious of you in the future. That can only worsen the situation." Old Two's words made sense. Maybe this old fox was not as bad as I had thought. Maybe he was trying to help me.

"Let me teach you a good way to get back at him, Ah-Juan. You are so silly. Why don't you ask for kickbacks from the foreign devils? Song doesn't even know a word of what you are talking about with them."

I hadn't expected this, and I pondered the idea for a second while Old Two fiddled nervously with his sleeves.

"Taking kickbacks? It's not morally right. Besides, would the devils give me kickbacks? What would they think of me? And what if Song finds out?"

"Ah-Juan, don't be stupid. Does Song think of you when he puts all the money in his own pocket?"

I shook my head.

"And as far as the devils go, they don't care as long as they can make money. Give Song a slightly higher quote, and ask the devils to wire the money back to you. And don't worry. I will help you to make sure Song doesn't find out. He trusts me, and I won't ask much. How about you just give me forty percent of the kickbacks you get?"

Now I knew why he was helping me, the old fox. But if he could help hide the kickbacks from Song, forty percent was worth it.

"Brother Two, forty percent is fair. I'm not worried about that. But are you sure this is going to be okay? I don't want to get into trouble. It's not right to take kickbacks."

"Nah, no worries. We're okay, as long as this thing is only known by you and me, the heaven and the earth. Don't tell *anyone!*" He pressed his finger to his lips.

My thoughts were muddled, and I couldn't make a decision right on the spot. "Brother Two, I just don't feel good about taking kickbacks. Let me think about it."

"Ah-Juan, be smart. Nobody else can take care of you in this world, only yourself."

I went to my bedroom and shut the door behind me. For a while, I sat on my bed, trying to clear my mind and weighing the morals in my head against the greed in my heart. I remembered what one of my elementary school teachers had said years ago: "Living in this world, don't lie, don't cheat; because if you do, you will get punished." An honest person would get rewarded eventually, he had told us, standing at the blackboard in front of the room full of children.

I wondered when Director Yip, the Zhou brothers, and Song would get their punishment. They cheated the banks, lied to the tax bureau, and betrayed their wives and employees, but they still got to drive around in Mercedes, bury their faces in shark-fin soup, and watch their businesses grow bigger and the number of their mistresses get larger. After seeing all the inequality, tears, struggles, and cruelty in life, was it possible to really believe in justice?

I called home. I couldn't think of anyone to talk to except my mother, who I was sure would convince me that only fools believed in truth and honesty these days.

"Mama, Old Two just told me a crazy idea of making money," I whispered to her on the phone, eyes glancing at the window nervously, as though there were eavesdroppers on the other side of the glass.

"What?" She was interested right away.

"Ask foreign suppliers for kickbacks."

"Is it safe?"

"It should be. I am the only one who talks to the foreigners. I just need to change the prices on the faxes before sending them to my boss, and then I can ask the devils to wire the money back to me. I know this can work. I could get a lot of money."

"Really?" My mother sounded more excited than I was.

"Yes. But I just don't think taking kickbacks is right. Only bad people take kickbacks."

"Don't be stupid. Nowadays, in this society, who *doesn't* take kickbacks? You have to give a few yuan to the head of a canteen when you sell a few chickens to them, and high officials and businessmen are putting thousands and millions of government money into their own pockets under the table. I don't know much, but I do know the seamy side of this society. You're a fool if you don't take kickbacks."

That night, holding the fax with the offer for KOKETT machines that Jacques had just sent, which I knew my boss would probably buy, I lost myself in my own train of thought for a while. Next to me was an earlier fax from Jacques, who had simply replied *No Problem!* to my request for kickbacks.

I took out the white-out bottle, shook it slightly, chose a number on the fax, and covered it. Once it was dry, with a black pen, I carefully wrote the number 1 on the white spot. I held the fax up before me and exhaled deeply. The quote for the KOKETT machines had changed from "$10,000 each" to "$11,000 each." I put down the fax and tried to relax. My hands were sweaty. I made a copy of the new fax and sent it to Song in his home town, then dropped into my chair, telling myself that I had just added another big dirty secret to my shoulders, one that I would carry for the rest of my life.

Song confirmed the price with me on the phone. "Book it! Thirty-percent down payment will be sent tomorrow from Hong Kong, as usual." After giving the order, he quickly hung up. I put the receiver back on the base, feeling ecstatic. I leaned my elbows on the desk, crossed my fingers, pressed them against my forehead, and told myself to calm down. I had made a lot of money in just a few minutes, but I shouldn't be so proud. After all, it was black money. Yet I couldn't help wondering: Am I rich now? Will I be rich soon?

I picked up the phone and called home to tell my mother how much money I had made.

"You don't have to ever worry about money from now on," I told her. "I'll wire a lot to you. You don't have to get up at three o'clock in the morning in the winter to sell vegetables any more. Song buys a lot of machines every year, and I will make so much more," I babbled to her rapturously.

She was delighted. "Really? I cannot believe this. Really? We'll be rich? But I need to sell vegetables. What if you can't make any more? Oh, I should not tell this to anyone. Oh, I cannot believe this."

I pictured her rough, wrinkled skin and trembling lips at the other end of the phone, and felt so happy, so satisfied and proud, that I told myself I could just die on the spot. No longer was I the useless daughter who couldn't plant rice shoots, couldn't cook, and hardly even talked. To think that my father had at one point disowned me. Miserable memories from home began to rush back to me, all the pain I had endured feeling like they hated me. I stood still, my immense joy quickly transforming into resentment.

"Mama, go to sleep," I said coldly and hung up.

One evening a few weeks later when I returned to the apartment from a walk, Old Two was waiting for me at the door with a pale face. He had found a letter from the Tax Bureau lying at the door. Xiao Xi had sent a letter to the government accusing our company of evading taxes.

She had even listed everybody's name: ". . . with the help of a girl called Shen Juanjuan. . . ." Old Two read the letter aloud, word by word. Then he put it down. "I told you how slimy she was. You didn't believe it," he whined. "You were her best friend, and see what she did to you?"

The heartache of being betrayed by my former best friend kept me quiet. Nobody was trustworthy, I told myself.

"Go start packing immediately," Old Two ordered. "We gotta move."

"Why do we need to move?" I protested. "Song told me the company is registered in his county, and he has been paying tax over there. We have nothing to be afraid of."

Old Two sucked his lips a few times and looked at me pityingly. "Ah-Juan, you're a smart girl, but why don't you have any street smarts? Song is nothing but a rich rogue. Even if he registered the company in his home town, he still needs to register the office in Xiamen and pay taxes here. And who knows if he has even done this in his home town? I certainly know that he hasn't registered it in Xiamen."

"He's been lying to me all along?"

"Just pack, and let's get out of here!"

In a hurry, we moved to the eighteenth floor of an even newer building, into a bigger apartment with fancier furniture that overlooked the manmade lake in the middle of the city.

Song came to Xiamen the next day, and his eyes turned glazy when Old Two told him about the letter. I had never seen him so disoriented.

"I will find a way to pay back the taxes in my home town and resolve this problem as soon as I go back," he promised.

"I hope you do," I said. I didn't trust this sleazy businessman, yet I felt powerless to protect myself.

SOON IT WAS April. The willow trees around the lake started to blossom, and people swarmed to the teahouses at the beaches, spending their days sitting lazily in the sun and sipping tea.

It had only been two months since Xiao Yi had been fired, but my life seemed to be completely different already. Work took only a few hours every day, and I was left with tons of time to kill on my own. Finally I had money, but I was extremely lonely.

In the afternoons I often sat in the parterre in the open yard in front of the new building, staring at the sidewalk and the street and getting lost in a trance. The sound of a lifeless recorded female voice announcing the names of the bus stations mingled with the loud chirping of birds and crickets in the flowering shrubs behind me. I remembered someone once telling me proudly that every bus in Xiamen ran on vegetable oil, and that was why Xiamen had been voted the cleanest city in China. So what? I thought to myself. The sense of novelty

I had felt when I first arrived in Xiamen, the pride of being somewhere so gorgeous and exotic, was long gone. Everything in my world seemed to have lost its original bright color. I was back to being a lonely, miserable creature who had a lot of inexplicable wrath inside.

A spatter of giggling interrupted my thoughts. I saw a group of young girls in tube tops and high heels brushing past me on the sidewalk. Their faces were as fresh as peaches, and their laughter was as carefree as spring itself. I frowned enviously and reached for my purse. I took out a cigarette and lit it.

Jennifer, my new friend, had just taught me how to smoke.

"A long, thin cigarette dangling between your fingers with red nails—what could be sexier and cooler than this? Every man likes bad girls who can smoke," she'd said.

I had gazed at her in the dim light of the bar she had taken me to, at her face painted with Shisheido powder and L'Oréal eye shadow, and hesitated for just a second. Nicotine's danger came to mind, but then I dismissed the thought. I should just be happy that a trendy girl like her was willing to hang out with me, I told myself.

Jennifer and I had met one afternoon when I was especially bored with wandering the streets. I had gone into a spa, thinking that now that I had money, I should fix my rough peasant skin, which Ah Mei had once compared to a chicken's. Just as I was standing over a giant bathtub and exclaiming at amount of the milk the girl had poured in—the kind of milk from real cows that was very hard to get in the hamlet—and vacillating about whether to get completely naked, Jennifer walked over in a lace bra and panties. She chastised the girl for cheating customers by putting in only three kilograms of milk instead of four as the price table stated. I gave her a thankful look, and we exchanged cell phone numbers and became friends.

Sitting in front of my building, I puffed out a streak of

smoke and looked at my bare fingernails. I really needed to get a manicure and go to the newly opened Le Printemps department store to get more clothes. Otherwise, I would never be able to keep up with Jennifer, although I doubted that I would ever be as stylish as she was. She knew all the cool restaurants and bars in the city, especially places where foreigners hung out, and where to find the best steaks and desserts.

Jennifer had opened up a new part of city life to me, a life intimate with Western culture. The previous night, she had taken me to the Oriental Bar next to the best hotel in the city, the Marco Polo. Almost all the customers were Westerners and Chinese girls eager to hang out with Westerners. She'd introduced me to Corona, Heineken, Budweiser, and her American boyfriend.

"This is Danny," she had said, pointing to the round guy sitting next to her with his arm around her shoulder. I'd looked at him curiously. Short and in his forties with a moustache, he looked a lot like the plastic statue of the Colonel that stood outside every KFC. The only difference was that he was wearing shorts and sneakers, with a pair of white socks pulled all the way up to his knees. If he had changed into pants and leather shoes and had been given a cane, he would have fooled every KFC-crazy Chinese kid in the city. At the thought, I'd had to cover my mouth to keep from laughing.

The sun was going down already. I glanced at my watch. It was nearly five o'clock. I had gotten myself out of my bed just two hours earlier, yet I was already feeling exhausted. I took out my cell phone.

"Hey, Jennifer, it's me."

"Hey, Caroline, meet you at KK around nine?"

"Sounds good. Shoot some pool after KK is closed?"

"Of course."

Jennifer had turned me into a night animal who wouldn't

go to bed before dawn. KK, the most popular disco club in the city, closed at four in the morning, but Jennifer and I lingered in all sorts of dim-sum places and pool clubs every night until the taxi drivers changed shifts at six, and the new drivers picked us up as their first passengers of the day.

I walked back to the apartment. Old Two was busy in the kitchen with dinner. In the living room, the computer's screen saver flashed *Caroline,* and I saw a few pieces of paper lying on the fax machine next to it. I sighed and grabbed them. Damn Europeans! Couldn't they start their days a little earlier than three p.m. my time? I sat down at the desk listlessly and started my daily few hours—or minutes—of work. After faxing back and forth for a little while, I signed a deal for $100,000 worth of KOKETT machines with a German company before Old Two called me for dinner.

In my bedroom, I unlocked the top drawer of my desk and took out my bank account booklet. Seeing all the wire transfers from overseas in Euros or dollars, made at different times and in different amounts, I felt my heart beating a little faster. I found it hard to convince myself that I was becoming a wealthy woman. It felt strange and surreal, like I had climbed to the top of a skyscraper and was now looking down at the street, feeling dizzy and perplexed.

At nine o'clock, my taxi pulled under the tall metal arch of the KK disco club, where crowds gathered, waiting for a chance to sneak in. The fifty-yuan entrance fee was a lot for most people. The air was filled with the familiar smells of grilled lamb skewers from the barbecue stands on the sidewalks and heavy cologne and deodorant from the foreigners, who didn't blink at throwing multiple fifty-yuan bills to the girl at the admission window.

I walked quickly toward the entrance, made of heavy metal and shaped like a giant tube leading to the club. As usual, several kids holding wilting flowers in their hands besieged me. Pulling my sleeves for all they were worth, they cried, "Sister, sister, buy some flowers from me!"

I kept walking. They followed me, tugging on my clothes with their dirty hands. At last I lost my patience and shouted, "I don't want to buy flowers. Let me go!"

"Sister, please buy a flower from me," one of the girls begged. "It'll only cost you five yuan. I haven't sold any today. My mother will be mad."

I paused and dropped my eyes to her little dirty face. "Stop selling flowers on the street. Go back to school."

"We don't have money for school," she answered right away. "We moved here from the countryside. Buy some flowers, buy some flowers!"

I looked at her and didn't know what to say. I wanted to reach for my purse and give her some money, yet a voice inside warned me: don't help these parents who use their kids to make money. As I was struggling with my conscience, one of the kids screamed to the others, "There's a foreigner over there. Let's go!" All of a sudden they let go of my clothes and dashed to a big-bellied American guy in a Dell T-shirt standing a few feet away from me.

I entered the club in an inexplicably gloomy mood. I spotted Jennifer's pale, delicate face right away. She was sitting on a leather couch in a corner, on the other side of the bar that occupied the middle of the room. I walked over and sat down. I said hi to Danny when he looked up from touching and squeezing Jennifer all over for a moment.

Sitting quietly and sipping beer, I watched the couple flirting. Holding Jennifer's leg up by her ankle, Danny ran his hand all over her skin and then bent down and kissed her ankle bracelet, which was made of tiny bells. Seeing him drooling all over her, I turned my head away. Jennifer was so pretty. Why was she sleeping with Danny, a man with a wife and three kids back in Cleveland? Working for Dell as a software engineer, Danny could live like a king in China. To Jennifer, he was probably just a sugar daddy. I wondered how much money he gave Jennifer every month. Five thousand, ten thousand yuan?

In the twinkling light of the club, I couldn't tell exactly what I was feeling—envy for her for sleeping with rich foreigners for money or loathing for her for sleeping with rich foreigners for money. Perhaps money wasn't the only thing Jennifer was getting. There was also jealousy from other girls and the prestige of hanging out with rich foreigners.

The DJ turned up the music, and suddenly the whole floor was shaking with the strong beats. The sound of Coco Lee singing "Di Do Di" blared from the giant speakers that seemed to be everywhere in the club. I grabbed the Corona bottle on the table and gulped down the awful beer, which cost ten times more at the club than it would have at a convenience store, and felt increasingly fretful in this drunk and dreamy world. There was a strong desire inside me. I realized that I hadn't been with a man since I had left the South. Now I felt as if a hand were reaching out from my body and trying to grab men on its own.

A tall man leaned against the big metal column at the bar, watching the dancing crowd quietly. His long nose, blond hair, and athletic figure caught my eye. A few minutes later, Jennifer introduced him to me.

"This is Hafs, from Finland. He works for Nokia. You know they have a big factory here, right?" She seemed to know every foreigner in the city.

I stared up at him admiringly. He looked like the model in the Calvin Klein ad in a Western magazine that Jennifer had shown me.

"You are the most handsome man I have ever seen," I said

sincerely. I didn't know how to be subtle. His eyes looked as cold as icebergs, but his haughty demeanor triggered something in me.

"Thank you." He smiled politely.

We quietly watched the go-go girls in tall boots dancing on the bar. He kept drinking and rarely spoke. All I learned about him was that he had a wife and two kids in Finland.

When it was almost four o'clock in the morning, the music started to become sluggish, as did the crowd. Hafs stooped and grabbed his coat from the leather couch, and then with a faint smile he said, "Time to go."

I watched his tall, broad back moving away from me in the crowd, and suddenly I felt a little lost. But after a few short steps, he paused, turned around, and asked, "Would you like to come with me?"

I hesitated only for a few seconds and then I followed him out of the club, into a taxi, and then to one of the most luxurious condos in the city. The view of the lake was supposed to be fantastic from this building, but I didn't get the chance to see it. Without wasting any words, Hafs led me directly to his bedroom.

He laid me down on his bed and slowly took off my clothes. In the dark he kissed my lips, then my chest, and then gently moved his lips all the way down. When he pressed them on my bare skin, I suddenly couldn't breathe. It was such a wonderful feeling, his lips kissing the most private spot on my body, a new feeling that I had never experienced before.

Hafs took a condom from his pants pocket and then, after putting it on, he slowly entered me. My body jerked with sudden pleasure. He held me tightly with his muscular arms, and I felt like screaming. But almost immediately, Hafs let out a groan and hunched his back.

"Sorry, I haven't done this in a while." He got up on his knees. I told him not to worry.

The next morning, as soon as I woke up and saw his cold blue eyes, I said a quick good-bye and rushed out of his apartment.

That night, when I saw Hafs walking in my direction at KK, my heart almost stopped beating. I gazed at him, ready to give him a sweet smile, but he passed by without looking at me, as if he had never met me before.

I looked around the smoky club blankly, deeply puzzled and hurt. Why didn't he even talk to me, after the previous night?

Night after night, Hafs passed me in the club as if I was a total stranger. I watched his tall figure from a distance. I saw him holding other girls' hands and leaving the club with them. Was I not good enough for him? That must have been it. Those other girls were flowers, and I was dirt. They were tall and slender, and I was short and chubby. I tortured myself with these thoughts in KK's deafening music.

Jennifer, who had seen enough of my eyes following Hafs all over KK, reprimanded me. "Come on, Caroline. Haven't you heard of a one-night stand? Foreigners, they sleep around. They play with Chinese girls. They never get serious with you. Be realistic. No need to get jealous of those girls who go home with Hafs. They just want money."

I was at a loss for words. I didn't understand why no one was ever serious, why everyone just wanted to play. Like Steven, who had fooled me with his deep voice and loving words. Like Hafs, who had taken me home and then treated me like a stranger.

I looked at the young girls in tiny shorts and high boots flirting with foreigners all over the club. I wasn't sure I was any better than them. Sure, I didn't need the money. I had enough on my own. But it didn't seem to matter. I felt empty, lost like a kite with a broken string. I drank a lot of tequila that night and went home with an Australian guy.

A few nights later I got drunk again and got into a taxi with a German guy. The only things that I remember about him are that he was tall and thin, like a man made out of paper; that he worked as an engineer for a German forklift company; and that he had a huge penis that hurt me like hell. But I didn't care. All I wanted was to get drunk and sleep with foreigners.

—

I started a befuddled new life. I slept like a log in the day-time and then wandered around the city like a ghost at night. I learned not to bat an eye when paying for a Ports skirt or Chanel lipstick. I sat outside and smoked as if there were no tomorrow. The total in my bank account book kept growing, as did the number of foreigners I'd slept with, but I grew sad-der every day.

I rarely refused to sleep with a Westerner. Like a sick person in need of his medicine, I longed for the moment when a foreigner asked me whether I wanted to go home with him. I was always nervous until it happened, clenching my muscles and holding my breath, as if my entire life depended on these moments and only if I got my dose could I breathe, eat, and sleep again.

I was a slut again. I cursed myself. It was bad to sleep around. But though I condemned myself, I couldn't figure out why I was doing it and what was wrong with my head. It felt as if I was trapped in a bog, and no matter how I floundered, there was no way to get out.

"Next time I come to Xiamen, I'll sleep with you," John, one of our American suppliers, told me in a commanding tone, pointing his finger at me and smiling.

How old was he, sixty? He wanted to sleep with me, did he? Fine, I thought. I'll sleep with you, but not for free. Your Japanese mistress could bear to sleep with you every night for big houses and a Mercedes-Benz. Why can't I do the same?

The old millionaire came to Xiamen the next month, and I spent the night with him in the most luxurious suite in the Marco Polo Hotel. I was sitting on the couch, looking down at the artificial but beautiful lake. He walked up to me and gave me a Dior lipstick, some Guerlain powder, and a gold bracelet. Then I felt his cold, wet lips. His mouth moved down to my chest. I looked at this head covered with white hair and felt nothing. When he asked why my underwear didn't match, I lied and said I didn't have enough money to buy many pairs. In the morning, he handed me five hundred dollars and said, "This is not much, just for some underwear. Next time, I want to see them match."

Next time? Would there be a next time? I chuckled to myself as I rode the elevator downstairs. I stopped at the Godiva counter in the lobby and bought myself some dark chocolate balls. I figured I should celebrate because I had finally pimped myself out successfully, and for a great price, five hundred dollars! I decided I should buy chocolate for myself from then on, since I didn't think any man would buy me Godiva in this lifetime. Or roses, for that matter.

I walked out of the lobby of the Marco Polo Hotel smiling to the sun and crying inside to the devil that had taken over my soul again.

—

I started to read the classified page in the daily newspaper and circled the want ads for overseas jobs. The air in Xiamen was still so fresh; the sun was still so enchanting; but I couldn't breathe freely there. I felt like all my organs were clogged up with filth. Weekly facials in beauty salons could only purify my skin, nothing more. I hung around in every club and bar in Xiamen with Jennifer, the bad girl, or with my other friend Ann, a good girl who had no idea that all the foreigners I had slept with could perhaps make up a mini–United Nations. All the martinis and bottles of Corona that I drank couldn't wash away the dust that had settled on me. I was backsliding. I was hypnotizing myself with alcohol and cigarettes.

Before I was completely eroded, I wanted to get myself out, out of this circle, out of Xiamen, and out of China.

One day, I read that a boat traveling between China and the Middle East was looking for wait staff. I rushed over to the office of the company. I followed the directions the captain had given me on the phone, and in a small lane I found the rundown building. I knocked on the filthy door.

In a stale conference room with a dusty navigation map on the wall, the captain told me to sit down and then handed me a piece of paper.

I held it up in the air and started to read. "'May I help you? Would you like a drink? This way, please.'" When I finished, I saw the captain's puzzled expression.

"Let me ask you something." He shifted in his chair and looked at me sincerely. "Why are you applying for this job? You know that we'll be on the sea all year around, right? And also, waitress is not the highest-level worker on the deck. It's really hard work too, to be honest with you."

"I know that. I don't care. I can take it." I shrugged.

"Your English is too good to be a waitress on our boat. You should be sitting in a fancy office building working for a foreign company making good money like all the girls out there—I mean, from your English and the way you dress."

I looked at the captain's aged face and gray temples and smiled wryly at him. He could tell there was something wrong with a girl with fine skin dressed in a silk suit and skirt who was willing to endure the harsh wind on the sea.

"Let me give you some honest advice. Go back to your work and enjoy life. So many girls must be jealous of you."

I started to talk to people at all the agencies in the city that helped Chinese citizens go abroad, but every time I told them I was single, they quickly shook their heads, especially those who dealt with visas or immigration to America.

"Americans rarely let single women enter their country on non-immigrant visas," one person told me bluntly. "They're afraid they would never leave. They guard their borders like dogs and don't let any inferior humans like us in. The best shortcut to get to America is to marry an American, and he'll be your ticket to America."

It seemed marriage might be my only bridge out of China. So I was supposed to just find a man and marry him? I wondered if it would be worth it to get married in exchange for a way out of the country.

After pondering this idea for many days, I faxed a personal letter to Carl and Jacques, our two biggest suppliers, who had become my friends, and asked them for a favor—to find a good man to marry me and take me out of China.

I was feeling desperate and suffocated, as if there was a cage around me: and this cage, in my eyes, was the entire country of China. All I could dream about was getting out of China and going to America, where it was said there was freedom and respect. There I could start my life all over again. Snakes could slough off their skin three times in a lifetime; why couldn't I?

Jacques and Carl promised me that they would do as I'd requested and find a good husband for me. My face burned with shame as I read their faxes. What kind of woman asked everybody she knew to find a man to marry her in exchange for taking her out of China? Only a woman with no morals or sense of shame would do that.

The summer was almost gone, yet the heat was still boiling inside me. September came. Soon I would turn twenty-four, and I couldn't sit around and wait for a man to drop from the sky to marry me any more. I was consumed by the idea of getting out of the country.

A teasing line in an ad in the evening newspaper caught my eyes: *Want to go to the UAE, a country where everyone is rich and dripping with oil?*

"We can easily get you out and send you to the UAE for twenty thousand yuan. You can get a job in a hotel. Many rich people go to the UAE, and you'll meet a lot of them at the hotel. But you need a passport," the lady at the front desk in the tiny, disordered office told me.

"How do I get a passport?" Chinese citizens were only given identification cards by the government, not passports.

"You need go back to where you come from, get approval from the unit you belong to, and then go to the local Public Security Office and apply for it. And the government will decide whether you are entitled to a passport," she explained.

Damn it, my identification still belonged to the middle school as far as the government was concerned. This stupid system with its ridiculous rules, I thought. Now I would have to go back to the middle school and beg the headmaster for his stamp on my passport application form. I had left the school two years ago, and I didn't belong there any more. I didn't want to belong to anybody, to any unit or any government. I wanted to belong to myself.

No matter how mad it made me, I had no choice but to yield to the rules in order to obtain a passport. I put on my sky-blue wool suit and high heels, and, with utter loathing in my heart, I returned to the Hope Middle School, the place I had fled from two years earlier.

I took a flight to Shanghai and then a taxi directly to Ba Jin. It was a shivery fall day there. Broken bricks and moss could still be seen everywhere in the town. The sparse bamboo bushes were still swaying listlessly around the school, and the teachers, whose faces I still remembered, were still running to the classrooms at the ringing of the bell with chalk dust all over their gray or black clothes.

I sat in one of the offices while several teachers stood around smacking their lips at me. It had been only two years, yet it felt like so long, like a lifetime.

"That necklace must be real gold, mustn't it? Is that sapphire too?" one of the female teachers asked admiringly. I nodded my head with a proud smile.

"How much are you making every month now, Teacher Shen? Oh, I should call you *Miss* Shen now," my former English team leader said.

"Well, my boss pays me five thousand yuan a month, not to mention bonuses," I replied briskly and shrugged my shoulders.

"Wow, that's how much we make in ten months."

I relished their envy. I smiled and kept quiet, remembering how they'd shaken their heads and admonished me when I'd quit.

The bell buzzed in all the buildings, giving everyone a start.

"Oh, I have to go to a class now." One teacher sighed and stood up.

"Yeah, I need to grab that little brat and give him a good beating on the palm," another said, grabbing a box of chalk and a ruler. All at once, they rushed out the door.

I went to the headmaster's office on the third floor. Fifteen minutes later, I walked out with a blood-red stamp on my passport application form, but there were five thousand fewer Yuan in my purse. It was the price I had to pay for my first step toward freedom. I had been blackmailed by the headmaster, yet I'd had to swallow it because once again he was the one who held the power.

I took a last look at the school, vowed never to come back, and then shook the dust off my feet.

The next thing to do was submit the application form to the county Public Security Office, fifty miles away from the school.

"It will take sixty days," the clerk behind the counter told me without showing any emotion on his face. "And I am not sure if you will be granted a passport. If the government thinks you shouldn't leave the country, your application will be denied," he warned me by rote while skimming through the application package.

All I could do was look at him helplessly, listen carefully, and pray that he happened to be in good mood and wouldn't tell me that I needed one more stamp here and another there. Getting out of China seemed to be tougher than climbing to the sky.

Nonetheless, I was still full of hope for going to the UAE. After I went back to Xiamen, I started to say good-bye to my few friends in the city.

One of them opened her eyes wide upon hearing my decision. "Are you crazy, Caroline? Do you know that the UAE is in the desert? You go out the door, and all you can see is sand and more sand."

"I'm not going there for fun. I just want to get out of here."

"The women there are all wrapped up in black cloth all year around, only showing their eyes. Are you going to live like that?" she pressed on.

I bit my lips. I could hardly imagine myself in a robe looking like a nun every day, yet all I could do was to pray that this would not be the case. You couldn't work in a hotel if you were all wrapped up, I told myself.

WHILE I WAS still waiting to hear about the passport, Song told me that he wanted Old Two and me to accompany him to the city of Harbin for a business trip. Although I was worried that I might miss some news about my passport application, I agreed to go since I knew my nerves would break down just like an overwound clock if I allowed myself to sit around immersed in my UAE dream for one more day.

So at the end of September, the three of us boarded an early morning plane to Beijing and then changed to another one for Harbin. A few hours later, we arrived in that dirty and disorderly city in the northernmost part of China. Black smoke came out of the many chimneys of the industrial compounds surrounding the city. People in heavy coats and ski masks biked around hurriedly, fighting with the harsh wind. We hopped in a taxi. After a couple of hours' ride, we finally reached our destination—a bankrupt warp-knitting factory in a small town somewhere close to the border of Russia. We looked around. It felt as if this town had been deserted years ago. The streets were empty, decorated sparsely with bare trees. The sun felt cold. The landscape looked like something from a dark oil painting by a depressed artist.

The head of the factory showed us the machines that were for sale, walking with hunched shoulders and arms folded inside the sleeves of his wadded jacket. Although it wasn't yet October, in this part of China it was already chilly like deep winter, and I could hear the sound of my teeth chattering.

We rushed back to Harbin that evening and checked into what was supposedly the best hotel in the city. In a lifeless restaurant, we had a much-too-salty and spicy dinner and then headed back to the hotel right away. The steam heaters hissed in the hotel room, but it seemed like they weren't putting out any heat at all. I crawled under the freezing quilt and felt my throat itching from the extremely polluted air.

Suddenly I missed Xiamen so much, missed the growing grass and the nightingales in the air, missed the gorgeous sunshine and the palm trees on the beaches, missed my small but warm room. I realized that everything is relative, and without comparison you could never tell what's good or bad. Why did I want to leave Xiamen so badly? I started to ask myself in the dark.

Three days later, the bargaining between Song and the head of the factory was finally done, and we didn't waste one minute getting on a plane back to Beijing.

We wandered in the shopping area of the Beijing airport to kill time during the two-hour layover. I saw boxes of moon cakes all over the counters, and suddenly I realized that the next day was the Moon Festival, a traditional Chinese festival when families gather together under what is supposedly the roundest moon of the year and enjoy these moon-shaped cakes.

I strolled along the counters looking at the rows of moon cakes in fancy packaging and marveling at the variety of cakes made these days. I remembered that when I was young, the only moon cakes available were filled with sweetened bean paste, but now I saw moon cakes with egg yolk, lotus bud, sesame, coffee, and even chocolate filling.

I stopped at a ruby-red tray with six cakes on it that was installed on top of a music box. Every time you turned the tray, euphonic music played. I immediately liked it and decided to buy it for my mother and mail it to her. Though the Moon Festival, with its expensive cakes, had rarely been celebrated in my family, a peasant family where everyone hated each other, I wanted to let my mother know that now everything was different, and the Moon Festival didn't just belong to city people any more but also to an ordinary family like ours.

Just after I handed the money to the saleswoman, my cell rang.

My mother's sobbing voice burst through the phone. Something was wrong again. I had thought that my family wouldn't bring me tears any more, now that I was making money and making them happy, but apparently I had been wrong.

"Your sister is pregnant," she cried.

A sick feeling started to spread through my chest. Spring was barely twenty.

"Whose baby?" I asked. I had never heard that she had a boyfriend.

"This bastard called Ming. He is married, thirty years old, with a kid," my mother bawled.

I couldn't believe it. My sister, my only sister, was pregnant with the child of a married man, just like five years ago when I had gotten pregnant by Pan.

"What are we going to do now?" I asked feebly.

"The little bitch thinks he will get divorced and marry her. Stupid bitch. Even if he is willing to, we will never let her marry him," she swore.

"Can I talk to her?"

"She won't talk to anybody! She thinks we're all her ene-
mies. First she ran to the road and wanted to get herself killed
by a truck. Luckily we pulled her back just in time. And now
she's locked herself in her room and won't come out."

"How did this all happen? Did you have any idea about this
guy before this happened?"

"How could we know what your sister was doing? She keeps
everything a secret. The guy told her he wasn't married, and
one day he sent his wife and daughter away and had your sister
visit the house, and when she wanted to leave he locked the
door. I gave him a good slap on the face when your father and
I grabbed him yesterday. He cried and promised to solve the
problem in a week. Now he's just disappeared. Nobody can
find him.

"Oh, God." My mother sobbed for a few seconds and then
cried out, "Little bitch, how could she ruin our lives like this?
She will never find a decent husband now. She's a broken shoe.
What are your father and I going to do now? We'll never have
a good family. We are doomed."

"Just calm down, Mama. I'll fly back right now. You need
to take care of yourself."

"How can I care about myself in a situation like this? Our
family is ruined. I was so upset that I fell from the top of the
stairs, all because of this little bitch. I cannot move at all. I've
just been lying on the bed!"

Her voice made my head ache. I leaned my forehead on my
palm. Tragedy was never tired of visiting our family.

"Son of a bitch," she continued. "We will take him to the
arbitration court and have him compensate us for our loss!" She
ground her teeth with hatred.

"I'll catch the earliest flight today."

My words seemed to comfort her a little and she fell into
quiet sobs. After a moment, she said, "If anybody asks you why

you came back, don't mention anything about your sister. If the villagers know this, they'll laugh at us until the day I go to the grave. Your sister will never be able to find a husband if word gets out."

So instead of returning to Xiamen, I boarded the next plane to Shanghai. With a heavy mind and the music box with the tray of moon cakes in my hands, I arrived home early in the evening, when the lamps in the Shen Hamlet had just started to go on.

I stepped over the threshold into our house and went straight upstairs. Seeing my sighing mother on the bed and my distressed father sitting on the floor with his arms wrapped around his head, tears came to my eyes. I felt the familiar, tense air that had accompanied me throughout my childhood and youth. I told myself to be strong, because right then I was the only string that was holding my family together.

I cleared my throat. "Could it be possible that they really do love each other and Ming will divorce his wife for Spring?" I asked my parents calmly.

"Never. Don't even think about it. I will never allow it to happen." My father raised his head and bellowed at me with a stiffened neck and red face. "The man is thirty. Instead of the thousands of single young men out there, why did she have to mess herself up with all these old married men? I would rather disown her than allow her to marry some divorced guy."

Suddenly I couldn't control myself any more. I glared at him. "Don't blame Spring only, Dad. Ask yourself, have you ever been a father to her? She wants old men, yes. Why? Have you thought about why? Maybe it is because you, her father, have never been there for her."

He put his arms down and looked at me, startled. "Are you saying—she misbehaves, she ruins herself with married men, all because of *me*?"

He was hurt. He didn't have the slightest idea of how much Spring and I had been wounded by my mother's affair and his retreat from our lives, how much damage they had done to us. He would never fully understand.

I left the room. I knocked on Spring's door gently, wanting to say something to her. There was no response. I stood there for a while. My sister was just on the other side of the door, yet I felt like she was so far away from me. I imagined her sitting in the dark in pain alone, and I wished that she and I knew each other better.

After a fruitless two-day search for Ming, who seemed to have vanished from the earth, we finally decided to take the matter to the arbitration court in the hopes that a summons from the government to his family would be sufficient to bring him out of whatever hole he was hiding in.

The next day, in the town's arbitration house, we waited a long time for Ming to show up. It was almost noon. Small Uncle was sitting on the long wooden bench along the wall with his arms crossed, his face boiling with anger toward Spring, who had brought such shame to the entire family. Our Aunt Jasmine, who had traveled here from her village two hours away, arriving early that morning, sat on the bench next to him, staring at the floor with tears on her face. Our mother's older brother, Big Uncle, who had left his fish stand unattended in the market, leaned against the wall smoking silently, still wearing his fishing boots. For a country family, a young girl pregnant with a married man's baby was humiliating and serious enough to gather together all the family members to try to come up with a solution. My parents were notably absent, though. My mother was too weak to come, and my father simply refused to be in such an official and serious place.

It was quiet, except for the drops leaking from the corner

of the ceiling in the old cement room and the sound of the arbitrator, Old Yao, taking long, loud sips from his clay teacup. If my family hadn't begged him to solve the matter quietly inside the arbitration house, Old Yao would have been on his bicycle riding all over the countryside searching for the "dirty little shit" Ming.

Spring was sitting motionless on one of the square wooden stools at Old Yao's desk with her back straight, staring vacantly at the Chinese rose swaying in the breeze outside the window. It was the first time I'd seen her since I'd flown back. Her eyelids were swollen, her face wan and sallow. One corner of her mouth was curled upward, the way it always used to be when she stood aside, watching our father beating me with the bamboo broom.

I wondered what she was thinking and feeling. I knew she must have been feeling scared, otherwise she wouldn't have told our parents about her pregnancy. But did she still hate our mother for forbidding her affair? Did she blame our father for threatening Ming and therefore scaring him away? Did she still believe Ming's promises? Did she expect him to prove he loved her today? I knew she hated me for flying home, hated Aunt Jasmine for coming all the way from her village, hated Small Uncle and Big Uncle for dropping all their business for her. I knew that she hated herself, hated everyone. But did she have any idea what her family was feeling, how much shame she had brought to them?

Gazing at her familiar thin eyebrows and flat nose, I suddenly had the impulse to clutch her shoulders and shake her until she came back to life.

The day before, while she was locked up in her room, I had bicycled down the coal-ash road for an hour to Ming's work unit in the hope of finding him. In the remote coal factory run by Ming's family, I had sat on a red bench for hours, waiting for his haughty uncle, the owner, to show up. The women outside the window had whispered loudly about what a bad, loose woman my sister was to have enticed the poor man, saying that our family, back to the eighteenth generation of ancestors, should jump out of their tombs for what Spring had done. I kept quiet with my head lowered. The owner never showed up.

The sound of a roaring motorcycle broke into my thoughts. Everyone straightened their backs and turned toward the door, except for Spring, who sat still. The round belly of Ming's uncle appeared, wrapped in a suit. He passed the steel security bars, followed by a short square-faced man with a hanging head and his hands in the pockets of a suit full of creases. From everyone's angry eyes, I knew that he must be Ming. I wanted to break his face and watch it crumble to bits.

Old Yao pointed Ming to a stool next to Spring's. Ming started to talk in a low, withered voice: "I told her from the very first day that I was married and had a lovely daughter. She might have told you that I held the wooden bar to the door, not letting her go. Well, she was lying. She slept with me of her own will. I can't get a divorce for her. This is ridiculous."

I was gratified to see Spring shaking, finally coming to life a little. Old Yao frowned as Ming continued with his story.

A woman with a stupefied grayish face walked into the room and stood behind Ming. She was so tall and thin that she reminded me of the compasses I had used in my geometry classes. I wondered if she was Ming's wife. Perhaps it was she who had cooked up this story, to humiliate that little bitch, Spring.

Ming finished talking and was now staring at the ends of his shoes. It was Spring's turn. She gazed at the floating green leaves in the tea glass in front of her. It looked like she was gathering her thoughts, while those of us who knew her were all worried that she might collapse. Abruptly, she grabbed the glass and splashed the tea in Ming's face.

Before anybody could react, the thin woman, Ming's wife, lunged at Spring and started to strangle her, her teeth bared and hatred all over her face. Standing closest to Spring, without thinking I pounced on the woman, grabbing the back of her striped coat and trying to pull her claws away from Spring's neck. Like a mad lioness, the woman turned around and attacked me. I had never even been able to kill a chicken, and soon my glasses were on the ground and the woman was pulling my hair hard. Small Uncle ran over and forced her arms down. Her body was still twisting, and her mouth was pouring out the most malicious curses I had ever heard. Before I had the chance to catch my breath, Aunt Jasmine was clutching at Ming's face while he was trying to knock Small Uncle's legs out from under him to help his wife, and Ming's uncle was wrestling with Big Uncle on the floor. Old Yao and Xiao Chen, a young mediator, were jumping up and down, flustered and exasperated, yelling at everyone to stop.

Furious, Old Yao shut my family outside the security bars while the other family stayed inside. Big Uncle and Small Uncle stood there puffing and blowing with their hands on their hips and giving Spring angry looks. Aunt Jasmine pointed at Spring, weeping and wailing to her about how stupid she was and how much shame she had brought to the family.

I clasped the steel bars with my fingers. I could feel warm tears flowing down my face, mixing with the blood from the bridge of my nose and my neck where Ming's wife had scratched it open. I was fighting alongside these illiterate peasants when I could have been sipping wine with my American clients in warm, civilized Xiamen. I could have been sitting on the Italian leather couch in the lounge of the Marco Polo Hotel as someone played Mozart on the piano and the waiter handed me a martini. Instead, I was stuck in the mad world of the Shen Hamlet.

I turned away from the bars, and through my teary eyes I saw Spring standing before me. We stood face to face, looking at each other silently. She reached out her finger, touched the scratched spots on my face, and gently wiped the blood off my nose. She was crying. On her chin I saw the tiny round black dot that I had left many years ago when I stabbed her with my ballpoint pen to stop her from pretending to cry to get our mother's attention. I saw the little pink scar on her forehead from a rock thrown by a man chasing her after she had stolen peaches from his trees when she was only seven. I saw myself holding her small soft hands when she was a little girl, as we huddled together in a corner when our parents were hitting and cursing at each other. I saw her growing up and coming to the crossroads of life on her own and trying to figure out which way to go. I saw her as another me, young but scarred, looking for love everywhere but making mistakes again and again.

I am sorry, Meimei, I thought.

A couple of days later, with the fifteen thousand yuan that Ming had eventually agreed to pay as compensation, my mother took Spring to the hospital two towns away for a secret abortion.

"Did she say it hurt?" I asked my mother as casually as I could manage after they had come back and Spring had gone up to her room.

"No, the little bitch is lucky. They used anesthesia. She said it didn't hurt at all."

"Mama, can you and Dad try not to call her 'little bitch' in the future and not yell at her for ruining her own future?" I suggested carefully. "It's like putting salt on her wounds."

"How can I not yell at her? Her face is still swollen from the motorcycle accident, and now she just had an abortion. How is she ever going to learn if I don't remind her?"

I sighed and said nothing. Spring had undergone a near-death accident and had had to get an abortion after getting pregnant with a married man. I hoped this would be enough to teach her to think more carefully from then on. But why should *I* expect her to learn? What about myself? Had I ever learned from my mistakes?

At least she wouldn't have to remember the feeling of the iron rod inside her for the rest of her life, and at least Mama had been outside the room when she was on the operating table. But it couldn't feel good to have our parents know about it.

After the abortion, there was finally some peace in the house. Spring went back to Zhenze to tend to her clothing shop. Still angry with her, my father remained uncommunicative as usual. I didn't feel I could just leave the family in this state, so I talked to Song and got permission to stay an extra week in the hamlet.

My mother and I often sat at the window, looking at the rows of vegetables in the fields and chitchatting with each other. Eventually, she stopped crying whenever she thought of Spring. I found that she had turned old overnight, as if transformed by a magic wand. With the sound of chickens cooing and dogs barking in the background, I told her about my life in Xiamen and tried my best to convince her that life could only get better, because I would make more money and Spring would behave now.

"Mama, where is Honor?" I asked her. I hadn't seen him once.

She sighed helplessly. "He rarely comes now. We're both getting old, and our children have grown up. His business is not doing well. Besides, your sister exhausts me. How can I have the energy to care about Honor now?"

I had mixed feelings. The ten-year affair between my mother and Honor had brought so much agony to everyone that I was relieved to see it ending, yet I wasn't sure I would get used to a home without him.

My mother liked the music box with the moon cakes very much. The six moon cakes filled with egg yolk and lotus buds were like treasures to her, and she ate each of them very slowly. She held the music box carefully in her lap and smiled whenever I turned the tray to make the jingling music play. Her dry, wrinkled fingers, which were used to touching only dirt, didn't match the vivid ruby-red tray. Her excitement and shy, almost girlish smiles made me feel like crying.

"Mama, I would like you to come to Xiamen with me."

She lifted her eyebrows high. "Uh, you mean taking an airplane?"

"Yes, take the plane to Xiamen and then take the plane back. You can stay for a month with me and have a vacation. I can take you to the ocean. You've never been to the ocean."

I saw her eyes flashing with excitement, but then she shook her head. "No, I'd better not go. Too much money. Nobody in the hamlet has ever been on a plane except that son of a bitch Beiling, and you, of course."

I responded with disdain. "Mama, don't mention that evil person. Everybody knows where his money comes from—embezzled from the Communist government. And who said that only he, Beiling, can step out of the rice fields and go to the beach? Nobody else can? No, I want to show people that you, Feng Lin Yun, my mother, an illiterate peasant woman, can board a plane and lie on the beach too! Who said that once you are born a peasant, you'll always be a peasant? I can't wait for the day when that son of a bitch goes to jail. Embezzlement, murder, plus all the women he raped. Maybe he'll even get a bullet."

My mother shushed me. "Lower your voice! Don't you ever say things like that in the hamlet. And don't ever tell people you worked as a secretary in the South. I always tell them that you worked with computers, translating. Otherwise people think you're making dirty money, like all the girls hooking in the South."

I thanked God that I had left this place and didn't have to give a damn any more about whatever was going on in these people's minds.

The night before my mother and I left for Xiamen, Spring and I shared a bed just like we had when we were little. For a while, we lay quietly in the dark and let our thoughts run free.

"Meimei," I called her gently. "Are you feeling a little better now?"

"I don't know. I don't know what I'm doing." I could sense her smiling in the dark, helplessly.

"Meimei, I understand why you like older men. It's because our father was never there for us when we were little, because we grew up in a broken family. You and I never felt safe and protected. Married men have families, and we're jealous of their families, so we want to have our own families." Having gone through so many men in my life and having condemned myself continuously, I had finally figured out why Spring and I were drawn toward married men like moths to a light.

"I feel the same way. I don't like younger men. They're reckless and unreliable," she said.

"I know. I understand." I was happy that she was finally willing to open up to me. I kept nodding my head, though I knew she couldn't see me. "Just don't feel bad about yourself, okay? It's not your fault."

"But society doesn't think that way," she said dryly. "Jiejie, I am jealous of you. You can leave the hamlet and be on your own."

"You can leave too, if you really want. In fact, you can come to Xiamen to stay with me for a while. Just let me. I'll pay all the expenses. You can decide if you like the outside world or the hamlet better." I paused. "Just remember, your fate is in your own hands. You can control it yourself if you really want."

She hummed in the dark, half confused, half understanding.

"Meimei," I said gingerly. "Don't hate Mama and Dad, okay?"

She remained silent.

I continued. "It's hard to believe, but whatever Mama and Dad do for us, they think they are doing it for our own good. After what I've gone through, I've learned that family is always family and will always be there for you, because we share the same blood."

"Jiejie, I'll be careful now," she promised me.

THE NEXT DAY, I took my mother with me to the Shanghai airport, where we boarded a Shanghai Eastern airplane. During the one-hour flight, my mother didn't close her eyes once. She sat in the window seat and looked outside the whole time. She was carefree all the way to Xiamen, like a feather floating in the air.

I led her into the fast, modern Otis elevator, which took us up to my spacious apartment on the eighteenth floor. She stared at the flashing numbers above the elevator door like a child trying to solve a puzzle.

Old Two smiled to my mother and welcomed her unctuously when we entered the apartment. My mother looked uncomfortable and cautious in front of this Shanghai man. Shanghainese are known for looking down on people from the countryside and condemning them as rude and dirty. But I swore to myself that I would not allow my mother to feel any snobbery as long as she was with me.

I smiled. "Mama, take a rest, and then I'll take you to a good seafood restaurant. You'll have the best seafood in the country tonight."

At dinner, facing a whole table of delicacies including lobsters, jumbo crabs, shark-fin soup, and roasted pig, my mother was so delighted that she couldn't keep her mouth closed. But remembering the tips that I had given her about table manners, she ate slowly and politely. She didn't chew the bones or drink the soup loudly as everyone did in the hamlet. Watching her carefully enjoying the dinner, I thought to myself: Mama is a smart and strong woman. If she hadn't been born into a poor peasant family, if she'd had any education, she would have been a different person.

"Mama, did my grandfather Lianshen ever think of sending you to school when you were a little girl?" I asked her curiously that night, when we were sitting on the balcony enjoying the starry sky.

"You silly child, your grandfather couldn't even feed his children, let alone send them to school. When I was six, he gave me to a family in the Lin hamlet as a child bride just to get some rice."

"Child bride? You mean like a slave who'll marry the son after she grows up?" I'd only read about child brides in books and was shocked to find that my own mother had actually been one. Then I realized that this would have been in the late 1950s, when the massive famine had struck China. Back then, although child brides were forbidden by the government, they still existed in the countryside.

"Yes." My mother recounted her memories painfully. "I worked like a slave there for two years. The Lin shrew whipped me every time I couldn't find enough grass for the pigs. My child groom always rode on my back and twisted my arms. I couldn't take it and finally ran away after two years."

My mother told me about her young life, history that I'd never had a chance to learn. It was a night with a full moon when she ran away from the Lin family, she said. The zigzagging path through the fields between the Lin and Feng hamlets seemed endless. Prickly bushes stung the wounds on her arms and legs. She ran for all she was worth, panting loudly and scaring away the frogs jumping around her feet. Her thin, patched cotton coat was soaked in sweat.

The mulberry trees in front of the Feng Hamlet looked like a line of glowering ghosts. Faint light from a kerosene lamp came through the small window of a shack set off a little to the east. She knew her father was inside, sitting at his desk with knitted eyebrows while her mother lay in bed coughing. She quickened her steps.

She pushed open the shack's wicker door. Her father leaped to his feet, shocked. She threw herself at his knees and grasped his right leg as firmly as she had held it two years earlier, before the Lins had pulled her away. She pleaded with her father to take her back. Looking at his second daughter's limp skinny body at his feet, my grandfather felt his legs shaking as if he too were going to collapse. He had never felt so weak in his limbs. That day, his only meal had been some bark and weeds his two boys had gathered. But despite his poverty, he couldn't turn his daughter away.

After several unsuccessful trips to the Feng Hamlet, the Lin family stopped searching for my mother. Using her bamboo walking stick, my grandmother took my mother with her from village to village to beg. My grandmother was always sick and could not walk for too long. When they came to a house, she would lean against the door and try to catch her breath.

Clutching the bottom of her mother's ragged clothes with one hand, my mother would hold out a dirty ceramic bowl with the other and chant, "Uncle, Aunt, Big Brothers and Big Sisters, please be generous and throw us some leftovers. My mother is ill, and I have two younger brothers waiting for food at home. We will pray for you day and night and wish that you live longer than Mount Tai." When it grew dark, Mama would cuddle next to her mother in a haystack or under a leeward eave and fall asleep with a smile on her face. Her mother was so thin that her body felt like a skeleton, but despite having rags for clothes and little in her belly and occasionally having to escape ferocious dogs, my mother wished life could go on like this forever.

It was dusk on New Year's Eve when they arrived home at the Feng Hamlet. Every family gathered at their table for the big New Year's dinner, and firecrackers could be heard firing from Zhenze. Inside the ragged cloth bag slung over my grandmother's shoulder, there were four steamed buns and a small sack of rice for the family. My grandmother knew that her children were waiting eagerly for their food, but after six months of drifting, her life was like the last dim flame in a dried-up oil lamp. Before her hands touched the wicker door of the shack, she fell to the ground.

My grandmother was confined to her bed, and she never got better. My mother's older sister, Jasmine, was thirteen then, old enough to follow her father to work in the commune, planting rice. Every day at noon, my mother would take her two younger brothers and the dirty ceramic bowl to the commune canteen, stand in line, and wait for the allotted porridge. It contained so few rice grains that they could see their faces on its watery surface.

Life was indifferent to my mother's prayers and diligence. My grandmother eventually grew so ill that my grandfather

Lianshen had to take her to the hospital in the city of Huzhou. Back then, the doctors and nurses were kind and didn't ask for a deposit. He returned to the commune and left my mother at the hospital to take care of my grandmother.

She stayed at her mother's bedside for a month, listening to her coughing hoarsely day and night, sounding as if she was going to cough up her lungs. The doctor in white overalls stroked my mother's head and praised her, calling her a wonderful girl, only twelve and taking care of her mother all by herself.

The smell of sodium carbonate from the doctor's cuff lingered in my mother's dreams the night they left. My grandmother shook her awake. She whispered that they had to get out of the hospital right away, because they didn't have the money to pay the bills. They walked on tiptoe to the end of the long, white corridor and staggered into the darkness. The six miles between the city and the Feng Hamlet stretched on forever. Mama supported her sick mother with her arm, and they had to stop so often that it was almost dawn by the time they reached home.

Two months after leaving the hospital, my grandmother died of tuberculosis, leaving behind nothing but debt. After burying her in a small tomb behind the Feng Hamlet, my grandfather moved the family half a mile away, to the Shen Hamlet where there were better fields and crops.

"And then my grandfather Lianshen started to carry on with Old Number Two and gave you away to Dad?" Our neighbor, Old Auntie Feng, had told me this when I was little.

"Yes." Mama nodded her head in disgust. "I'll always hate your grandfather for that. He could've carried on with any woman, just not that dying old bitch."

"Mama, I had no idea you went through so much." Mama, I wanted to say, this is all in the past. The future will be much better. I will take care of you. I will make sure you have food, even if I have to starve.

The next morning, I got up early and went to the eatery downstairs. After breakfast, I sat at the computer and waited for my mother to wake up. Soon her sleepy voice came from the bedroom. "This is the first time in years I slept more than two hours in a night!"

I entered the bedroom, put a pillow behind her, helped her sit up, and then handed her a bowl of congee.

"What is it?"

"It's congee with preserved egg and lean pork. It's delicious."

Her eyes became moist and glinted in the room's pallid light. "Did you get this for *me*?"

She was that moved just by a bowl of congee. Probably no one had ever done even such a small thing for her as bringing her breakfast in bed.

I lowered my head, avoiding her eyes. Then I waved my arm in the air and said hurriedly, "Yeah, have it while it's still hot."

I rushed out of the room, running away from my mother's tears like a hare fleeing from a hunter. I knew now that my mother had suffered greatly, and I had secretly forgiven her for all the things she had done to me when I was a child, but I was still not ready to break down the wall between us.

The next three weeks flew by. I took my mother everywhere in the city—downtown, to the beach, and to the famous tourist spot, Gulangyu Island, a small island five minutes away from the city by ferry. It's also called "Piano Island," as there is a piano in almost every residence on it. We strolled leisurely through the small lanes on the island where motor vehicles were prohibited, enjoying the classic European-style architecture while breathing the extremely clean, fresh air. My mother was very excited everywhere we went. It was the first time in my life that I had seen her laughing genuinely, without a hint of sadness.

We took rolls of pictures together, and I had all of them developed as soon as possible so that she could take prints with her when she went home.

About a week before she left, I went into the bedroom with a Kodak envelope in my hand. "Mama, the pictures are here!" I yelled gleefully.

I sat on the bed and took the pictures out of the envelope. My mother moved closer to me. We laughed together when we saw the picture of her struggling to take her shoes off in the tide at the beach.

She put her arm around my shoulder, but when her skin touched mine, it shocked me like electricity. I felt uncomfortable, as if a bug were crawling around my neck. I shook her arm off and moved away from her.

She looked at me with a helpless but amused smile. "You're a strange child. Ever since you were a little baby, you always hated me even laying a finger on you. Other mothers and daughters are not like this at all."

She clearly did not remember how she'd neglected me. So many times, she had held Spring and left me in a corner. Now she blamed me for avoiding her touch. But I didn't mention any of that. "I just don't like to be touched," I said.

We continued going through the pictures. Holding a picture of me standing on the beach looking at the camera happily, my mother heaved a sigh and said regretfully, "If only Spring were like you."

I found I couldn't control myself any longer. All of a sudden, the question that had haunted me my whole life came out of my mouth like a firework shooting into the air.

"Mama, why did you love my sister more than me?"

She raised her head and looked at me, utterly confused. "What are you talking about?"

"Why did you love my sister more than me? Why did you pay so much more attention to her than me? Why did you never care about me?"

"Oh, you silly child. You're the older one. Of course we needed to pay more attention to your younger sister. We were so poor at that time. Your Dad and I worked in the fields day and night like two dogs. We barely had time to care about ourselves."

That was it? That was the reason why she had loved my sister more than me? It was just because I was the oldest? I didn't know if I could accept that.

"Why did you and Dad beat me with the broom all the time, but you never beat Spring? You didn't raise your voices to her once."

"We were so poor at that time. Don't you remember? Some days we had nothing to eat. I was always in a bad mood. When you didn't listen to us, of course we would beat you."

So all the beating, yelling, and abuse was just my illiterate parents disciplining their child. My entire childhood had been twisted and ruined because my parents had been raised in the same way by their parents. So I had been wrong all these years, thinking that my mother didn't love me?

"Silly child!" my mother continued. "Are there any parents who don't love their children? Both you and Spring are my children. Why wouldn't I love you?"

Her words made sense. My mother loved me. She and my father were just peasants who hadn't known any better. I didn't know if I fully believed it, but for the first time I began to allow for the possibility that my parents really did love me.

We kept flipping through the photos. I saw a large picture of my mother and myself leaning together and smiling happily on Gulangyu Island. I held it up in the air. "Mama, why don't I look like Dad at all?" I joked.

"What are you talking about? Nonsense."

"I'm serious. I can see that you and I have similar noses, but Dad and I look like total strangers. My face is meaty; his face is flat—"

"Stop it," she snapped.

"Mama, what's wrong?" I asked. "Why are you so nervous?" Suddenly some dim thoughts that I had had before flew into my mind. Why had the villagers always joked that I didn't resemble Dad at all? "Is Dad not my father?" I blurted out.

"Don't be crazy. Of course your Dad is your father." She clasped her hands tightly in her lap.

"No, Mama." I tucked my knees under my chin. "Why are you avoiding me, Mama? Dad isn't my father, is he?"

"I'm not going to talk to you any more." She turned her back to me, got up, and walked to the other side of the room.

"Mama, talk to me. Please, talk to me. I want to know. Dad isn't my father, is he?" I sputtered.

"I told you not to talk about this. Why are you being so stubborn?" she yelled at me angrily.

Nervous and flustered, I ignored my mother's temper and kept pressing her. "Dad isn't my father, is he? Who *is* my father, then?"

"Stop this nonsense," she said harshly. "Of course your Dad is your father. He raised you."

My mind was rattled. "Who is my father, then? Who?" I thought quickly, images of all the men in the Shen Hamlet running through my mind. One seemed to fit. "It's him, isn't it? That son of a bitch Beiling!"

She didn't budge, glaring at me like a warrior. My stomach turned. The man I had hated in my childhood was my biological father.

Mama moved closer and sat down on the bed. Eventually she began to speak. "That bastard. He sent your father away to guard the boats for the commune and then . . . it was only a month after your father and I got married. . . . He sneaked into our hut at night. . . ." Slowly she explained, twisting her fingers in her lap. She looked like she was being forced to swallow a bowl of sour medicine.

"He raped you?" I cried out. "Why didn't you tell the commune and the police?"

"Silly, he *was* the commune. He *was* the police. He was the head of the commune. He decided how much you were going to eat, what kind of work you were going to do. Would anybody listen to me? Every woman in the commune, as long as she was not ugly, was raped by that son of a bitch. Look at him today. Isn't he still the most powerful and rich?"

"So you gave birth to me? And then you never loved me? Why did you bring me into this world and let me suffer?"

"No!" She looked at me with anxious eyes and said, hastily, "Don't think like that. Every mother loves her child. This has nothing to do with that. Really, we were just too poor for love."

"Does Dad know this? Does anyone else know this?" I murmured.

"I've never told anyone except your aunt Jasmine. When you were young, your father once joked that you didn't look like him at all, but he never asked anything."

But maybe he did know, and that was why he had never loved me.

"Does that son of a bitch know?" I asked her tensely, feeling all the muscles in my body cramping.

"After you went to college, once he came into our house. Your father wasn't around. The bastard smiled and asked who I thought Juanjuan resembled—him or your father. I didn't say anything. He grinned and said of course you were more like him since you were such a smart kid. I threw him out." Staring into the air, she spoke without emotion, but her eyes were full of shame and anger.

"Is this why he always smiled to me when I ran into him on the asphalt road? Is this why he always peeked into our house when passing by? Is this why his wife always glared at me as if she wanted to eat me alive? Is this why you never liked me?" I rambled angrily.

"No. I told you I love you as much as I love Spring, and your Dad is still your father," she said in a flurry.

Before she could say more, I fled the bedroom. I ran to the iron anti-thief gate, opened it, and stormed out of the apartment.

I walked out of the elevator with a crowd of people and exited the building. The sun hugged me with its warm arms, but I couldn't think or feel anything. Everything my eyes could see seemed to be mixed up and blended together, the sky, the earth, the trees, the shops, the buses, the people, the bikes, the air, the breeze. I looked back on my life, and it seemed like a dream. In this dream, I ran and ran with all my might to find an oasis. I walked across rivers, climbed mountains, trekked through deserts, and finally I got to my oasis. I lay down under a lush apple tree, but as soon as I closed my eyes, I woke up to find that none of it had been real.

The dream had lasted twenty-three years. I felt so exhausted, cheated. I wanted to drop to the ground and howl loudly. I wanted to laugh to the world hysterically. So I walked along, laughing for a while and then crying for a moment, and then I paused, staring into space, feeling lost because I didn't know whether I should laugh or cry.

It is said that fairness always prevails, that the truth is always better than a false reality. But it wasn't fair that my life was doomed to be miserable just because I was conceived during a rape. It wasn't fair that my mother didn't love me just because of the way my father was chosen when I'd had no chance to refuse. It just wasn't fair. I laughed dryly to myself. What should I do now? I wondered. How was I supposed to live my life from then on, having just discovered that my entire life up to then had been nothing but a big lie?

Hours later, I dragged my feet back to the apartment and went straight to my computer. Fortunately, Ethan, the American friend who I knew only through Yahoo chat windows, was online. He had become the only person I could share my thoughts with since Steven and Xiao Yi had disappeared from my life.

"I am very sad at this moment. I have just found out my father is not really my father, and my real father is a rascal who I hated my whole life." I typed out my message of despair and hit send. My mind was buzzing like a swarm of June beetles.

"Oh, I am sorry, Caroline," Ethan responded right away. "It must be very hard on you, the truth."

"I don't know what I should do now. My whole life is a dream. I hate my mother. She should've told me this a long time ago. Instead, she just didn't love me." Warm tears poured down my face. Twenty-three years of grievances were bursting out.

"Maybe she didn't tell you because she wanted to protect you. You shouldn't hate her. Every mother loves her child, in different ways. Maybe your mother loves you in a way she thinks right. Perhaps she did her best under the circumstances."

I pondered Ethan's words. They weren't genius, but they magically cleared my head. Maybe my mother didn't know how to love because she had never been loved herself. She never smiled when I was little, but I remembered she had always tried her best to either make or buy me a new piece of clothing every New Year. She had made me a bag for my first day of school. She had visited me at college. She had cried both times I left for the South. She had never hugged me or said she loved me before, but since the day I was born she had been like an octopus wrapping around me with her endless and seamless care.

My mother loved me and perhaps always had. And even if she hadn't, it didn't matter any more, because I knew I had her love now. Why should I blame her for the past? And it didn't matter any more whether my real father was a criminal guilty beyond forgiveness or a man without emotions either. That only determined where I had come from, not who I was today.

I left the living room and gently pushed open the bedroom door. In the dim light, I saw my mother curled up under the covers like a shrimp. I saw her gray-haired head on the pillow. She was barely fifty, but the beautiful, tempestuous woman of my memory was gone. Now she was just an old, frail mother who needed love and caring.

She sat up when I entered the room and looked at me, concerned. "You're back?"

"Yes, Mama. Don't worry. Everything is fine. Go back to sleep. When you wake up, I'll bring you congee again," I told her gently and then closed the door.

EPILOGUE

EVENTUALLY I GOT my passport, but I didn't go the UAE. The agency returned my money after months of trying to obtain a visa for me. I was spared a life in a robe. I was actually relieved.

My mother returned to the hamlet with two big suitcases of gifts and souvenirs. She had told me that she hardly ever saw Honor any more, but, nonetheless, I put two cases of cigarettes in the suitcase for him, something I knew he would like. I will never forget what that man did to my family, and for my family.

Spring visited me subsequently. I sent her to a beauty school, where she could learn all the advanced techniques of hairdressing that she wished. A month later, after she had finished the lessons, she decided to go back to the hamlet. City life was not for her, she said. Soon my mother called and said that Spring had opened a small barbershop in Zhenze, and my mother was very worried about several male customers who frequented it.

Sure enough, the next time she called, she told me that Spring was seeing a divorced man in his forties.

My life continued in Xiamen, a life filled by shopping in the daytime and barhopping at night. I consumed cigarettes and alcohol every day, but not strange Westerners any more. That was not the right way to find love, I told myself. Through the Internet, I had become incredibly close to Ethan, the Saab mechanic who might have had grease under his fingernails but who seemed to be the person who was born to understand me. For months, we chatted for five or six hours a day. One day he told me that he had bought a ticket to China to come see me, but a week before his scheduled departure he suddenly told me that he couldn't talk to me any more and then cut off all contact.

It was surprisingly painful to get the message. I had fallen in love with Ethan without knowing it. I dealt with this blow by drinking and sleeping around again. At this point, I was willing to marry anyone in order to get out of China. I even considered a sixty-year-old man from California who knew me through the Internet, but he eventually disappeared just like the men before him.

Six months later, just when I thought I would rot in Xiamen, Ethan started talking to me online again. I forgave him instantly. He flew to China, and we finally met face to face at Xiamen airport. This time I knew I had found my love.

In 2000, a year after our lavish wedding in the hamlet, which would remain a legend for a long time, Ethan took me to America, the land of freedom that I had dreamed of for years.

Before we left, I gave some of my money to my parents and put the rest into a condo on an island close to Xiamen. This proved to be a disastrous investment, and there is very little hope of its being recovered.

In America, reality soon settled in. Ethan had closed his

garage. Neither of us had a job with a steady income. The struggle to live an American life began.

I realized that the first thing I needed was a formal college education. Fortunately, the inexpensive University of Massachusetts at Boston accepted me. For two years, I traveled from one end of Boston to another to attend classes while adapting to life in America. With Ethan's love and nurturing, I gradually developed self-respect and learned to think of myself as a human being just like everyone else.

In 2002, Ethan got an entrepreneurial opportunity in Shanghai that he couldn't pass up. I didn't want to go back to China, a place of nightmares for me, so I remained in Boston and learned how to survive alone in America, how to call the phone company, how to go grocery-shopping, and how to deal with life without my husband.

I never felt settled at UMass. Living in Boston, I saw Harvard with my own eyes. If I could go to Harvard, then I could finally prove to the world that I was the best, I thought, still like a competitive child. So I applied to transfer to Harvard and also to a school called Wellesley College that my English professor strongly recommended as a backup.

Wellesley quickly sent me a package offering the warmest welcome and generous financial aid. I visited the school, and the gorgeous campus and the friendly people I talked to all appealed to me strongly. Two months later, the rejection letter from Harvard made my choice easy. I went to Wellesley, and my life was forever changed.

I put my hair up in a ponytail and joined all the eighteen-year-old girls around me in receiving the greatest education a woman can get. Only after so much suffering and so little guidance in life could I truly appreciate a place like Wellesley. I felt like a fish put back into water, as I told people. I absorbed everything like a sponge, the knowledge, the atmosphere, the sisterhood, and the self-empowering air floating around the campus. In my second semester at Wellesley, I started to write this memoir in an attempt to come to terms with my past.

But peeling off the layers around the wound was so painful that it immediately threw me into a depression. I often wrote with tears and ended up drinking a lot of hard liquor and then sobbing like a baby. I suffered through many nights of insomnia. At this time, my long-distance marriage with Ethan was floundering. We were still best friends to each other. However, all these chaotic and unstable elements in my life and the enormous fear of not being able to make ends meet every month only added to my depression. During our numerous fights, Ethan and I often screamed at our computers on opposite sides of the world that we wanted a divorce. I thought of ramming my car into a cliff many times, and finally I walked into the counseling office at Wellesley.

By then, Spring had chosen to marry an uneducated and stupid young man. He hit my mother during a minor fight, but, after begging on his knees, he was let back in the house. My mother was extremely distraught. As usual, my father was not protective of her. Spring, who had found herself pregnant, decided to continue with her rushed and unhappy marriage. She had suffered three miscarriages already. There was little I could do from such a distance except comfort my mother on the phone. I could only tell her that I would work really hard to finally bring her to America one day. "I want you to come back to China," she said. I couldn't possibly say yes to her. I had no intention of going back to China, the land of constant struggle. I asked her angrily why she and my father had let this man back into the house. "I don't want the villagers to say I broke up their marriage," she told me. It still amazes me how backward the Shen Hamlet is. As I move farther away from it, the distance between my family and me grows too, both physically and mentally. No matter how much education I receive, I will never learn to truly communicate with my family.

In 2004, things finally turned around. I became a U.S. citizen and graduated *magna cum laude* from Wellesley, and I was offered a research job by one of the best economics consulting firms in the country. In January 2005, I started my career of being a professional woman in America. It might not have been a big deal to most people, but for me it was momentous enough to bring tears to my eyes.

Later that year, Ethan finally decided to end his fruitless business in Shanghai and come back to America. In the summer we purchased a small but beautiful house in a suburb of Boston. Finally I had a home in America.

I went back to the Shen Hamlet in early 2006 to see my little nephew Tiantian. He is a healthy and naughty boy who finally brings smiles to the family. He has become the focus of everyone's attention, especially my mother's. I love him with all my heart. In my eyes he is innocent and pure, with no history or flaws, someone I can love completely. I hope his fate will be different from everyone else's in the family, that it will include less suffering and struggle. Spring is clearly not happy with her incompetent and sometimes even feebleminded husband, yet she stays with him because of societal pressure and out of concern for Tiantian's happiness. No matter how much I try to encourage her, she won't leave him. But I know it will not last forever. China is changing so rapidly, and one day my sister will be brave enough to stand on her own. After all, we were born into the same peasant family in the same tiny village in rural China, and if I can change my own fate, so can she.